Daughters & Mothers
Making It Work

Dorothy Firman and Julie Firman

Health Communications, Inc.
Deerfield Beach, Florida

www.bcibooks.com

Library of Congress Cataloging-in-Publication Data

Firman Dorothy.
    Daughters & mothers : making it work / Dorothy Firman and Julie Firman.
      p. cm.
    Originally published : New York : Continuum, ©1989.
    Includes bibliographical references.
    ISBN 0-7573-0124-X (tp)
    1. Mothers and daughters. 2. Interpersonal conflict. 3. Self-help techniques.
  I. Title: Daughters and mothers. II. Firman, Julie. III. Title.
  HQ755.85.F565 2003
  306.8743'3—dc22

                                      2003056628

©2003 Julie Firman & Dorothy Firman
ISBN 0-7573-0124-X

HCI, its Logos and Marks are trademarks of Health Communications, Inc.

Publisher: Health Communications, Inc.
           3201 S.W. 15th Street
           Deerfield Beach, FL 33442-8190

Cover design by Lisa Camp
Inside book design by Lawna Patterson Oldfield

Contents

PART II • The Present

Preface

When this book was first published fourteen years ago, we knew so many women who called out for help in finding more satisfying ways to be with their mothers and daughters. We also knew that paying attention to these simple but deep truths—knowing and loving yourself, taking responsibility, communicating and never *ever* giving up—would support, guide and help almost every woman.

We came to this work because we were both psychotherapists, and through our work with women of all ages and life situations, we saw that the mother/daughter relationship had an impact on adult women in almost every aspect of their lives. We also saw that healing that primary relationship helped women grow into the person each dreamed of being.

What we didn't know was that so many years later the cry for love and understanding between mothers and daughters would be stronger than ever. For twenty-five years we have given mother/daughter workshops, and every year, the workshops are filled. To our great delight, women have come back several times; first with their mothers, then years later with their daughters. Three generations have come. Sisters have come. Daughters with their mother-in-laws have come. Women alone have come and come back again. Each woman has come for the same thing: acceptance, understanding, forgiveness and love, not only of their mothers or daughters, but also of themselves.

Julie is in her eighties and Dorothy is in her fifties. We face different issues now than we did when we first started this work together. Our mother and daughter roles are sometimes reversed and our years of caring and working on our relationship have prepared us for this change. We share many joys and see life as a constant challenge. We have grown in so many ways.

We are especially excited as we watch our youngest family member, Sarah Slade, who we cherish as a daughter, granddaughter and great-granddaughter. Her excitement in learning new things and her natural ability to love herself and others warms our hearts and reminds us of the inherent wonder of the human being.

We are extremely pleased to be offering this book to the public once again, and we hope that each of you who reads it will move one step closer to your own deepest wisdom. It is an honor for us to be part of the growth of women.

Dorothy and Julie Firman

Acknowledgments

Thanks, as always, to our families: Win Firman and Ted Slawski, our husbands; Frances Salorio, Tom Firman, Lore Firman, Jody Slade, Kendy Slade, Sarah Slawski, Chris Goodbar and Tom Slawski, our children; and thanks to the lineage of our mothers, extended back in time.

A special thanks to Sarah Slade, the newest daughter in the line.

Thanks also to HCI for reprinting this book and for having really wonderful people helping at every step of the way.

May all who ask for healing, find it and may all who have love to give, give it freely, in search of a safer, fairer world for all.

Introduction

WE ARE ALL DAUGHTERS

We are all daughters, and that fact alone includes us in a world full of many things: pain, fear, expectations, anger, hurt, love, pride, joy, disappointment, fulfillment and much, much more. Being a daughter and having a mother is one of the most profound experiences of a woman's life. It can be a wonderful, empowering experience or a frightening, disabling one.

"You know, my mother is definitely the weak point in my life in this world. It's just the most confusing, most unfulfilling relationship I have. I work on myself so much and have so many beautiful, loving friends, it just doesn't seem right that I can't reach my mother, that I can't show something real with her, you know. It just doesn't seem right that I can't communicate with her at all."

"I realize how much emotion there is attached to my mother. What I'm really experiencing is just intense, intense abandonment from her. It reminds me of so many times when she wasn't there. Times when she didn't show any interest, when she didn't take me seriously."

"I feel so much guilt and pain. I need to stop acting like a doormat for my daughter. I come from a very insecure place in relation to my daughter . . . maybe because of my relationship to my mother."

"My daughter is far away. She has no need or want, no desire to be with me. I still function. I go about my life. But the hole is the hole and the longing is there, and I feel bad about it."

"I'm angry and resentful and guilty. I'm playing both roles, pleasing my mother and my daughter. I need to bridge the gap between the generations and find my own identity in the middle—between my mother and daughter. I'm lost. Can I find my separate identity?"

How can there be so much pain in these women's lives, brought on by that most crucial relationship: a relationship in almost every case based initially in love? These are not unusual comments. These are not unusual feelings and problems. The hurt that these women feel is all too common in the mother/daughter relationship. It permeates and colors this essential connection, and it does not end there. The hurt and pain experienced in the mother/daughter bond is carried into the whole of a woman's life, a burden from the past—haunting, limiting, debilitating.

But this does not have to be the case. As adult women—daughters and mothers—we have a unique opportunity. We can turn and face our lives in a way that will change us. We can transform the mother/daughter relationship and we can transform ourselves. For every woman who experiences the pain of the mother/daughter relationship, there is the promise of finding the joy.

"My mother died of cancer several weeks ago. She had a relapse from the lymphoma we thought was cured. As she became sicker, she recognized the right to loving treatment and I recognized the joy in giving it. I remember thinking, *You've been guilty long enough, Mommy. Now you just get love.* We found out she was dying only ten weeks before she died; we didn't know it would be quite so short. I said to myself that I never wanted to be one of those people I'd seen in group therapy, telling a blank wall all the things they wished they'd told their dead mother. I knew I only had so short a time to settle all the scores, to end at peace after so many stormy years, to make sure my mother died knowing how deeply I loved her, to find a gift worth giving her in her dying. I knew she had always wanted and not had enough in her life.

"I began to care for her lovingly. I would stroke her head and feet, rub her stomach when it hurt. As she lost the ability to speak and began to be more and more dazed, I would sit with her and tell her how much she was loved. My mother died really knowing how much I loved her. I know she understood and was at peace with all the joys and pain of the relationship we had had, having forgiven and blessed each other."

It is the movement from pain to joy that has inspired us to write this book. We are a mother and daughter. This work is the culmination of our own journey together. Like the many women we have encountered, we sometimes found ourselves immersed in pain, alienation, confusion and longing. We struggled to transcend this impasse. We began to talk, then we began to communicate, then we began to find our love again. We have, since that time, shared this healing journey with thousands of women. We have never met a woman who did not long for the reconnection to loving and being loved. We have never met a woman who was unable to move closer to that love, and so to her own wholeness.

If you are a woman between the ages of seventeen to one hundred, you will find yourself in this book. Whether your relationship is difficult or wonderful, current or long past, a next step awaits: one that will take you closer to the truth of your best self. And if you are a man who cares for women, you will find out more about us. We offer this work to all who choose to grow and become more whole.

Readers' Guide

USING THIS BOOK ALONE

The mother/daughter relationship is one of the most intense relationships a woman ever experiences. It is strong and it is primary. Although your mother may no longer be part of your daily life, you still carry her with you, for better or for worse. This first and essential relationship has a powerful, though often subtle, effect upon your current dealings with your mate, children, friends and *yourself* for without thinking about it, or even knowing it, we are bound and conditioned by our pasts—and, most deeply, by the mother/daughter relationship.

The purpose of this book is to help you, the reader, sift through old behavior patterns, feelings and thoughts so that you can continue to grow beyond your limitations into a more integrated, freer and more fulfilled person. You will be able to do this not by placing blame but by taking responsibility for your own actions and reactions, and for your own potential. This book is primarily a workbook with practical steps to support you in your process of growing. You need not be a mother or have a daughter. The book is for you because you are your mother's daughter.

As individual psychotherapists and as a mother/daughter team specializing in mother/daughter workshops, we have seen many women take this journey to achieve greater acceptance, love and harmony in their personal relationships. In this book you will hear from and about these women. The stories, letters and comments that we include tell about actual and composite experiences and situations, in forms designed to protect the anonymity of the women involved. Our own stories are told as well, so that we may share a piece of how we worked toward our own growth as individuals and with each other. "Dorothy's Story" will tell of the experience of the daughter in our pair and "Julie's Story" will tell of the mother's experience. The workbook sections will offer you a chance to do this same work. We will ask you to delve into your innermost self to let your angers, resentments, fears, confusions, joys, hopes, needs and values surface. Each can be examined in order to see which ones are unhelpful, childish and restricting, and which ones are beneficial, worth keeping and valued. We want you to recognize the good in you and to heal the hurt, so that you will be your best.

We hope that you will not only read this book, but will do the exercises as well. It is this personal work that will support growth and healing. When we suggest that you write, it will be far more effective to do so than to just think about the answers. We suggest that you acquire a journal that you can devote solely to the exercises in this book and for recording your own thoughts in the process of working on your relationship with your mother/daughter/self.

USING THIS BOOK IN GROUPS

Over the years many women's groups have used this book as a group experience. This creates an opportunity to be with other women and to share deeply. If you are part of a book group or women's group, or if you choose to gather a group of women friends together to share the experience of this book, we encourage you to do so. Our best advice is to talk about each chapter after the individuals in the group have read that chapter and done the exercises. This will allow for conversations, not only about the ideas in the book, but about the personal experiences that each of you brings to your adult life.

SUGGESTIONS FOR USING THIS BOOK

We would like to offer a few more specific guidelines that may aid you. The first is:

❧ **Trust Yourself.** *This one, above all other guidelines, is the most important. Your own process is unique. If you trust yourself, you will guide yourself in the direction you need to go. In other words, remodel exercises to suit your own style, stay longer with one than another, expand an exercise, and do whatever works for you.*

❧ **Follow the Order.** *The exercises are presented chronologically to move you through past issues into present and future potential. The work will be most effective if you do all the exercises in the order given.*

❧ **Take Time.** *Some exercises will take only a minute; others may take considerable time. Make sure you have the time to do an exercise in a relaxed, quiet way. You will probably have the greatest success if you read and work when you are alone.*

❧ **Mother Substitute.** *Apply the information and exercises in this book to anyone who filled the "mother" role in your life. This may be more than one person.*

❧ **Be Specific.** *Whenever possible, keep the content of what you are writing concise and specific. Narrow down broad generalizations into definitive thoughts or responses; i.e., "I was always scared as a kid" is too general to be helpful and too big to be dealt with. "I was scared when Mother yelled at me, because I thought she would leave" gives you a real issue to work on.*

❧ **Be Honest.** *The more you let yourself know about yourself, the more you will be able to grow. We have all, unfortunately, learned to hide ourselves, even from ourselves. This journey is an opportunity to let illuminating thoughts and feelings out of hiding.*

❧ **Allow Feelings.** *If sadness, anger or fear begin to surface in you, let them surface. Remember to trust your own integrity. We have an uncanny knack for protecting ourselves from anything dangerous. Feelings, generally speaking, are not dangerous and want only to be experienced.*

❧ **Create Safety.** *Choose the place where you can read and work on the exercises with privacy and comfort foremost in your mind. Have a friend or relative or professional helper to turn to for support, if it is needed.*

❧ **Have Fun.** *Life is a serious proposition — perhaps too serious. Take this personal journey as an opportunity to grow and to have fun. We will ask you to explore your pain and your joy, as well as the adult and the child in you. Take this journey seriously and lightly, with deep caring for yourself and a willingness to grow.*

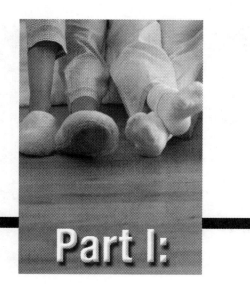

Part I:

The Past

CHAPTER ONE

Conditioning
and Uniqueness

You may give them your love
but not your thoughts,
For they have their own thoughts.
You may house their bodies
but not their souls,
For their souls dwell
in the house of tomorrow,
Which you cannot visit,
not even in your dreams.

—Kahlil Gibran

BEING A DAUGHTER

We are all daughters. We all had mothers. But how much are we affected by that relationship? How much influence did our mothers really have? Did it end when we grew up and left home? At times it may seem as if we are simply the product of our life with her: We carry the fears, doubts, images and ideas that were created at her

9

side; we react to life just as she did, or in complete rebellion to her; we still try to please her, or we are still angry with her; we wait for her to appreciate us, or we wait to prove something to her; we see and feel her ghost in almost every waking minute. While it may feel at times as if we are no more than the clay that she molded, that is not the case. Each of us plays a large part in deciding who we will be. Each of us has, from the time of our birth, influenced our own lives tremendously. We have certainly been conditioned, but our individuality—our uniqueness—has never been lost.

Being an adult woman is the result of both the conditioning and the uniqueness. The conditioning includes all that influenced us as a child, and high on the list is, of course, mother. Yet even with this powerful influence, our own styles and differences played an equally important part. The genetic makeup, the chemical and physical components of each newborn, the special gifts and skills, the strengths and weaknesses, all these make a person unique. No matter what our conditioning has been, our uniqueness shines through. *Uniqueness + conditioning = the way we are in the world.* We find ourselves, as adult women, both the product of our environment (especially our mothers), and the result of our own special "me-ness."

To get the most out of life, we need to understand this formula. The more we know about both our own uniqueness and our own conditioning, the more we will be able to grow into healthy adult women. It is too common to give most of the weight in the above equation to conditioning, allowing us blindly and unconsciously to live out the effects of our relationship to mother. In so doing, we lessen our individuality and allow ourselves to become simply the product of our pasts. It is time to step into our true selves.

As we begin to unravel the mystery of the mother/daughter relationship, we might look first at why that relationship is so powerful—perhaps more so than any other parent/child relationship and, in some ways, more powerful than any other relationship in life. As a girl child of a female parent, we are not only protected and nurtured by mother, as is her son, but we also model ourselves after her and see our impending womanhood in relationship to her. The son, on the other hand, turns his attention to dad as the image of himself and as the image of the man he will become. Daughters get a double dose of mother as nurturer and role model. This affects women in profound and important ways.

Mothers, while raising both boys and girls, are in the position of raising *and* modeling for their daughters. And no woman can help but see herself in this little female that she has borne. The mother's own identification with the daughter adds an increased two-way intimacy to that special relationship. While a mother nurtures and protects her son, she cannot quite imagine being him, or expect him to be like her—which is just what she does with her daughter.

There is a long and complicated history that is brought to bear on a baby girl. It includes not only the mother's personal history, but the societal roles, rules, mores and expectations that mothers pass on to their daughters as part of the job they have. Much has been written about the subject of the societal impact on women and it is not our intention to focus on this complicated topic, but only to give it a moment of our time to add it to the picture we are developing of this powerful and complicated mother/daughter relationship.

It is all too clear to most of us how society has limited women's roles in certain ways. We have been seen as nurturers, caregivers, wives, mothers, helpers, etc., but much less as people, as individuals, as "selves." And yet growing up female has to mean growing up to be *a person and a woman.* Ideally, we are supported in being both, but often we have been taught to sacrifice ourselves and our potential in order to take care of others. We have been taught to be females, in the entire limiting stereotype, rather than people. One teenager sadly stated that she wished her mother were more of a mother and less of a person. This mother had struggled to balance her personhood and her mothering and yet her daughter responded to the Ozzie-and-Harriet view of the all-giving woman who has no life outside of her role as mother.

In most cases, no permission or training is given to girls on how to balance these two crucial needs. Our mothers may never have thought of themselves as people independent of their identity as women/wives/mothers. Their lives may have been tied up in their roles rather than in their individuality. The "empty nest" syndrome points to this problem for women. When we have devoted our lives to raising our children, and they grow and leave, who are we then? This is a ripe time in women's lives for depression, confusion, doubt—and an opportunity to look where we haven't looked before: at ourselves as people.

爰 Rebecca was a doting mother, a product of old and traditional values. She felt completely fulfilled by her role as wife and mother. She raised her six children to be hardworking and devoted family members. But she had no influence over the changing values in the world. Rebecca had lived near her mother and brothers and sisters all of her life and they had weekly and sometimes daily contact, and her expectations were that her children would follow the same pattern. But life changed and gradually her children left the Midwest and ventured into varying and sometimes unusual occupations.

When the youngest daughter left to pursue a modeling career in New York City, Rebecca found herself severely depressed. She cleaned each room in the house over and over again; she called her children too often and felt only dissatisfaction after talking to them. The children felt guilty for failing mother and so contact between them became even more strained. Finally Rebecca decided to find a job for part of each day. She found just the niche for her skills in a nursing home and, once again, she felt needed and able to give the caring that had been so much a part of her life. Rebecca never thought in terms of her own *self* as a separate identity, but she did find a solution to her hunger for nurturing. And to her surprise, she also discovered hidden talents and gifts that slowly but surely blossomed, helping her to become more whole.

As a backlash to those generations of conditioning, many women have chosen to sacrifice meaningful aspects of their mothering role in order to preserve their greater identity as a person. That sacrifice may prove to be as painful and limiting as the original stereotype that so often defined women.

Jean's mother raised her in a very traditional way—modeling woman as homemaker above all else. But Jean hit adulthood at the heyday of the feminist movement and radical political thinking. Her college experience in political groups validated all the dissatisfaction she had felt as a child washing dishes with mom while her brothers helped dad paint and fix the car. And through her political involvement Jean found a life that had meaning: working to change the world. She married and had her first child while heavily involved in political activity. "Of course, I put Sandy into childcare, full time, when she was a few weeks old. We all did. Our work was so important to us, more important even than our own families. I missed her and felt badly sometimes at the long hours she was away and the meetings at night, but I wasn't like my mother. I knew that much. I was not, and would never be, a perfect homebody." When Jean came into therapy three years later, both she and her husband were "burned out" with all the work and lack of time for themselves and family. Jean worked toward a more balanced way to be with her new baby and with her family and herself, while still maintaining a deep commitment to social change.

For women who are living in only one dimension, life will be difficult. Rebecca faced this difficulty when all that she had made her life to be, as a mother, slipped away from her. Jean's life grew hard when she faced the pain of her loss of self as a family person. For a daughter whose mother has learned how to be both a mother and a person, the rewards are great.

❧ Simone had grown up in Chicago with a professional mother and father. Both were professors and constantly in demand for lectures and seminars. Simone watched her mother study and heard her mother speak out for things that she believed were important. Simone grew up knowing that women were important and independent. She had also experienced the love and tenderness that mother gave her in the times when they were together. Simone looked at life as a challenge and felt that all doors were open to her as she grew into adulthood. She, too, chose over the years of her life to devote time to family and personal interests, realizing, as she said, that, "Sometimes it feels as if life is hard, balancing this and that, but at other times I realize that anything is possible and that I can play whatever game I choose."

We may recognize some of our own limitations in these stories and get a glimpse of how we may have been raised. Regardless of our personal story, each woman has been conditioned at many levels. At the feet of our mothers, lessons are learned, ways to be and not to be are taught, rights and wrongs are elaborated, permissions and denials given. So we are conditioned—powerfully, subtly and usually with the best of intentions. But remember that even the deepest sources of conditioning, which may be societal, religious, multigenerational or personal, are not insurmountable. However we were raised, whatever bent or perspectives or tendencies guided us, we all faced growing up female: growing up as women and people. And our goal is to discover how to be that in the most complete way possible.

The Chain of Conditioning

A Tale of a Tail

Grandma came from the old country. She and her family had very little and so were frugal. The highlight of the year was Christmas, and the highlight of the dinner was Christmas ham. As Grandma prepared the many dishes that were part of dinner, her daughters helped. From the time they were little, they would spend those precious days in the kitchen with their mother, each doing what she could to help. When the ham was brought in from the butcher, the mother would ceremoniously sharpen her big knife, cut off the end of the ham and place the ham in the pan. Dinners were wonderful affairs, and leftovers made meals exciting for days afterward.

The daughters went their ways and grew to be women. Anna continued the family tradition of ham for dinner, though her life was not nearly so frugal. She had only one daughter, Jean, who also worked in the kitchen to help her. Anna still bought a big ham, fresh from the butcher, cut off the end and baked the ham. Jean waited for the day she would be old enough to handle the big knife. When Jean grew up and married, she too continued the tradition of ham on Christmas. It was harder to find a real ham, but she did. Jean had no daughters to help in the kitchen so her son, Tom, helped. He enjoyed the cooking as well. When the ham was opened, Jean cut off the end, as always. Tom asked, "Why do you cut off the end?" Jean didn't know. She called her mother. Anna said, "Well, the end is always cut off. Mother used it for soup. I give it to the dog." Jean called Grandpa. Although feeling silly to ask such a question, Jean finally asked: "Grandpa, do you know why Grandma cut the end off the ham at Christmas time?" "Of course," laughed Grandpa. "Because her pan was too small for the whole ham."

This simple story indicates how easy it is to accept dictates from the past, without thinking, without even knowing that we are doing so. What we have to discover is whether old conditioning serves us or harms us. Unconsciously taking on attitudes, behaviors and truths from our pasts can lead to distorted thinking and inappropriate behaviors. This is true for individuals, families, groups and societies. At the personal level, unconscious conditioning leads to an inability to know ourselves, whether it is knowing why we cut off the end of the ham or knowing why we can't get along with certain people, why we have such strong feelings about this or that, why we are hurt or are blocked or afraid. At the social level, unconscious conditioning leads, at its worst, to bigotry, group arrogance, lack of compassion, competition, feelings of superiority, and the justification of violence, oppression and abuse. To understand the conditioning that we have received, we must explore our pasts: our mothers' and our own. In this way we will be able to free ourselves. The past has conditioned each of us in powerful ways, and our past with mother has had a particularly strong and extensive influence.

In order to be sure of mother's love and protection, we adapted ourselves to do, think and behave in ways that would be pleasing to her. She, in turn, was conditioned by her own past and undoubtedly was trying to please her mother, her culture, her partner and, as a result, often acted out old, deeply buried messages within herself. The chain of conditioning is long and unconscious. A young girl is especially susceptible to the power of her mother's conditioning, for her mother serves a double role: She is her daughter's life support and primary role model. For an infant daughter, mother is the focal point of her life. In infancy, mother's nurturing and care keeps the child alive. The relationship is symbiotic; that is, mutually dependent. The child's life and sense of well-being hang in the balance, and the mother, in her turn, is fulfilling an important function in her own life. The two are inextricably bound with each other and the power of that bonding shows throughout a woman's life.

By the time we are adults, we have been filled with the dictates of the past. Our life with our mother will affect our lives across the board. It is likely that we will raise our own children through the model of our own mother, either by adopting or rejecting her way of doing it. But it may be surprising to find out that our relationships to men, women, authority figures, and other significant people are colored (often adversely) by unknown ghosts from the past. As adults, many of the ways we think and behave are patterns formed in childhood. We continue these patterns without thinking about when or how they started, and frequently we are not aware of the influence they have on our lives. Our mother has been so near to us over the years that we carry her with us in most aspects of our lives.

Raising kids is the first place we may notice mother's influence. It is quite common to raise our children in a way opposite to or significantly different from the way we were raised. We want to compensate in the areas in which we felt hurt or deprived. We want to protect our own children in ways that we did not seem to be protected. However, much of how we raise our children, in this effort to compensate, is *reactive* and *unconscious*. Without studying our behavior, our choices or even our thinking, we simply shy away from anything that feels like mother's way. This often creates an intergenerational hopscotch game. Patterns get repeated in every other generation, each one reacting negatively and unconsciously to the preceding one.

What doesn't work in this practice is that we are still unknowingly responding to conditioning. We have not chosen, for ourselves, how to raise our children. We have chosen in response to mother. In our efforts to protect our children from our childhood pain, we may well create the opposite pain in their lives. And, even in our attempt to make right our hurts, we create for ourselves new hurts. By not creating our lives consciously, we still don't get our needs met.

ﷺ Sharon, mother of four grown children, came into therapy when her last child left home for college. Her anxiety and pain were expressed over and over again. "My mother was never home for me," said Sharon. "She was never there with warmth and love. I have made my children my life. By loving them and touching them and doing for them, I found a way to do for myself and give myself all that I missed growing up. Now I don't know how I'll find a way to have that contact that means so much to me."

Sharon attempted to assuage her early life pain through her children, and her efforts worked—temporarily. When the children left, however, the early pain was rekindled and it was still unhealed. Sharon had never considered what was best for herself and her children except in the context of her own painful relationship to her mother, and when her children grew up she found she had neglected her own autonomy along the way. She was a lonely, abandoned child, and now, she was a lonely, abandoned mother.

While this style of *opposing* mothering is often the source of pain, we can be just as conditioned in raising children when we raise them compliantly, mimicking our own mother's style. It is equally painful to raise our children as we were raised, hoping to recreate the magic of our childhood or hoping to keep or win our mother's approval by raising our children "right." Any relationship that we have to our children that is still bound to our own pasts in an unknown way can hurt and limit us.

Julie's Story

❧ "In the year before my birth, my mother had lost two brothers and a sister during the flu epidemic, her own mother had a stroke, and my father was in France in World War I. So I imagine that when I was born, my mother was not very happy. I can remember watching her take care of my grandmother while I sat on the bed. Mother was tender and gentle with her mother, doing everything necessary for her. I was very happy being with the two of them. Then my grandmother died and we were all sad without her. When I was about six, my sister was born and Mother left to go to the hospital. She developed phlebitis, which in those days was life threatening. She was gone for a long time and I grew more and more anxious about her. When she finally came home from the hospital, my relief was tremendous. Ignoring the new baby, I can vividly remember running to greet Mother, with eyes only for her. 'Don't worry, I'll always take care of you,' I whispered to her. And I did, for years and years, experiencing my love through my desire to be sure she stayed alive.

"When I had daughters of my own, they behaved just like little kids—it never occurred to them to take care of me. And sometimes I found myself thinking, *Why don't they love me the way I loved my mother?* I was still basing my definition of mother love on being taken care of. That was how I had loved my mother and she had loved hers. It never occurred to me in those years that I was never sick. I never needed to be taken care of in that way. My daughters never experienced the threat of losing me. But it was not until they were grown, and I was in therapy, that I discovered how distorted my thinking was. It was wonderful to see that distortion, because then I could be free to see the love that my daughters really did have for me, expressed in their unique way."

Those of us who are mothers may want to explore how much we are still lost in our own mothers. Some questions we might ask ourselves:

ꙮ *Am I raising my kids in opposition to my mother?*

ꙮ *To please her?*

ꙮ *What things do I do with my kids that don't come out of my own well-thought-out values?*

ꙮ *What things do my kids do that hook me? (Does this relate to my own mother?)*

ꙮ *Have I thought about what it means to me to be a mother?*

If we scratch the surface, we can see that it is not simply with our children that this conditioning has its effect. In every aspect of life we may discover the unconscious remnants of our early lives with our mothers. When we relate to our mates or lovers, acting out the needs we had with our mother, the results can be disastrous.

Dorothy's Story

ꙮ "One of the ways my marriage of twenty-five years works is that I can be 'little' with my husband. I live most of my life as a strong, out-in-the-world person. But every once in a while, my world seems to cave in. When it does, I know that I can go home and be three. I sometimes find myself thinking or saying, 'I want my mom.' Because I know what it is that I really need and feel, I am able to get those needs met. In my first marriage, when I felt little, needy or confused, I would begin to feel clingy and demanding—my way of trying to fix that 'little' feeling that I was unconscious of. My husband felt threatened and moved further away. Neither of us knew what was happening. I just felt little and acted unconsciously. He felt endangered. It didn't work. Understanding it has made it possible to honor that need, without confusing or threatening the marriage."

And we carry our mothers further: into friendships, into relationships with authority figures and into our professional lives. Whatever
patterns we acted out with our mothers—patterns of conflict, competition, manipulation and appeasement—are often duplicated in
other walks of life.

Debbie, a thirty-four-year-old professional woman, has pro-
jected her unresolved relationship with her mother into her
work situations, with unfortunate results. Before she discovered this pattern in herself, she said: "I have never had a woman as a boss without
giving up or losing my job in a short time. They have all been so picky
and critical. Once I thought I had found the perfect boss; she was everything I wanted her to be. She greeted me warmly every day, praised my
work and even invited me to lunch. Then a new person joined the
office and she did the same things for her, and I knew I had to leave the
job because she didn't really care for me. I wonder if I'll ever advance
in my career if I have to keep changing my job?"

Debbie did not realize the implications of her frequent job
changes. Unconsciously she was searching for someone to give her
all the reinforcement that she had not received from her mother.
Once she was aware that her boss did not have to assume the role of
a mother, Debbie began to free herself to pursue a career in the way
she wanted.

The depth to which our conditioning can affect our lives is seen in
therapeutic settings over and over again, as well as at the kitchen
tables of women everywhere. We tend to act in subtle and deeply
rooted ways, as if our mothers still had all the power. We often feel as
if we are only six, even when we are sixty!

Elise was a wonderful artist, sixty-five years old with children and grandchildren, a happy marriage, and most of what she wanted in life. Her art was shown in various places and was quite extraordinary, though often sad or disturbing. She came to therapy because she wasn't painting anymore. "Mother didn't approve of my art," the artist said. "She wanted me to be a musician. I still feel sad when I paint, not to be pleasing her." "Has your mother reconciled herself with your choice of careers?" the therapist asked. "No, she has been dead for twenty-five years." Tearfully, painfully, slowly, a small child emerged still desperate for her mother's approval and love. Her mother had profoundly colored her life for sixty-five years. Even in Elise's art—her most private world— her pain and confusion about her mother were manifest.

Our mothers can be with us everywhere. Certainly they are deeply buried within us, affecting our experiences of the world and of ourselves. Like some ancient goddesses once worshiped and feared, now discarded, they float through us like ghosts in many ways we may not realize. As we have seen, mothers can affect us everywhere, but most importantly, our lives with them affect our sense of self. The conditioning in our pasts may be so strong that it overshadows our uniqueness, and we may be left still feeling, thinking and behaving in ways that are really responses to our mother. This situation can be sadly painful and deeply destructive.

Louisa was told over and over again by a hard and frightened mother that she must improve, do better and be better. "The world is a dangerous place for women," her mother said. "You are only safe with a man, and you must try to find one. But you are so dirty, a tomboy, rough, you'll never make it in the world." Louisa was a deeply unhappy woman. She herself was hard and critical, like her mother, criticizing others and driving them away, and criticizing herself, moving deeper and deeper into depression. In her late thirties, she took in a foster child, having never found a relationship that lasted, although having desperately tried for all those years. The child was her last effort to reclaim herself, her love of others and of herself. But her response to the child was as critical and unloving as her mother's had been to her. She saw this and felt trapped. Only in that greatest despair did she look for help to try to find herself again.

Louisa was conditioned so deeply that she barely found a way to reach outside of her pain for help. While the power of the conditioning we received at our mother's side is undeniably great, it need not be overwhelming. Even in the most painful situations there is a way out, if only we can find the door. Beginning to be conscious will make all the difference. When we look at our lives and ourselves and ask, "How is Mother with me now?" we can begin to find out and start to overcome the limitations imposed by our conditioning. We can keep what works and choose to leave behind what doesn't.

THE SELF THAT SHINES THROUGH

While we may be all too painfully aware of the conditioning that still influences us, we must notice that life is more than a one-sided affair, with a mother doing all the conditioning and a daughter receiving blindly. A child's own uniqueness adds an important dimension to this process of growing up. No matter how she is raised, a daughter manages to interpret, discriminate and react in ways that are hers alone. And without a doubt, there is always the spark of that child's self that shines through.

But what does this mean, our uniqueness? The old nurture/nature question has never been answered and leaves us wondering whether we are anything more than our conditioning. More and more, it seems that human beings are discovering an essential nature in themselves, a place of uniqueness, and a *true self* that is a perfect expression of each being. The self that we are assuming here is an inherent quality of being that defines one individual as different from another. Just as each physical being is unlike any other, expressing in her body configuration a unique style, look and presence, so too is the emotional being, in thinking and in personality; each is unlike any other, and each expresses, from the start, a style, a way of being and personality of her own.

This unique way of being might be considered the building material that we are given to start out with. Some start with special gifts or talents, with personality styles, with dominant traits or tendencies, with certain qualities that define that person. We have always heard of the "easy" baby and the "difficult" child. And we've too often heard the attributes our mothers have seen in us: "my shy daughter," "the studious one." But the real definition of ourselves is an internal one, not based on behavior or others' perceptions, but on our felt sense of who we are, essentially. *Who is it that has gone to sleep and woken up every night of my life?* I am not a different me than I was ten or twenty years ago, though much of my presentation has changed. Others might not recognize me many years later, but I always recognize myself.

There are certain truths about each person that stand out in their whole lives, certain qualities that represent them. There are "ways to be" in the world, felt internally and expressed externally, that draw on a seemingly infinite variety and combination of qualities: love, wisdom, creativity, humor, intellectual insight, curiosity, movement, appreciation, awe, inspiration, perseverance, power, strength, skill, receptivity, etc. Each woman is a unique combination of these and other qualities, and her way of growing up was also an expression of this essential direction or tendency within her. It is not, to be sure, that we are fated to be a certain way or do a certain thing. On the contrary, we are only given building blocks and with these we can create anything. Remember the simple equation that defines the building that we do in our lives: *Uniqueness + conditioning = the way we are in the world.* To honor and support our true self, while coming to terms with our own conditioning creates the greatest opportunity to become whole and fulfilled that is available.

Arabelle is a twenty-eight-year-old student. She is one of four daughters. Her mother is a powerhouse, running for political office—aware, independent and assertive. Arabelle says, "I'm not fully equipped. My sisters all know how to be in the world, but I don't. I'm considered the weak child, the needy one. I always ran to my room for protection and never could stand up for myself in a fight, with my sisters or my mother. I wonder why I was dealt the bad hand?"

Was Arabelle dealt the bad hand? When asked if she would prefer to be one of her sisters, there was an unequivocal "No!" As she explored that certainty about choosing her own being, she discovered that she was not ill equipped, just different. Her strengths were in a more inner-directed modality. She was introverted, creative, compassionate and sensitive. In her present life she valued deeply her social consciousness, her efforts at personal growth, her intimacy and caring for friends. Even her confusion was finally honored, as she realized that "to think you know everything that's going on doesn't leave room for any more growing." Arabelle's problems in her childhood were the result, in part, of her own uniqueness. In such an extroverted family, she was seen as weak. The conditioning she received caused her to call herself "not okay."

Our own uniqueness, even as children, has a powerful influence on our relationship to mother. Arabelle's introverted style caused her mother alarm and worry, even anger. Her other daughters more neatly fit into the mold and mother's reaction to them was quite different. Quite often, two daughters in the same family are likely to be distinct, seeing life with varied, even opposing outlooks, and experiencing their mother as two entirely different people.

It is important to understand that we internalize our childhoods uniquely. The ghost that stays with us is, in each case, a different ghost. And we may carry several ghosts. Learning about life as children, we may see and hear several different mothers and internalize elements of each. The classic split is "good mother/bad mother." Sometimes one daughter internalizes a good mother and the other a bad one. Sometimes one daughter experiences and internalizes both. The factors that create our differing experiences are vast. Mother is different, the situations are different, and the uniqueness of each child is crucially different.

Julie's Story

ᏍᎧ "I, as the firstborn, carried the view of being not only my mother's sole interest, but also my grandmother's. I saw my role as a daughter to be a special privilege. In addition to my being the firstborn, my health was also a factor. I was a four-pound baby and needed to be fed and held much more frequently than a full-term baby. When my sister was born six years later, she was a strong, healthy baby and did not receive or need that extra nurturing, nor did she have the advantage of having a grandmother around. Therefore, when my sister and I talk about our mother, my sister remembers Mother as not being there most of the time and I remember her as never turning me away. We are perhaps basing our views on a very early experience that we have carried throughout our lives.

"We still carry these perceptions into our relationship. But it wasn't only the changing situations that affected our relationship to our mother. I believe that I had a cheery, positive outlook on life from the start. Even when I was gravely ill as a child, the world looked good to me and I felt safe and loved. My sister seemed to take things much harder. I think my cheerfulness allowed me to receive Mother's love and ignore the rest."

On the other hand, there is Delma, who did not find it easy, as her sister did, to understand and accept their mother's changes of mood and seeming loss of love.

Delma says, about her childhood, "My sister was fourteen months younger than I, yet when Mother yelled at us or hit us, my sister just took it and ran off to do whatever it was she wanted. I cried and cried and hung around, hoping Mother would say she loved me. I often wondered what made us respond so differently. Somehow my sister seemed to have a stronger sense of survival than I did. I believed that if Mother got angry enough, she'd never take care of us; and I still respond to life that way."

What can be learned from these stories? Was Delma's mother "bad" to Delma and "good" to her sister? The important lesson is that we have always had a certain degree of choice available to us. Delma's sister chose to run out and play. Delma felt sad and scared and chose to stick around her mother. If you can begin to think about having always had choice, that realization will change your life. It will allow you to know that today and every day you have choices. What Delma was not realizing in her understanding of herself was not only that she had some choice, but that the choices she made reflected not only her fear and need, but a piece of her self. Delma, as we might guess, even from that brief story, is a sensitive person, her sister much less so. Delma is also deeply committed to people. She is drawn to roles in which she can be supportive and help people. As Delma begins to see the positive side of her childhood pain, as she begins to own and honor her uniqueness, allowing it to have some power in the equation of her life, she can respond to her style and way of being so that her conditioning is not a drawback anymore.

We might say that every story has its opposite side, every cloud its silver lining. In every story that shows the power of conditioning, and even those that show the depth of pain in a young child's life, there is a quieter story of strength, determination, of a self shining through. When a mother and daughter come to experience, each on their own and each in the other, their own selves shining through, joy is created.

WORKBOOK

Discovering the balance of conditioning and uniqueness in our lives is the first step in freeing ourselves and learning to grow into our own greatest potential. Are you overly identified with conditioning, having adopted consciously or unconsciously the laws and dictates of the past? Have you forgotten, or never acknowledged, what is unique about you? Do you allow yourself to know what is just yours, in terms of feelings, beliefs, thoughts, hopes, styles, or do you try to fit into accepted molds and conventions? In any case, there is more to know about yourself. These three exercises will offer you the opportunity to explore all the ways you are, to identify the "ghost" of mother that hangs on in your life and to own and acknowledge the gifts that are yours. Enjoy the journey!

❧ Who Am I? ❧

This exercise is designed to develop self-awareness. It is based on the assumption that we experience ourselves as many things: as mothers, daughters, women and much, much more. Each of these images or ideas about ourselves makes up our sense of who we are, but often these concepts are negative remnants from the past. The layers of who we are may well cover up our uniqueness and keep us from experiencing our greatest potential. The first step is to find the many answers to the question "Who am I?" and in so doing begin to peel away the layers.

This exercise can be repeated frequently to go deeper into the answer. Select a place for this where you are quiet and undisturbed. With your paper and writing implements (crayons or markers will be a nice addition) near you, create a quiet mind state and ask the question, "Who am I?"

Allow every answer that comes to be written down, both the obvious and the obscure answers. When you have run through most of the verbal answers, ask the question again and allow an image or images to appear that also answers that question. Take time to draw these. Remember, it is crucial that you not be an artist in this moment. The drawing is for your own inner purposes only. Ask the question again and go back to writing. Stay with this process as long as you feel you can gain information from it. After a time, look at your answers and drawings and see if you have written anything that surprises you, angers you, pleases you. Are there ways you want to change, based on these answers? Are there aspects of yourself that you feel you have inherited from the past that no longer serve you? Take some time to think about what you've discovered and what it means.

≈≈ Mother's Ghost ≈≈

We've talked about "mother's ghost" as the internalized part of mother that we carry around inside of ourselves, whether mother is alive or dead, living thousands of miles away or in our own homes. Mother's influence affects us in our lives in many, many places, and when unconscious, it may cause us pain and confusion. This ghost is the conditioning that we have adopted without yet being conscious of it. It is cutting off the end of the ham without knowing why. Taking time to search out the conditioning will allow us to reconsider the ways we are and the things we do and to decide whether, for us, the end of the ham needs to be cut off.

Close your eyes and take time to get relaxed and quiet. Spend some time following your breath as it moves in and out. This will help you to settle into the quiet space. Allow your thinking to slow down—to stop if it will—so that you have a blank mind screen. In this quiet space get an image of your "mother's ghost," a symbol that reminds you of that conditioning. Think about these questions that might help guide you in this quest:

- When do I feel mother's ghost most?
- Do I carry this ghost with me to work?
- Does this ghost affect my relationship to my children? friends? lovers? bosses? mate?
- When I look in the mirror, is mother's ghost there?
- Is she in my kitchen?
- Do I take her to bed with me?
- Is mother's ghost supportive, encouraging me in difficult situations, or is it negative, critical, demanding?

After you have come to understand some more about mother's influence in your life, take a moment to think about your power to choose your life now—the way you want it to be.

&c Will the Real Me Please Step Forward! &c

We've seen in our first exercise the many, many answers to the question of who I am and we've also seen mother's ghost creeping into our lives, even into our sense of self. So who are we, really? What's behind the conditioning, the roles and the ideas about ourselves? It's important to begin to find out about our most essential selves, about our uniqueness, about that aspect of our being that is not created in response to the outside world, but that is our birthright. Answer the following questions quickly, with the first thoughts that come into your mind. Keep your answers brief.

- When I was a child, who was my hero/heroine?
- What did I want to be when I grew up?
- What were my favorite activities?
- What was my most positive assessment of myself as a child?
- As an adult, whom do I admire? What is it about that person that I admire?
- What has meaning to me in my life?

Now, from the following list, check the qualities that you feel really represent you.

❑ Acceptance	❑ Creativity	❑ Intelligence
❑ Beauty	❑ Curiosity	❑ Joy
❑ Calmness	❑ Detachment	❑ Light
❑ Goodness	❑ Enthusiasm	❑ Love
❑ Goodwill	❑ Faith	❑ Order
❑ Gratitude	❑ Freedom	❑ Patience
❑ Positivity	❑ Friendship	❑ Playfulness
❑ Power	❑ Generosity	❑ Serenity
❑ Sensitivity	❑ Harmony	❑ Service
❑ Compassion	❑ Humor	❑ Silence
❑ Cooperation	❑ Inclusiveness	❑ Simplicity
❑ Courage	❑ Insight	❑ Truth

❏ Understanding   ❏ Wholeness   ❏ Wonder
❏ Vitality   ❏ Wisdom

Write down several more qualities that reflect your true self.

Take some time now to go over what you have written and notice what qualities, attributes, styles and preferences are expressed in all the questions. Compile this data into a list or summary that will represent a partial definition of your uniqueness. Make sure that you include information gained in all the questions. In other words, when you look at the qualities of the people you admire, put those into your list about you; so too for the styles and qualities of the heroines you may have had. *After all, it is only that which is within us in a very deep way that we can see and admire in another.*

Sally, a young woman who as a child had felt lost in her family, had been conditioned to stay invisible, be good and have no needs. She was not used to commenting positively on herself or even allowing herself to deeply know many important truths about herself. In this exercise she drew from the qualities of her childhood hero, Robin Hood, as well as from her childhood dreams to be an actress and an astronaut and from all her current models and thoughts about herself. She put together a beautiful piece that expressed many of her known and many hidden qualities.

"I am a person who expresses herself easily through vibrant physicality. I have a great deal of positive focus and many avenues for creative expression. I have deep commitment to personal growth and learning and considerable gifts of diplomacy. I am a social being capable of deep and rewarding relations and am grounded in the simplicity and solitude of the natural world and ordinary home life. I have vision and integrity about my place in the universe. I have a lot of fun with my playfulness, resourcefulness and independence."

CHAPTER TWO

Growing Up Female

A SON IS A SON TILL HE GETS HIM A WIFE.
A DAUGHTER'S A DAUGHTER THE REST OF HER LIFE.

—*Old folk saying*

STEP BY STEP

By the time we find ourselves as adult women, we have been through a long journey. To become the most we are able, it will help us to see some of what that journey was about. Let's begin with our births as daughters. We can assume that we are already conditioned to a degree by the environment in the womb, both the physical and emotional environment. Mom is happy or sad, well or ill, stressed or relaxed—and probably all of these at varying times. We feel this and our bodies already begin to respond to that environment in the way we develop and grow. Yet we most certainly already possess elements of our uniqueness. At birth, the conditioning and uniqueness formula is already in play. And labor and delivery are the first beginnings of our relationship to our mother.

"When I saw that she was another girl, I was crushed. I couldn't bear to have another girl when we so much wanted a son."

"My mother had tuberculosis while she was pregnant with me. As soon as I was born she was whisked off to a sanitarium. I have never felt close to her and I know I was a burden."

"My first child had been the doctor's baby—a clear-cut surgical procedure in which I wasn't in the way. I didn't hold her for a day. My second child was my bab—natural delivery and touch from the minute of her birth."

"My mother died in childbirth. An aunt who loved me as much as her own child raised me. I wonder if I could have been closer even to my biological mother."

When we enter into the world, total dependency is our first experience. In most situations that dependency is on our mother. It is a healthy, biological dependency: a symbiosis. This initial bonding sets the stage for the continued development of the daughter, who must move, inevitably, but with greater or lesser success, out of symbiosis and into separation. As the child grows and needs less life support, her dependence decreases. And finally a daughter leaves her mother as an independent person. The ideal mother, in perfect timing, relinquishes control and supports autonomy in a graceful dance with her growing daughter.

Each daughter, in this process, will learn about trust of herself and of the world; about her feelings; about thinking and being in the world. She will find out about initiative and intuition, self-confidence and impulse control. She will learn about giving and receiving, about sexuality, choice, power, curiosity, creativity. She will have explored and come to understand much about her own needs and she will know about aloneness and togetherness, about love and autonomy. This life with her mother will be her most important education.

Ideally, the young woman who leaves home will have developed a working and satisfactory identity. This is the perfect dance between mother and daughter.

However, we don't dance the dance perfectly, and the movement from dependence to independence that is so natural in lower life forms will be fraught with pain, confusion and lack of resolve in the mother/daughter relationship. Many of the essential qualities that lead to personal identity will be threatened: Some will not be taught; others will be incorporated in a disjointed or distorted way; others will be denied, not allowed. Every woman will gain independence to a certain degree. The nature of our aging, and ultimately our mother's death, will support this. But this may be only physical separation and not emotional independence. It may not be healthy, fulfilling or complete. For adult women who have not achieved their autonomy in a clear way, there will be issues reflected in all walks of life. Much of how we may experience ourselves as adults will still be in childlike ways. We may feel like a victim, helpless or frightened. We may feel as if we are only playing grown-up, relying on a false front that just barely covers our lurking feeling of inadequacy. We may shut off parts of ourselves, our thinking, our feeling, our ability to be intimate, to be sexual, to be a success. We may not allow certain aspects of our being to be expressed. The lives that are lived denying their full range of potential are many and painful. Sadly, we often don't even recognize how we have limited ourselves.

Helena was a dutiful daughter. She took care of her elderly mother and gave her everything that she possibly could. Mother expected this behavior and would have been deeply surprised if Helena had done for herself rather than for her mother. Helena didn't ever consider the possibilities in her own life: relationship, challenging career, adventure, creativity, independence. She said, "Mother will die sometime soon. Until then, she needs me. I don't really mind giving her so much time and energy." Helena had been working from that premise for most of her forty years. When she began to really mind, she felt trapped and unable to change. She said, "Even if I could get help for Mother, I wouldn't know what to do. She's been my life." Helena's seventy-five-year-old mother was destined to be around for a long time. While Helena flirted with the idea of having a life of her own, she had the perfect excuse not to face herself.

Helena was robbed of some of her potential in growing up. She never knew that she had a right to a life of her own or even who she was as a separate person.

Somewhere in the building blocks of each woman's life, there was a glitch in the system. Something did not develop perfectly. Everyone has these glitches. Are they mother's fault? It's tempting to think so, but the answer is a resounding "No!" Laying the responsibility on mother is just a piece of misinformation that we have absorbed.

Mother played her part. She brought her whole life's experience into the role and we can assume that she did the best she could. Certainly she was a product of her own conditioning. Her limitations, faults, weaknesses can be traced, in large part, to her life as a child. Each woman experiences the new role of mother in her own unique way. And each attempts to do this job in a way that seems "right" to her. The role of mother may have allowed one woman to feel powerful and dominant with her daughters, as she may never have felt anywhere else in her life, while another might have felt inadequate and frightened in this awesome role. One may have seen her job as provider for her growing daughter while another saw herself as trainer of a future woman. Each does the best she can with what she has and what she knows. Women in the role of mother are faced with an ever-present demand to be all-nurturing and protective in those early months and years and then to relinquish this power and control in later years. "Give up your life for this child" is the first commandment; "Let the child go" is the second. No wonder mothers sometimes think they can't win!

Society sits right in the backseat, adding to the mother's dilemma. Different periods of history have reflected society's tendency to emphasize one or the other commandment and to blame mother for being too much of one or the other. We are as familiar with the idea of the "smother-mother"—overprotective, holding too tightly, never letting go—as with the cold, aloof mother, never giving enough. Mothers are simply expected to do it all perfectly: to be everything for their child and then to adjust their letting go in perfect time to the daughter's growing independence. Mother's job in supporting the daughter's gradual emergence into adulthood (and independence) is an enormously difficult one. The task is no less difficult for the daughter. Can anything replace the feeling of security that we may have had as an infant? Can we ever truly feel big, after feeling so little all those years? Can we find a way to leave our mothers without losing our mothers?

Most of the problems encountered in the mother/daughter relationship and many that adult women face in their own lives stem from this awesome task of being bonded and dependent, and of having to grow through that into separation. Each and every mother and daughter struggles with her unity and her separateness. And every daughter shares a common set of needs. Simply stated, these needs are to be nurtured, protected, and given the opportunity and safety to grow into a functioning, complete adult.

In the Beginning: Life as a Newborn

The first months of the mother/daughter relationship are often like a honeymoon. Like young lovers, the mother and daughter are bonded and bound to each other. The dependence is mutual and mutually protective. The mother's investment in her daughter, and her love and desire to protect, cause her to want to be there fully for her daughter. The child's helplessness demands that involvement. The daughter will experience tenderness, physical gratification and interest from the mother. The daughter, in turn, will be more responsive to her mother than any other adult, turning her head more readily to the higher-pitched female voice and learning to recognize mother's smell at a very young age. Although an infant is dependent on her mother for life, the infant also gives to her mother, for both infant and mother feed each other's emotional state and live together by bonding.

In the first days, weeks and months of a child's life, when all is dependent on the nurturing protective mother, babies begin their education. They learn about themselves and their environment through their relationship to mother. Early on, it is the mother's job to think for her daughter and figure out what she needs. She must learn to distinguish each cry and its meaning and to meet needs that are often hard to assess and even harder to satisfy. Mothers are doomed to fail a certain amount of the time. As mother nurtures her daughter, the mother's beliefs about raising children, her view of how and what girls and women are meant to be, her own feelings about herself, and her thoughts and feelings about this particular child determine what her responses will be. If a mother believes her baby is strong and healthy, the mother's touch and method of holding and caressing will be different than if she believes her baby girl is weak, helpless and fragile. If she thinks women are meant to be givers, she may resist allowing her daughter to be a receiver of her care and affection. If she thinks it is a dangerous world, she may overly protect her daughter from real and imagined fears. If she is unhappy, frightened, insecure, angry; if she is criticized, overworked, sick; if she is confused, ambivalent, uncertain, all of this will affect her parenting. Growing up is a difficult task under the best of circumstances and in whatever way the mother expresses her own imperfection, the task will be made more difficult.

> "Penelope was a tiny baby. I had a lot of trouble keeping a baby full term. I'd lost three before her. I took such good care of her. I never realized how overprotective I was until I got to know other mothers and children in public school. The things they let their kids do! I think Penelope was developmentally and socially slow for years, as a result of my pampering, protecting and worrying ways. I'm so sorry I did that to her. But I didn't know any better."

The daughter receives all of her mother's teaching—the good, the bad, the conscious and unconscious—like the most willing of students. She has no choice!

There is a sequence of learning for children that takes them through all the developmental stages that they face, and it is in these learning experiences that the child comes to know herself and her world. As an infant, a girl is learning about trust and her place in the world. Is this world safe or not safe? Does it work or not? Do I have any say in what happens?

All early learning begins with a need. For an infant these needs are about hunger, cold, tiredness, loneliness, touch and exploration. The little girl lets others know of her needs by expressing through noise and movement: loud cries, whimpers, screams, moans, coos, wiggles, clenched fists, rooting, etc. If a mother appears and helps meet her daughter's need, the baby experiences success and learns that she does have power, that the world is safe, that people are reliable and helpful and that suffering can be alleviated. A baby who is never allowed to cry or express herself, who is taken care of so quickly that she doesn't know her own needs, might well grow up to be passive and dependent.

On the other hand, a baby who is ignored and neglected when she cries might tend to think that she does not count, that people can't be trusted, and that there is no sense in expressing wants and needs because nobody will pay attention anyway.

☙ Grandmother was the unchallenged matriarch of her family. When her daughter Janine came home with her newborn, grandmother insisted that the baby learn to sleep through the night. She had Janine move Elsi's crib into the far end of the house. She shut all the doors so they couldn't hear the baby. Janine fed her when they went to bed and then again when they woke. For several nights faint cries could be heard from the far end of the house, but after the sixth night the cries were no longer heard. Janine believed that she had trained her daughter not to want to eat for those long night hours as grandmother had said she could. But as Elsi grew, friends, relatives and neighbors saw a child that had little sense of her own body: She never seemed to know if she were hungry, cold or tired, but let others tell her when to eat, go to bed and put on warm clothes. Somehow, that early lesson in denying her hunger pangs had taught Elsi a stern lesson about her own needs—ignore them.

The baby needs so many things, even this early. Some are obvious needs, like Elsi's need to eat. Others are subtler and hard to recognize. It is not enough to be fed and clothed. Long ago, it was discovered that a baby could (and probably would) die without being touched, even if all the biological needs were met. Affection, touching, hugging and stroking are as important in a baby's growth as food, safety and shelter. When a mother can express unconditional love, it will help the daughter to create a positive perception of herself and allow her to grow up with a strong sense of self-worth. If that love is conditional, in any way, or perceived as conditional, it will alter the ease with which a daughter can feel good about herself. And truthfully, can any of us as mothers not see the shades of condition that we had for our children even at this early stage?

The greatest mental and emotional "dis-ease" suffered by adults is likely to have originated at those earliest stages, when our first experience of being in the world took place. And yet, even in very difficult childhood experiences, most children come out intact, able to grow and work through whatever limitations existed. We are so adept at coping and managing our lives that we learn to survive, even in extremely difficult worlds. As children we made the best of the situations we were in, and in that process we learned ways of being that came to limit us in our adult lives. Our true and unique selves have gotten partially buried along the way. Our education with mother, while it has served to keep us alive, has also served to limit us.

Particular traumas or confused learning at this earliest symbiotic stage may show up in adult experience as generalized feelings of being discounted (not important, not existing), of not having a sense of separate identity at a very basic level ("I don't know who I am without . . ." [spouse, mate, parents]), feeling disconnected from our bodies (out of touch with bodily sensations, needs), severe lack of trust, struggling with feelings of too much or too little ("smothered" or denied baby), inability to recognize or ask for our needs to be met, or a sense of ourselves as bad without a reason.

&e Rita came to couples counseling to decide whether she and her husband should have a baby. Her opening statement was "I'm not sure I'm good enough to have a baby." As our work progressed, she came to a profound sense of feeling "not good enough" even to be alive. All through her life she had wondered whether her life was worth anything. "When I was ten, I figured out how much money my parents spent to keep me alive and I realized that if I were dead they'd have much better things to spend it on." Rita's pain felt to her like a hopeless, bottomless pit. She recalled her mother saying what a bad baby she had been, and she felt inside of herself that she had been born worthless. It will take a long time before Rita can overcome those early negating messages that she received from her parents. When she manages that, she'll be able to decide whether she wants her own child and she will be able to love that child in a way that she was not loved.

In the beginning of our lives, the stage is set, by accident, by our parents' intentions, by the best and worst of our mother, by our own efforts to grow. All the factors come together. We begin to grow up and we begin to experience and create what it means to us to be an individual. Our education is well under way.

STARTING TO LEAVE: LIFE AS A BABY

Our greatest task as a child is to become an adult. And while our body goes naturally along on its way through childhood stages, our emotional and mental world is hard put to do this job so easily. But the urge to grow and attain independence is insurmountable. Every mother knows it as she sees her child one day, crawl into another room without so much as a backward glance; and every child moves in that direction, unconsciously at first, and then consciously. Starting with the earliest games of peekaboo, the infant explores leaving and returning. Mobility, wriggling, crawling, then walking all support this movement to independence. Baby starts her earliest interest in separation at only a few weeks old, and by six or eight months each little girl has begun a full-blown investigation of her world through exploration.

Curiosity, the ability to move, growing motivation and desire to express all support the baby in her task of starting to leave. She has newfound control of and interest in her body. Playing takes on primary importance. Life is exploration. High on the list of strategies in this exploration stage is practice in leaving mother and returning to her. These are dress rehearsals for autonomy. The ideal process for this baby to explore her growing independence has mom sitting endlessly in her chair while baby leaves and returns. Baby would always know where security was and she could explore without threat of loss. Later, mom would follow baby down every path the daughter wanted to travel. And later, mom would stop and start, come and go at baby's command. At least this would be ideal from the baby's point of view. But mom doesn't stay in her chair and so little girls' exploration is fraught with uncertainty. Danger in the exploration stage is of two kinds: too much independence and not enough. Mothers walk the tightrope between the two. This precarious balance that mothers attempt to achieve lasts from that first crawl to daughter's early adult years. During all this twenty-year span (and then some) daughter is practicing, preparing and training for, and retreating from and leaping toward adulthood and autonomy.

Somewhere in this process the daughter's sense of herself as separate from her mother develops. Starting as a newborn, the daughter discovers that her mother's body is not an extension of herself, and her exploration of herself as separate continues into her adulthood, as she constantly compares and contrasts herself to her mother in her efforts to get a solid answer to the question, "Who am I?"

Life seems to support the mutually beneficial nature of timely separation. Mother and daughter both enjoy the games of peekaboo that take the daughter away from the mother, and mothers tend to feel pride, not fear, as their daughters exhibit all types of growing-up behavior from crawling, to talking, to first dates. The process of separation is naturally supported in all the stages of growth. But, inevitably, this natural process gets thwarted to one degree or another somewhere along the way. Like every flower that blossoms, a perfect unfolding is impossible. There are always rocks in the way, bugs eating the leaves, dogs running through the garden. Flowers and children have setbacks as well as advances in their growth. Even this early, a baby's efforts to begin to separate and establish an identity can be hurt. A young girl, even at one or one and a half years, can be conditioned in some pretty limiting, and sometimes frightening, ways. The results of our experimentation with exploration will stay with us for life. We may go on to feel that the world is safe, that exploration is great, that our curiosity is a good thing, or we may internalize the opposite.

᎒᎒ Betty, a thirty-four-year-old teacher from a large city, faced each new task in her life with great fear. Recently she had been so afraid of moving about in her hometown that she came for therapy. A story emerged of the eighteen-month-old, crawling through her mother's bedroom, finding and swallowing a small bobby pin. Mother gasped, grabbed her child, screaming, and rushed her to the emergency ward. In a panic she demanded they remove the bobby pin.

Betty doesn't remember what happened in the hospital, but she was there, alone, for at least a day. "Could this affect your feeling of safety in the world?" I wondered out loud. "Well, yes, but my mother saved my life." Betty couldn't help but notice my slight smile. "Are you sure you were actually in danger?" As I elaborated on the many objects discovered daily by mothers in their babies' diapers, having been swallowed and eliminated, she was shocked. When she checked out what had happened at the hospital, she found that they had just watched her for a day. Betty had not actually been in danger. Her mother had overreacted and Betty was convinced that even the most harmless possibilities were fraught with danger. Her willingness to explore had been seriously jeopardized and every movement into newness had been painful and slow for her.

Betty was overprotected. Moving toward independence and autonomy was not highly valued in her family, and her mother's fear of the world was internalized by the daughter at a very early age in a frightening and dramatic way. Another child may be given too much autonomy. With each new exploration, mother leaves her on her own. She's nowhere to be found when baby goes back for a safety check. When she hits a shyness stage, mother laughs at her, "Don't be silly, nobody's going to hurt you." For that child, exploration means abandonment: "If I go out on my own, Mommy will be gone." Another child can be endangered by lack of protection or "smothered" by too much, or taught to fear this or that, or taught not to be discerning enough. So much learned, so early.

GETTING STRONG: LIFE AS A TODDLER

If mother had trouble letting go of her baby, the toddler's more overt struggle toward independence, epitomized in the "terrible twos," will add a new dimension to the dance. The toddler, with her growing sense of power often expressed through stubbornness and defiance, challenges her mother to let go a little. Those "no's" that are the constant refrain of the two-year-old are not ultimately a problem in the parent/child relationship, though they often seem to be. Essentially, they are a way to help that child become a more individualized person.

A very important aspect of the daughter's search for self-identity comes during this first stage of defiance. At this time "no" is simply a way of saying "I'm not you." Toddlers will often say no to something they want while taking it happily. This stage, in its hardest moments, pits mother and daughter against each other in a battle of wills from which no winner emerges. But here again the daughter begins to learn some very significant lessons about the world and her place in it. Earlier, she learned about trust and the safety of exploration. The education she is receiving now is about power. The scenarios for how a baby gets messages about the world at this stage run the gamut from the child who becomes terrified of her own power because mother crumbles in the face of her daughter's anger, to the child who is forcibly put down at any evidence of self-assertion, to the child who is covertly taught that her power is bad and dangerous.

Julie's Story

🥀 "I know that I wasn't allowed to have anger as a child, nor to have power except by doing what I was supposed to. I grew up thinking that being powerful was basically not okay and anger certainly wasn't. Niceness and harmony were all-important. The bad news about that is that I didn't advocate for myself a lot in my life. When I had the right to demand something, I usually didn't. The good news is that I didn't get angry with my kids, even when they were expressing their newfound power in difficult ways. I thought they were cute and I secretly was thrilled that they could stand up for themselves. When I saw my daughter Dorothy dealing forcefully with doctors and hospital staff, advocating her own child's needs, I knew that her power was a good thing. I still feel lacking at times when I don't have the reserves of confidence and a feeling of justification for pursuing my needs."

If we are excited by and have faith in our daughter's growth toward womanhood, the twos are not so terrible. They may even be terrific as we see our daughter already trying on, in childlike fashion, her soon-to-be-adult roles. As the toddler continues her growth, the urge to do things on her own creeps into the pattern of living: Whether it is to feed herself and make a mess, to dress herself, to walk alone, or to go to bed when it suits her, the young girl soon tests her own limits and the mother is challenged to allow and support her daughter's growing power and autonomy. Letting go—which a mother must begin to do—is not pushing the baby from the nest at the first sign of wings, but letting this daughter explore what it means to be her true self.

The developmental building blocks are being stacked up for the child. In the years before school, she continues to play out most of her world experience through her mother. It is here that her education is gained. The toddler, who has already learned about trust and safety, not only has to learn about power, but also about control. Control of impulses and biological functions become issues for the growing person and for the mother, who again is forced to walk a tightrope between control and the granting of autonomy. And mother, of course, is filled with the rules and conditioning of her own life, all of which weigh heavily on the child as she is taught (allowed, encouraged, forced into . . .) toilet training, social rules, discipline.

As if this weren't enough, at the same time the little girl is learning about her feelings. Most mothers support the experience of joy, happiness and love in their daughters. After all, that really does feel like a lovely reflection of us as mothers. But how much harder it is to deal with our daughter's anger and rage at reasonable and unreasonable things. Mother may not have any permission herself to feel anger and so will deny it to her daughter. Or she may be overwhelmed and fearful at her little girl's power. And a daughter's sadness may be the hardest because it goes right to the heart of the mother who knows, remembers and deeply feels her own sadness. We often cannot let that feeling exist in our daughters. In that we may experience our own guilt and our own failure.

Dorothy's Story

ꝰ "I remember that my whole childhood I was happy. I always thought I was happy, anyway. And I can remember my mother saying, 'All I want is for you to be happy.' If that is the greatest demand a mother has on her daughter, it doesn't sound so bad. She didn't expect me to perform, be good, be neat, but she did expect me to be happy. . . . and until my teenage years I mostly was. Even in those later years, my mother tended to bail me out of every painful situation. I lost the skirt that I had made for sewing class. It was due the next day. I was miserable, of course. So Julie stayed up and helped me sew another one. I loved this, at the time. I felt that unhappiness was not appropriate. Being sad meant something was wrong. And I felt that mother promised me, in overt and covert ways, that I would never be unhappy. Well, it was inevitable that I'd have to face other emotions, and when my first marriage became so painful that I was faced with divorce, I chose to take my baby to my brother's home instead of my mother's. I somehow knew that I didn't want her to make it okay. It wasn't okay and I wanted and needed to experience that deeply. I'm much more inclined to let my children have their whole range of feelings, though it is often extremely painful for me not to save them."

No formula can be given for the specific how's of raising a toddler or child at any age. In the end, a mother's authenticity and love will be her best guides. Knowing a little bit about what makes this toddler tick may help, however, in sorting out our guidelines. A toddler is busy being concerned with herself as separate from her mother and her family. Anything that supports her growing autonomy, while continuing to offer her safety and nurturing, will help her on her way. As mothers, we must still guide and socialize this next generation of women, but we need not control and dominate them. We might ask ourselves whether we can allow our daughters to separate and whether, in fact, we can help them do so. If a mother does allow and support her daughter's natural urge to separate, she will face not being the most important thing in her daughter's world at times ("You'd rather go with Daddy?"), dealing with her daughter's feelings (sad, scared, and angry), allowing her daughter to set some of her own limits ("Do you want one or two cookies"?), letting her daughter be important to herself and have control ("Mine, mine, mine!!"), and having her daughter begin to face the consequences of her actions (not bailing her out of everything she creates). This is her education in these years. So much is learned before we ever walk into a schoolroom. These early years at mother's side set the stage for all the rest of our learnings.

HI HO, HI HO, IT'S OFF TO SCHOOL WE GO: THE LIFE OF THE CHILD

From the preschool through elementary school years, the daughter begins to actually be away from her mother's influence more and more. The stage has been set by her mother, and mother is still a dominant force and will be for many, many years. Important developments are happening for the child in these years and everything that she learns in the world will be filtered back through her relationship to mother. Mother's influence becomes subtler, but equally powerful. As the preschooler learns to think and take in information, mother's perspective will infiltrate her growing mind. Who will this child be allowed to play with? What will she be allowed to do? How will she be encouraged or limited as a thinker? How will her sex affect the way she is raised? While male role models become much more important in this stage, mother is still the model of the same sex for this female to deal with and it is at this tender age that *gender identity* is explored:

- 👾 *What is female as opposed to male?*
- 👾 *Is there a difference between boys and girls?*
- 👾 *What does it mean for me that I am a girl and not just a person?*
- 👾 *What does it mean that I am a girl, like my mother is?*
- 👾 *Am I just like her?*
- 👾 *What does a girl do? ("I better watch Mommy and see.")*

This is the beginning of an endless list of questions and concerns that start for the girl child in these early years. And the answers will be worked on for a very long time. The answers will be easier for the girl if mother represents a positive model of females. Is she happy with her sex? Does it work for her to be a woman? Is there anything she can't do/be because of being female? How a mother answers these questions by her life example will have much greater impact than her verbal responses will. Mother, as a woman, will deeply influence the little girl's sense of herself as a thinker, as a female, as a person—for better and for worse.

👾 In the play group to which her daughter belonged, Martha could not help feeling out of place. She dressed Carol Ann in dresses, every day, while most of the kids wore jeans. She asked the teachers over and over to help keep her neat and was always distressed that she came home with paint or dirt on her dresses. Another mother suggested that she put Carol Ann in jeans and Martha responded that it was Carol Ann, not she, who insisted on dresses. And if you asked Carol Ann, true to her mother's word, she would request a dress.

Carol Ann, at age four, already had a firm image of what a female should be and she wanted to be that. Her instincts to play and explore conflicted with her image of being female. While she struggled to stay neat, her creative urge kept leaking out and she would find herself knee deep in mud or paint, enjoying herself thoroughly, only to be confronted at a later time with how she had violated her "femaleness." Carol Ann became more and more conflicted, her mother more and more concerned. Martha didn't see that she had made the decision for Carol Ann by the values and emphases she placed on how to be a girl. Only when she actively supported her daughter in being other than a "neat, good pretty girl" did Carol Ann's conflict lessen. For Carol Ann and every one of us as children, the building blocks of our lives are firmly in place by the time we venture off to school. Each stage of our life, with its new experiences, builds on our old foundation.

The elementary school years take the girl to new focuses. She is concerned with friendships, belonging and accomplishments. This is largely a period of how-to's in life. How to: be a friend, have a friend, deal with school, feel good about myself, please my parents, break away a little more from my mother (and keep her close by, as well), how to survive mistakes, how to concentrate, how to be giving and how to get, how to be a female, how to be me, how to be. . . . Mother's input will continue to be felt and daughter will start making conscious choices about herself that will ally with her mother or put her in opposition. But these will be minor. For now, playing at being a woman is a major strategy for learning. Playing "grown-up" will take many forms, from the way girls stick together, to the clothes they wear (or wish they could), to the make-believe games they play, to their secret hopes and dreams—all of which point to their impending emergence as adult women.

Dorothy's Story

᪥ "By the time my daughter was ten, she and her friends didn't play 'house' anymore as they had when they were younger ('You be the mommy, I'll be the daddy'), nor did they play with dolls. But they did play 'women,' a variety of games that put them in women's roles, ranging from poor, homeless women (a favorite outdoor game), to maids, to rich women with maids, to rock stars, to business owners. Men were only hastily sketched background figures in their play. These games were about being adult women and all of what that might mean. It was often a joy to watch them, but sometimes quite frightening as I saw them struggling with some pretty big issues (abuse, poverty, sexuality, war)."

The struggle with big issues intensifies for the girl child who moves into adolescence and young adulthood with a tremendous need for her mother.

APPROACHING WOMANHOOD: THE LIFE OF A YOUNG WOMAN

The struggle for independence and adulthood takes its hardest turn in the teenage years, when mother sees only too well that her daughter is leaving, and with that she faces all her fears—for herself and her daughter—and she puts out her concluding effort to help her child. Mother is so important at this stage because it is her last chance, in some significant way, to have an impact on her daughter.

To do this a mother may serenely or, in panic, use this time to get in her final two cents' worth. She may try to mold, teach, train, control, discipline or scare her daughter during this period—in the name of helping! Daughter sees all this, too. Her fear is matched with excitement and anticipation. She deeply feels her adulthood coming and the need to leave her mother becomes more and more pressing, even though this may well be as hard for the daughter as it is for the mother. At this stage all of the younger woman's images of mother and of woman begin to coalesce. Her years of playing dolls, and modeling adult women in any way that she could, begin to be defined into ideas of what a woman is, how she should be, how much of mother she wants to be like and not be like, what other models she can find to draw on.

This is an age of best friends and role models. Best friends serve to nurture the impending adult by giving girls a place to talk, share and fantasize their lives as women. Both consciously and unconsciously they play more and more into adult ways. This is also the age of role models. There are female idols (big sisters, teachers) and subtler role models (book characters)—all of whom begin to be taken in as possibilities. There are also villains: females (models and in real life) who are seen as what it is not okay to be. These influences begin to mold the consciousness of the soon-to-be woman in ways that will become visible as she steps into that adult role.

🐝 Janet's mother, a feminist before her time, raised her daughter from her youngest days to be autonomous, nondependent, powerful—as she herself was. Janet bought the line, talked a good show and left home when she was seventeen, with mother's blessing, to go create a meaningful life for herself. But her meaningful life ended up being a never-ceasing attachment to one man after another, several ending in unwanted pregnancies, all ending in feelings of anger and abandonment. Janet had only learned how to pretend to be a grown-up woman.

Whatever we adopt as guidelines in these formative years will set the stage for how we are as adults. Janet mimicked her mother, as Carol Ann had. What her mother had expressed and believed in may have been authentic for her mother, but it was just a fraud for Janet, who had never come to know herself. The answers to the questions that she asked were too pat. Mother made it look too easy, too one-sided, and put too heavy a burden on Janet to be the right way.

All of what it means to be an adult is put on the line during these last years in our mother's home. And the questions and answers should not be taken lightly. Sex, money, career, relationships, religion are all part of the exploration. Sexual attraction begins to emerge. And the daughter, facing the whole new world of adulthood, autonomy and sexuality, is also reviewing—in fact, recycling—every other childhood stage she has been through. The need to play it all out again is done as a way of internalizing learnings, righting earlier wrongs, checking on mom's continued role in our lives. As a daughter plays out this "regrowing up," she may well make mom the bad guy a fair share of the time (not the terrible twos again) or she may ask mom to rescue her. She will certainly struggle with the limits that are placed on her, reacting particularly to mother's limits, looking for, in mother, both an ally and a foil for her growing up.

In truth, this teenage person is beginning to have her own set of values, her own ideas about the world and herself, a real, deep-seated sense of her uniqueness that cannot be squashed. Her moral sense; a personal experience of spirituality; the true ability to see through another's eyes and to respond for another's sake and not for one's own; and a burgeoning sense of right and wrong, of meaning and value, and of personal integrity develop in these teenage and early-adult years. This developing sense of morality, conscience and spirituality, as well as each young woman's uniqueness, blends into the crucial need to solidify ego and personality, to become a strong individual, to fit and to make it in the world. Efforts to balance internal concerns with external social and identity needs can be quite painful. The outer pressures from peers as well as family may deny or oppose inner truths. "Can I express my true self [feelings, beliefs, talents] and still be accepted?" All of these factors play into the need to define this self that she is (as woman and person) and it is no easy matter. And in the background, mother still looms large: as a model or villain or some of both, as someone to hold on to in order to soothe the troubling waters of life, or someone to get away from to save oneself.

What does it mean to you, the reader, to be an adult woman? Every answer that you can come up with is part of what the child/now teenager/now young adult must begin to understand. Some of what she needs to know will have been taught her, but much of what she needs to learn hasn't been learned yet, or has been taught through mother's eyes and is in conflict with the daughter's own sense. Finally, this teenage girl sets her life to answering every important question that can be asked about herself—as a woman and as a person. And the next ten or more years are the search for and creation of those answers.

PLAYING WITH BLOCKS

By the time we are twenty-one, we have gone through many stages of development, each one with its own tasks, its own needs, its own set of learnings to be gained. If we think of them as blocks, we will know that a tower constructed solidly, evenly and consistently will serve us best. Each block will rest on the other; each learning becomes a foundation for the next. But the tower may be tilted, some learnings lost, the foundation shaky. The tower may be at risk of tumbling down or perhaps the stack of blocks, while crooked, will still be solid and unique.

A young woman learns about: • Values • Choices • Loving • Sexuality • Inclusion • Scripts • Identity • Ego	**What doesn't work for the young woman?**
A schoolgirl learns about: • Thinking • Reality • Gender Identity • Pleasure • Giving and Taking • How-To's	**What doesn't work for the schoolgirl?**
A toddler learns about: • Separation • Feelings • Anger • Limits • Control • Self-Importance • Power	**What doesn't work for the toddler?**
A baby learns about: • Exploration • Motivation • Curiosity • Expression • Playing • Her Body	**What doesn't work for the baby?**
A newborn learns about: • Trust • Comfort • Needs • Sensation • Feeding • Safety • Having an Impact	**What doesn't work for the newborn?**

With each stage of development, different areas and abilities come into focus for the daughter to explore. Each child, as her tower of blocks is built, needs to learn everything necessary to become an adult! The syllabus is endless, but the major tasks include learning about:

trust	self-importance	assessing reality
comfort	feelings	(versus fantasy)
sensation	pleasure	mistakes
safety	love	both sexes
exploration	imagination	learning to do
motivation	thinking	creating

impulse	friendship	work
needs	belonging	values
curiosity	giving and taking	loyalty
bodies	authority figures	spirituality
separation	logic	personality
limits	the ability to argue	intuition
exploration	choices	meaning
power	gender identity	and more . . .

The struggle toward independence is shared by mother and daughter. The mother has her own views and beliefs about how and when a daughter should grow up and the daughter asserts her own version of how to do it. The best development assumes a compromise, in which the daughter's urges toward growth, autonomy, separation, and adulthood are supported and honored in an environment that is created to be safe by the mother. No matter how the process unfolds for an individual, patterns of thinking and behaving develop in our growing years; decisions are made in the child's mind with the available knowledge, and many of these carry over into adulthood as unconscious ways of looking at the world and the people in it. It is in these years with mother as our teacher that the deeply buried roots of our conditioning are formed, nurtured and, in all too many cases, set in stone.

WORKBOOK

We may have little actual memory of our early childhood. Often, the clearest images are those from photographs or from the stories told in the family as we grow up. We are more likely to have a "felt sense" of childhood, and vague images and memories may float in and out of awareness. It is not crucial for our work in uncovering and growing that we have clear memories. It is enough that we know ourselves today. The detective work we do, stemming from our own present experience, will give us all the information that we need. As you work in the next two chapters on issues from the past, allow yourself a lot of leeway in exploring. If you have ideas, memories, thoughts, suspicions or fantasies about your childhood, let them come out. Each one points to an experience you have internalized, even if it does not represent an actual, factual memory. So trust your process in this work.

☙ My Mother and Me ❧

In this exercise we invite the child within you to reemerge. She is not so far buried as you might think. The adult you, with all your thinking about childhood, would do this exercise in a very different way. This one is for the child. In letting your inner child speak, you'll get a deeper sense of your own uniqueness and the conditioning that your childhood brought you. You will begin to feel and know the steps that your life involved, so many years ago.

Use crayons and a pencil for this one and give yourself plenty of time to enjoy it.

First, think about yourself as a child between the ages of three and eight. If you can get an image of that little girl, do so. A photograph from that period would be particularly evocative! When you have a sense of that little girl—what she looks like, her age and the name she was called—imagine that you are that child. Say to yourself, "I am _____, I am _____ years old. I live _____," etc. Fill out the picture of yourself as a child. Then with your nondominant hand (this is most important: righties, use the left, lefties use the right) draw a picture of yourself and your mother: a picture of yourself, the little girl, and your mother as she was to you when you were little. This is kindergarten and that's the assignment. Draw it any way you like, draw any mood or feeling, draw more than one picture if you like. One rule: Don't edit! Let the picture come easily and playfully from the child.

After you've finished your picture, write a story to go with it. Write it in the language and experience of the child.

When you are done, shift back to your adult self and think about this experience. What do you know about your inner child? Was she sad? happy? confused? outgoing? Take some notes about yourself as a child. Can you view this child compassionately and without blame or do you find yourself having a harsh and critical attitude toward her? Think about this child lovingly. It is crucial that you find acceptance and love for yourself. And remember: Every child deserves to be loved!

🙠 How Was I Built? 🙢

The building blocks of our lives help us learn everything we need to know to be an adult. As we have noticed, in ourselves and in the world, most lives are not built perfectly. When we think about the developmental stages that every child goes through and the important learnings that we need in order to function as whole human beings, we are sure to notice areas of weakness, distortion and confusion in ourselves. Take this opportunity to speculate about your own development.

Perhaps you will be able to right the blocks that are out of alignment when you begin to see what they are.

Look at the block image below that sums up an ideal development. In the blank blocks, starting at the bottom, fill in your development as it corresponds to the stages listed. Note what you learned and didn't in each phase. Be aware of stages that you need to learn more about. Mark in areas of hurt/ "stuckness"/confusion. When you are done, spend some time assessing what you need in order to strengthen the developmental tower. What do you need to learn or relearn or unlearn as an adult?

A young woman learns about: • Values • Choices • Loving • Sexuality • Inclusion • Scripts • Identity • Ego	
A schoolgirl learns about: • Thinking • Reality • Gender Identity • Pleasure • Giving and Taking • How-To's	
A toddler learns about: • Separation • Feelings • Anger • Limits • Control • Self-Importance • Power	
A baby learns about: • Exploration • Motivation • Curiosity • Expression • Playing • Her Body	
A newborn learns about: • Trust • Comfort • Needs • Sensation • Feeding • Safety • Having an Impact	

❧ A Woman Is. . . . ❧

Wherever our exploration of being a woman went when we were children, it certainly created many of the images that we hold today of what women could and should be. Some of these images serve us and some limit us. Does our image of Woman primarily point to the roles that we have been taught or does it allow for individuality and uniqueness? Does our image include being a person and a female?

This exercise requires a few magazines, anything that you can cut up. Cut out images from magazines of women and anything that women relate to. You may want to cut out, as well, words that represent the meaning of being a woman. When you have a bunch of images, make a collage that represents your image of Woman. Let your imagination run the show, and don't bother to think about this. Cut whatever draws your attention, and paste in the same way—jumbled or organized, logical or illogical, it doesn't matter. (An alternative is simply to draw many of the images and ideas that you have about being a woman.)

When you are done, ask yourself a few questions:

- What does this image of Woman say to me?
- Is this image of Woman limited in any way?
- What are those ways?
- What strengths and potentials are seen in this image of Woman?
- How would I like to change this collage to make it represent Woman in her greatest potential?
- What do I want to keep, inside myself, from this image of Woman?

If you want to, change the collage in any way that helps it represent an ideal model of Woman and let yourself know that you are always growing toward that ideal.

CHAPTER THREE

Many, Many Messages

"MOTHER, MAY I GO OUT TO SWIM?"
"YES, MY DARLING DAUGHTER. HANG YOUR
CLOTHES ON A HICKORY LIMB, AND
DON'T GO NEAR THE WATER."

—*Folk rhyme*

MOTHER TALKED ABOUT EVERYTHING

In the course of our growing up with mother, she gave us many, many messages. Mother may have talked about everything or she may have avoided talking about some things, but we received messages from her all the time, about almost everything. Mother was always onstage, modeling for her daughters the complete range of experiences that life has to offer. A mother's every act is a message, whether witnessed by the daughter or not. The messages mother sends, consciously and unconsciously, are taken in by the daughter as her own way of understanding the world and her own role in life. Messages come in all disguises: verbal and nonverbal, direct and

indirect, overt and covert, clear and ambiguous. They come as statements, gestures, commands, modeled behavior, omissions, attitudes
and more. Messages are directed at who we are, how we are, what we
should do, what our potential is, and what our mother wants and
doesn't want from us and for us.

Messages come from all directions and sources to bombard and
shape us as children. Messages a father sends to his daughter during
certain stages in her development have great power in shaping her
sense of the opposite sex and her potential for relating to men.
Cultural messages she receives from society play an influential role
in how she thinks she should be, especially when those messages are
supported by parents or significant others. Siblings, teachers and
friends all send messages, but in most cases the strongest and potentially most limiting or expanding ones come from mother.

A daughter, so often considered by her mother as an extension of
herself, is the logical target for mother's hopes and expectations—and
all of these are passed on in some form of message. Even during her
pregnancy a woman dreams of her baby and makes plans about how
to raise her. Who and how mother is will determine the thrust of the
messages that she gives her daughter. Depending upon her feelings of
self-esteem and self-worth, her values, her conditioning and her limitations, as well as her own internalized messages and her uniqueness,
a mother will give or withhold tenderness, love, nurturing, care,
appreciation, joy, interest and more. She constantly indicates acceptance or rejection of her daughter by the messages she gives. From the
first, the daughter must and does tune in to cues and clues about how
welcome she is and in what way she is most acceptable to her mother.
Her safety depends upon reading those messages correctly.

While we heard messages about everything, the most important
ones were those that dealt with us, in one way or another. Those messages form the core of our feelings about our self-worth and ourselves.
They are the basis for our conditioning and it is with these limiting

or negating messages that our work to change must be done. How a child internalizes, and thus believes, a message she hears depends upon the intensity and frequency of the message, the age of the child when she hears it, the power of the giver, and whether the message is contradicted or challenged by another message.

Messages may be clear, straight messages or they may be conflicting. Mother may say that girls are meant to be wives and she may validate this by her commitment to her husband. She may reinforce this message by discounting and not appreciating the daughter's achievements in other areas of the child's life. As hard as that message is to take and as limiting as it is to the daughter, nevertheless it is a clear message and at a later time the daughter may well be able to override it. However, a mother may say to her daughter, "You can be anything you want," but when she does nothing to support that message and, in fact, opposes it in overt and covert ways, the daughter will be left with an even more confusing view of herself and the world.

❧ Frances is a twenty-three-year-old teacher. She had this to say about her own messages: "My mother said that she was interested in what I did and how I felt, but she never came to school when I was in a play. She never heard me sing in the choir, and when I won the athletic award in seventh grade she didn't even come to the ceremony. I guess keeping the perfect house and playing bridge were more important to her than I was."

When a daughter receives conflicting or mixed messages, which is she to believe? In most cases the nonverbal, underlying message will be the more powerful. Frances experienced this in a painful and limiting way. From her extroverted, outgoing manner in junior high, she changed and became more withdrawn and therefore limited her own possibilities. Frances was responding to that sad and defeated feeling that she expressed above. She finally learned by her mother's omissions—not her words—that she was not very valuable or important as a person.

Luckily for mothers and daughters alike, every word we say, every outburst or regrettable comment is *not* internalized. In fact, our daughters have a great capacity to ignore, or push away, much of what we say. The messages that finally hurt are the ones that represent a *real* theme or pattern in the child's life. Mother's consistent presence will, like the blows of the hammer, nail certain messages firmly in place. These messages may reflect the best or the worst of mother and so may be expansive or limiting to her daughter. Remember Rita in the last chapter. She had deeply internalized the message that she was a bad baby, so much so that she believed this to be true even as an adult. Her mother's ever-present negation ate away at Rita. Amy, on the other hand, had her mother's positive influence to offset a hostile, abusive father.

> "My father was often nasty and critical to me, but Mom was always in the background telling me I was okay, supporting and stroking me. I feel anger at my father, but I don't feel crippled by him. When life is hard, it's Mother's words I hear."

The messages that are most important to decipher are the ones that unconsciously continue to limit and hurt us as adults. What messages did we get as children? Were we told we were smart or stupid, good or bad, capable or incapable? Was it okay to be a girl? What limits did being female place on us? What was our role in relationship to men? to other women? to ourselves? In the building blocks of our lives, we learned about being female, about sex, money, God, about life, danger, values, clothes, food, children, bodies, men, women, love, death and more from messages given overtly and covertly. It's not hard to pull some of those messages to consciousness and to see their effects.

Sandy is thirty-eight years old and works in the peace movement. Her mother always corrected her as a child and told her how important it was that she look good, not only physically but also in every impression that she made on people. Her father had abandoned her mother when Sandy was four and she had raised Sandy alone in difficult financial circumstances. Her mother thought that finding a new husband to support them was terribly important. She groomed and presented herself to this end and constantly groomed and presented Sandy in a similar "perfect" manner, until Sandy lost all confidence in her inherent self.

When Sandy was still a young woman, struggling to make it in the world, she chose to have herself sterilized. It was clear to her that children were a burden in one's efforts to make it in the world. She had been a burden for her mother, who never did manage to remarry. Sandy believed that she couldn't afford such an extra burden in an already difficult effort to be "perfect." In therapy, Sandy presented herself saying, "I need help to become a better person." What was rapidly revealed was her deep sense of insecurity and inadequacy. The message she had received was that she was not and could not be enough.

Sandy had learned how important it was to "look good" in the world, and she had added her own interpretation to her mother's message: that children made that impossible. The combination of her mother's clear and limiting messages and her own interpretation, based on her hurt as a child, added up to a powerful and painful reality for Sandy as an adult.

As we begin to sort out our internalized messages, it is important to find out how our own uniqueness, our beliefs, desires and our confusions colored the messages that we received. Remember, we are not just the product of our conditioning. Sandy's mother gave her some hard messages, but didn't tell her that she shouldn't have children. Out of her own pain and sorrow in childhood and her efforts to understand how to be, Sandy added to the equation and made an early decision that would affect her the rest of her life. To free ourselves, we also need to know mother's intent in passing on that message. Why did she treat me that way? Did I misinterpret her intention? What life circumstances affected that message? Does the message really mean what I think it does?

Lena and her sister began to sort their hurtful messages out and so began to be free of them, free to act for their own best interests, not solely in opposition to their mother, and free to love their mother in ways that they had been unable to before because of their reaction to early stifling messages.

ᘍ Zelda came to a workshop with her two daughters, Lena and Ursula. Zelda was miserable, angry, scared. Her daughters felt guilty, angry and resentful of her demands. Zelda didn't like her daughters' "radical" lifestyles. Her eldest daughter had married, "My God, a Buddhist," and her youngest was a "hippie." The daughters, of course, were protecting their right to make their own decisions. Often their decisions were made just to feel free of their mother's demands. The messages they had always received were about the *one* right way to do things. The relationship had deteriorated almost to the point of no return.

Zelda began to talk about her early life in Germany under Hitler, her gnawing fear, her loss of her mother in the war and the ferocity of her efforts to protect her daughters from the horrors she had experienced. Both daughters began to change their view of their mother and of her messages. They began to be able to review those messages in an open way. They let go of a great deal of their anger toward her and were able to be with her in a new way, not blindly and reactively, but with compassion.

It was still hard for Zelda to allow her daughters to be themselves. She still felt so much pain and fear, based on her own cruel conditioning. Even though they all still struggled with the conflicts in beliefs and values, this understanding of intention and conditioning opened up a great world of love and caring to each one of them.

The messages mothers send, like Zelda's, are rarely sent with a conscious intent to hurt, undermine or confuse daughters. In most cases the messages come from an unconscious thought process. All of these messages, given with varied but generally good intention, can and often do create limiting outcomes for the adult woman. Yet as adults, we are able to come to know and change whatever messages we received.

Dorothy's Story

"I believed, as surely as I believed in the rising of the sun, that having a baby would be the most meaningful experience of my life and that it would erase all traces of doubt and anxiety about my place in the world. I don't think my mother told me this would happen in so many words, but in her behavior, in her stories about her life, and in how important I perceived myself to be to her, I came to think this was absolutely true. When my son was born, I faced a crisis of meaning. With all the love and commitment that I felt toward him, I felt a painful lack in my life. This caused me to suffer. And, I sadly suspect, it hurt my son—on whom I had placed the great burden of bringing meaning into my life. Being a mother wasn't enough. It was then, when my son was quite young, that I embarked on a career path. I was fortunate in being able to understand what I needed and to sort out those needs in relationship to old messages. This balance of parenting and career seems to represent who I truly am more fully than either alone could."

We can learn about the limiting messages we received, as Dorothy did, and we can re-choose. We do not need to be limited. We are not fated to repeat old patterns, or live out unconsciously internalized messages. To peel away the conditioning that exists in these messages we will have to know the messages. To do this we may be helped by looking at the various types of messages that may limit, condition or define us.

Shoulds and Oughts

"Shoulds" and "oughts" comprise, unfortunately, a large percentage of the messages that children hear, and these come in two varieties: the shoulds and oughts about behavior and the shoulds and oughts about being.

Injunctions are strong forms of shoulds and oughts that relate to the core of the child's being. Everyone has many no's in a lifetime and these are necessary for society and growing up; however, an injunction, aimed more at a child's being rather than her doing, is the most powerful message given. "Don't think you're so smart." "Don't think you are better than your mother." "Don't wear pants, you look more like a boy than a girl." These are injunctions that infiltrate children's thinking systems and insidiously alter the concepts they have of themselves. The injunctions a mother gives us set the stage for our future lives.

ॐ Lee is in therapy because of relationship issues. "I heard my mother over and over again saying, 'Don't be trapped, as I was. Don't trust men.' I was never sure what I wasn't to trust about men, so

I just avoided them. Now I realize that I like men, but I have a long way to go before I learn how to be easy and comfortable in their presence. I wish I hadn't wasted so much time." Lee's mother had been married to an alcoholic who had deserted the family. It was no wonder that she felt this way. But in tracing the family history we discovered that Lee's grandmother had also been wary of men. Lee carried a long-standing message into her own life as an adult, without even understanding it— but acting on it all the same.

Many injunctions are passed down from grandmother to mother to daughter. They are values that have been swallowed without reflection and later pop up as strong commands on how to live. They may be moral beliefs or personal idiosyncrasies. Injunctions have a powerful influence because they are believed so completely by the person who says them. They are not open to discussion or consideration, but are considered to be truth. Often, injunctions are given in anger or with strong emotion, especially when a mother sees her daughter straying away from her own beliefs and values. Our memory of childhood injunctions may lie dormant for many years, but a particular incident can push injunctions into the foreground during adulthood just as if a switch had been turned on.

🙝 Bea has come to understand the injunctions that still define her behavior. "We lived in war-torn Greece when I was growing up. My mother never raised her voice in anger, but I could feel her fury and fear if I shouted or made noise. The don't-make-noise, don't-be-noticed message was strong and necessary for survival. But today when my children shout or play loudly, I feel that same fury and fear and I do raise my voice unreasonably and really threaten them. It's almost as if I have no power to stop myself."

Injunctions run the gamut from "Don't exist," the most detrimental injunction possible, to the more superficial injunctions about every aspect of life. All of a child's needs in life, the stages and aspects of development that she goes through, will be met by mother with either an injunction, a "no," or with a permission, a "yes." When a child receives a "Don't exist" message, she will play that out by being invisible, insignificant and unimportant; and if the message is strong enough, she will die. Some of the whoppers that we may have thrust upon us, and which will alter the course of our lives, include:

- "Don't feel"
- "Don't think"
- "Don't be who you are"
- "Don't be a child"
- "Don't grow up"
- "Don't succeed"

The variations are extensive. Here are a few of the common ones:

- "Don't be your sex" ("Girls are not okay")
- "Don't be sexual" ("Sex is not okay")
- "Don't trust men" ("Men are not okay")
- "Don't trust women" ("Women are not okay")
- "Don't fail" ("Be perfect")
- "Don't be happy" ("Be serious")
- "Don't be sad" ("Feelings are bad")

The list is infinite. And the variations are uniquely created by the message that the child receives.

꿈 Blanche is fifty-three, the mother of three grown children, divorced. She works as a librarian, owns her own home, is working on a doctorate. Blanche's father was the bigwig in the family.

Mother passed on the message overtly that women could be good in music and the arts, but not in other areas, and certainly they couldn't make it on their own. The covert message was that women were to be dependent, like children, and her messages to Blanche were "Don't grow up" and "The only happiness is in a good marriage." Blanche's marriage was painfully unsuccessful. Unconsciously rebelling against her limited permissions, her beginning career as a concert pianist fell flat as she first confronted the message about her inability to succeed. She finally left her husband, bought her own home, developed a satisfactory career, and enjoyed her music as a pastime. She started to override the early childhood injunctions that she had seen as the only way to lead her life. Even at the height of her successful, fulfilling life, she would sometimes find herself feeling like a child, thinking she was unsuccessful, and feeling afraid of making it on her own. When the old messages would suddenly and painfully creep back, Blanche had to keep rethinking and reaffirming her new lifestyle and writing new messages that supported her in her life today.

Whenever we say or think "I can't" or "I should," there is a strong possibility that we are responding to internal parental messages that we have hidden in the recesses of our minds. Those areas of life that we dare not approach ("I could never write a book"), those goals that we wouldn't take on for ourselves ("I'd love to be athletic, but I know I couldn't be"), those negative feelings and experiences that seem inevitable ("Well, I'm just not a happy person; that's just the way I am"), those roles and ideals that we feel inevitably bound by ("Really, I am only a mother, and that's what I do well, so I'll just keep doing that")—deep-seated beliefs that define our lives—point to injunctions that are still in effect.

Many of these injunctions, these "shoulds" and "oughts" will haunt and stifle us for years unless we take time to sort them out. The key to unraveling shoulds and choosing our own values and beliefs and our own sense of ourselves is to think each through and evaluate it. Injunctions are the same as any unfounded, unconsidered stance in life. They are the cornerstones of prejudices. As societies support injunctions, they become the "isms" that are so limiting: sexism, ageism, racism, classism, heterosexism. . . . After all, what are these other than injunctions: messages received and repeated about the way things are—false and inaccurate messages. Individually, injunctions define and limit a woman's possibilities. When we fail, feel inadequate, doubt ourselves and our worth, operate in constricted or frightened ways, we are likely to find an injunction lurking within us, a strong inhibitor that puts us in a cell.

WHAT'S SHE LIKE? (WHO'S SHE LIKE?)

While injunctions come at us like well-aimed arrows, messages that affect us equally strongly are often covert. The thoughts and ideas that our mothers have about us are often expressed in ways that even they don't realize. These subtle messages, called attributes, often reflect some of our mothers' deepest feelings about us. These are the guerilla warfare of messages, so fast, so quick to sting that they are barely noticed. We are encouraged to be a certain way simply by being told repeatedly that we are that way. Being given attributes, negative or positive, is somewhat like being hypnotized. If we are hypnotized and told that we are thirsty, we will begin to feel that way: We are not given the opportunity to assess whether we are thirsty or not. A similar process takes place when attributions are hammered into a child.

Julie's Story

"'Julie is so sweet and helpful. She does everything for the family and even her friends.' I heard this all my life. My mother said of my brother, 'He's so smart,' and of my sister, 'She's so cute'—but I was 'sweet.' For a long time I interpreted this to mean that it didn't matter about my intellect or ambitions; being sweet was enough. And I think it was enough for my parents. But that is only being half a person and very empty. What I thought or created was never important, only that I was sweet and took care of people. That attribute was so firmly in place in our family that when I suggested to my mother that I quit college one week before I was to graduate so I could have a June wedding, she and my father readily agreed. It wasn't until I was a longtime wife and mother that I began to appreciate myself as something other than sweet. I went back to school then, and I remember the joy I felt when I was told that I was a clear thinker."

Everyone is subjected to attributes, but girls are likely to be given certain stereotyped attributions that attempt to define their behavior in "good girl" ways or comment on their physical being from the "beautiful women" standpoint. As a child, these models will often be the reference point from which attributes are given to us, in a conscious or unconscious effort to create in us these "perfect" ways, or as a response to any indications that we are not these "perfect" ways.

Girls who are made into "beautiful women" and are admired just for their beauty often see themselves only as adornments. Who they are and what they can do never seem as important as how they look. Doreen often says in anger, "Don't tell me I'm beautiful, tell me that I'm smart and clever and competent." Girls given the opposite message suffer equally: Lea says, "I know why I'm not married. I'm not good-looking, and that's what men see first. I never will be either."

Girls' behavior is attributed in the same way: "My daughter is not only sweet, but neat. How lucky I am!" "Gail's a tomboy. I don't know what to do about her!" "I know you want to make your mommy happy, sweetie." The power of even the subtlest attributes can be seen over and over. Attributes come in many forms: how our mother refers to us, who she says we are like, qualities that she attributes to us, names that she calls us. And mother, often unconsciously, is mimicking her culture, the messages she received and, in this day and age, the ever-present media that limits girls and women with a whole host of painfully limiting injunctions.

Do you think of yourself as being "just like" someone in your family (or *unlike* someone)? When the family, and especially mother, lets you know that you are just like, or not at all like, your Aunt Gertrude, your sister, your father, the minister, your married cousin Linda, the bad girl next door, "my father, who was a bum and a no-account," etc., the message has deep relevance.

Everyone "loved" Hannah's Aunt Mary, and thought Hannah was quite a bit like her. Mary had been a rebel in her youth, had challenged the limits of women's roles and was just a bit eccentric. Aunt Mary was also single and, by the time Hannah was in therapy, Mary was eighty, still single, embittered and more than a little crazy. Hannah was in her late thirties. She had also been somewhat of a rebel, had stretched the limits of women's roles and appreciated about herself her unique qualities (eccentricity). But she had fears about never having a relationship and finally came to see that she had almost bought into the model of Mary—lock, stock and barrel. When she realized that, she was understandably worried about her future and took some positive actions to conquer the negative sides of those attributes that she had adopted. She didn't want to be "like her Aunt Mary" anymore.

Attributes fill our lives. Even the name we were given is likely to have a meaning that attempts, in some way, to define us. Names are one of the first messages that we receive and our names often have a tremendous impact on us.

Dorothy's Story

"I was named after a great aunt, a woman revered and respected in my family. She was a churchwoman and missionary. The name means 'gift of God' and the qualities that I associated with that name were love, acceptance and service. I appreciate the heritage passed on to me through that name.

"But the problems it created were also intense. My family bought into the idea that I was the peacemaker in the family. The name and associations to it affirmed that role and I often played it out, neglecting and denying my own feelings and needs."

The names children are given may indicate the parents' confusion about the child, any ambivalence they might have toward the child's sex (usually directed at girls), or the parents' concerns with themselves rather than the child:

"I named my daughter after my father, James. He was such a great man: strong, successful and a great comfort to me. I want Jamie to be just like him."

"I never cared what I was called because there were five girls in my family and each of us had first names that began with B. I ended up being called 'Baby' most of the time."

"My mother named me after her. I am Susanna, she Suzanne. But she never called me that. It was always 'Silly' or 'Sassy.' I always felt unworthy of her name."

"I named my daughter Faith. She was my last child and my only daughter. I really needed a girl to feel whole."

Not only the name itself, but also the continuing and varying uses of the name are messages to the child. First, middle and last names, as well as nicknames, all carry a message, especially as the parents empower the message by using the names to affect the child. How often we see a friendly nickname dropped in anger in favor of the full name, or a nickname used to tell the child covertly a feeling that the parent has. Even as an adult woman you may not have come to terms with your name. It may still ring in your ears with the sound of your mother's voice. You may have rejected the name altogether or altered it. You may be adamant about its being used in one specific way.

"I can't stand to be called Elizabeth, because my mother only called me that when she was furious. So I'm still 'Betsy,' even though it doesn't feel adult."

"Never call me Dotty!"

"I finally changed my name, 'Leaf,' because it just didn't work in the stock market."

"Neither 'Barb,' 'Barbie,' 'Babs,' or 'Barbara' worked for me—and I've tried them all. My name just reminds me of my confusion."

"I hated my nickname, 'Nutsy.' It was a takeoff on my last name, but it hurt, especially when my mother laughed if I told her to call me Janet."

And sometimes a name becomes an active struggle in a family: One woman will have her own choice about how to use the name she is given; another will meet with resistance from her mother or daughter, who will try to maintain the status quo, keep power, and hold on to the attributes she values for the other.

❦ "My name is Katherine—that's my given name—and I've always liked it. When I was growing up I was called 'Kitty,' which is also my great-grandmother's nickname. I never liked the name Kitty, but I lived with it for quite a while. Then, seven years ago, I chose to be called Katherine for the first time, because I felt that I had grown into the magnitude of the name. Now, the only person who hasn't adjusted to the change of name is my mother, and she still calls me Kitty. It's like having an incredible struggle. She just won't change. She will not grant me my identity. Why not? Why won't she let me be Katherine?"

❦ "My daughter would never call me by my first name, even though I asked. She called me 'Mommy' at cocktail parties and had her kids call me 'Grammy,' even though I wanted them just to call me 'Lisa.' I don't understand it. I don't want to be just a mother anymore."

Katherine's question, "Why won't she let me be Katherine?" more deeply stated, is "Why won't she let me be me?" So, too, for Lisa, who wasn't allowed to be the way she wanted to be. In just one name, we have seen the pain and struggle of a mother/daughter pair. All the anguish, love, pain and confusion played out in the battle of Kitty/Katherine, the battle of Mommy/Lisa!

Attributes are everywhere. It would not be possible or desirable for a mother to give her daughter none. We would have to walk around with our mouths closed, with our thoughts and hopes and dreams stifled. An attribute is a problem only when it is limiting. A limiting attribute is one that is repeated often, that does in fact express a true (though perhaps partial) sentiment of the giver, that does not allow for alternate perspectives:

- "My daughter is *hopeless*."
- "She'll never make it."
- "Alice is *so* pushy."
- "This is my *shy* daughter."
- "Bibi's like her *crazy* sister!"
- "She's smart, but *not* very *pretty*."

One-liners, like these, given as a message in oh-so-many ways, will be terrible, limiting attributes.

SOME THINGS ARE OKAY WITH MOM

However, for all the bad news about messages, there is some good news as well. If we are alive to read this, then we are more than the injunctions and limiting attributes that were given to us. Mom must have given us some permissions and these are significant. We have permission to exist, probably to think, maybe to be inquisitive and to grow. Permissions come in various ways, ranging from the direct, such as to go swimming or to college, to the subtle, those implying that it is all right to behave or think in a certain way. And in order to accomplish anything in life we need a permission to do so. Originally we need these from our parents and, particularly, our mother. Those that mother gave us will likely have profound and long-lasting value. If mother didn't give us permissions that we needed, we will have had to find another way to get or give ourselves permission for each new task that life offers.

"What permissions do we need?" we asked a group of women in a workshop. In a few moments they began a list that could go on and on. "We need permission," they said:

"to do for myself,   to have needs and express
to be in a good relationship,   them,

to be angry,
to disagree,
to please myself without
   feeling guilty,
to take risks,
to feel little,
to not always be the problem
   solver,
to be an adult,
to think,

to be sexual in whatever
   way I want,
to be single,
to have children,
to not have children,
to choose my own religion,
to be successful,
to cry,
to not have to cry,
to be me."

Permissions in the form of positive messages are often direct words and actions allowing the child to think and behave in a specific way: "It's all right for you to make mistakes." "You can wear whatever you want." "You thought that problem out well!" Each permission gives an expansive, rather than a limiting, view of the daughter who hears it. The message is: "You are okay. You will make it in the world."

We watched a mother and daughter in a grocery store one day. The girl was about seven and she had a shopping list. The girl looked at different cereals and then chose one that suited her. She followed the same process with other items and spent time picking fruit that was ripe and firm. By her actions it seemed likely that the mother had given this girl permission to be successful, not simply as a shopper, but as a person whose tastes were acceptable and whose choices mattered.

Mothers often try hard to give their daughters permissions that they never had. This is one of the great outcomes of learning about ourselves. We are able to change consciously the messages that we pass on to future generations.

 Sally tells of her own efforts to change limiting messages. "My grandmother was always so overtly controlling and my mother would react in ways that I considered fragmented. Grandmother managed to control both of us, and I never had any permission to upset the apple cart. I still find it hard in my life to do anything that threatens the family status quo, but I have given my daughter permission to do her own thing, whatever that is. Recently, my daughter, Susan, who is nearly six, and I visited my grandmother in Florida. My grandmother tried to control my daughter the way she always controlled my mother and me. When my grandmother fought over the way Susan chose to dress and tried quite persistently to make her change her clothes, Susan said, 'I'm not gonna wear that yucky dress!' It was incredible. Susan just didn't get sucked in. She didn't let my grandmother control her. I saw the old patterns: exactly what had happened to me when I was Susan's age. But I saw how different my daughter was. She asserted herself. She didn't give up her sense of self for that dominating force. It was a heavy scene because my grandmother was upset, but I was happy for Susan and for myself when I saw it happen."

Most mothers try to give their daughters the permissions that they themselves didn't have, as well as ones that they think we need to get by in the world. It is important for us, as daughters, to view not only the limiting messages given, but the expansive ones as well. There is a sad fact to be reckoned with by many of us: We may not allow ourselves to own the permissions that mother did give us. If we reject her upbringing out of hand, then we throw out the baby with the bathwater. The worst possible scenario for a daughter is that she has believed the negative, limiting messages that she was given and discounted the positive permissions given. The worst of both worlds! Since we are alive today reading, thinking, ready to take another step, we must acknowledge what worked in our lives and what worked in our relationship with our mothers. If we let ourselves look at the positives, subtle as they may be—we will start the process of growing toward our own wholeness and toward a better relationship with our mothers.

Julie's Story

"My mother died more than twenty years ago and I still miss her. I often wish that she could see my house and garden and the paintings that I do. I thank her over and over again for her permission to dare to do new things and to dare to risk failure. She had lots of fears about people, but none about her ability to create. One time when I was a teenager, I picked out wallpaper that had lovely little dark blue flowers on it. In the book, it looked delicate and dainty, but on my wall it looked like a million dark spots that made me dizzy. I was crushed, because we couldn't afford to redo it. One day when I came home from school, I found that mother had painted every dark blue flower in that room a soft, pale blue, and the room looked exactly how I had hoped it would. Being able to dare, to fail without disaster, to risk, these were permissions set in stone for me in this incident."

Dorothy's Story

"Julie gave me permission to think and I never doubted my ability to do that. I didn't get that same permission to be creative with my hands, however, until Julie was much older. Julie responded to my *uniqueness* by supporting my thinking, and she was balancing her own life by giving me the permissions she didn't have."

WORKBOOK

No one can be blamed in the passing of messages, for the chain of conditioning is long and deep and is held and passed on unconsciously. Understanding the way messages were given to you and sorting out what you swallowed whole and digested without thinking is a first step in freeing yourself. Articulating messages will allow you to see them objectively, to analyze them in relationship to your own uniqueness and sense of values, and to choose to assimilate those you want to keep and drop those you know to be untrue for your life now. All the messages, in all their many forms, are with us today—some limiting, some supporting our true self. As we reveal the roots of how we experience life and ourselves, we will become free from limiting messages and will be free to accept and create the permissions that we need to grow.

ℛ The Name Game ℛ

You may or may not like your name. You may have changed it, reclaimed it, lost it or found it. The following exercise offers an opportunity to explore your name so you can begin to sift through the messages that may live in it.

Part 1: Fill in the following sentences and phrases:

My full name is _____.
My mother called me _____ when she was angry.
My mother called me _____ when she was loving.
My friends called me _____.
What is the message in my name?
How did I feel about my name as a child?

What was my nickname as a child?

Did I like that?

Who chose that nickname for me?

Am I called by any nickname today?

What does it mean to me and what does it mean to others?

In what way has my name, or for whom I was named, had any part in determining how I think of myself?

Have I ever talked to my family about my name?

When I say my name to myself, what do I feel?

Am I willing to accept the way people say my name, or do I feel anger, resentment or hostility when I hear my name or various forms of it?

Can I choose my name as the right name for me and wear it proudly?

Part 2: Many adult women still call their mothers by a maternal name: Mom, Mama, Mother. Others took to calling their mother by her first name somewhere along the way, with their mother's acceptance or rejection of that change. Mothers may also continue to call their adult daughter by little-girl versions of her name, or they may refuse to call their daughter by her chosen name. We may, in fact, be stuck in our use of the names we call this significant other in our life, thus limiting our way of being with her. Perhaps, in the end, there may be several names to call our mother or daughter that can express a number of different ways that we relate. This reverse of the name game will give you just a little peek into other aspects of yourself and your relationship to each other.

The Daughter's Exercise:

When I was a child, I called my mother _____.

Now I call her _____.

Why do I, or don't I, call her the same as I did when I was little?

How do I feel when I call her?

What do other adults in her life call her?

What would it be like to call her by her first name?

Does the way I refer to my mother make me feel like an adult? See her as an adult?

How would I like to change the name(s) that I call my mother?

The Mother's Exercise:

When my daughter was a child, I called her _____.

Now I call her _____.

Why do I, or don't I, call her the same as I did when she was little?

How do I feel when I call her?

What do other adults in her life call her?

What would it be like to call her by her chosen adult name, even if it is different than her given name?

Does the way I refer to my daughter make me see her as an adult?

How would I like to change the name(s) that I call my daughter?

ᐦ You're Just Like. . . . ᐦ

To help clear your thinking about yourself and attributes that might have been given to you, experiment with the following exercise over a period of time. Think of adjectives that have been used to describe you, such as shy, bold, talkative, creative, selfish, rude, dumb, aggressive, cautious, smart, creative, hopeless, worthless, timid. List not only the actual words you have heard used to describe you, but the words that have been used by implication to describe you. "She's just like Aunt Mary" (who is eccentric, single, etc.). List as many of these as you can. When the list is done, go back and assess the accuracy of those attributes, and define and limit them as they actually apply to you.

Julie discovered that "sweet" was a strong attribute in her

life. When she explored the validity of this attribute in her life now, she wrote: "I am sweet when I think my help is needed. I am sweet when I'm with little children. I am sweet if someone is sick. I do not want to pretend to be sweet when I am really angry. I am not sweet when I am thinking. I can be sweet when I want to, and I do not have to be sweet to be acceptable."

Rita, after recalling the oft-repeated message that she was bad, says: "I am not bad and worthless—ever."

By doing this exercise, you can begin to expand the ways that you think of yourself and the many ways you have of being in the world.

🌿 The Many Commandments 🌿

All of the "shoulds" we received as a child are like commandments that define one version of the perfect person. This version may or may not be in line with our own unique and essential vision of our ideal self. Whether we respond to those commandments compliantly or rebel against them, they define us—until we know them and choose for ourselves. Imagine your mother sitting you down and stating outright all of the commandments that she thinks you should live by. Using her words, list all of them that you can think of in sentences that all begin with "You should or should not. . . ."

When you have completed that list (and it will probably be long), ask yourself about each one, "Is this right or true for me now?" For every "should" that fits your values and uniqueness, rewrite the commandment as "I choose to. . . ." For every one that is not right or true for you, rewrite it as "I do not choose or need to. . . ." Take your rewritten versions and consider the implications in your life of choosing your own commandments.

꽃 I Must Have Learned Something ꕦ

Stop now and think of the areas in your life in which you feel good about yourself today: your intellect, friendships, physical ability, beauty, nurturing qualities, skills, etc. Now ask yourself who gave you permission to be, feel, think or act in this way. Who praised you for this? If you have difficulty, fantasize a scene early in your life when this quality that you like about yourself was recognized. Now take a minute to thank the person who reinforced your own desire to be this way.

If the person who gave you this permission was your mother, ask yourself if she, too, possessed this quality or if she helped you choose a path that was suitable to your life. Acknowledge to yourself all the permissions that you have. Write them down. List, as well, permissions that you still need, and practice giving yourself those permissions.

Rita continues her work in sorting out messages: "I have from my mother permission to be alive, to grow up, to think. I need and give to myself permission to feel, to be angry, to be spontaneous, to have and meet my needs!"

CHAPTER FOUR

The Story of Our Lives

WHAT A MOTHER SINGS TO THE CRADLE
GOES ALL THE WAY DOWN TO THE COFFIN.

—*Henry Ward Beecher*

THE DRAMA

Life may well be considered a drama, or perhaps a comedy: Life has often been likened to a production. Yet that idea can mean many things, positive or negative. We may think that life is pointless or predestined or that we are helpless to change, that we are just a hastily sketched background figure in a great drama over which we have no control. Or we may think that we are the star of the show and the director of the drama, and that it has been written just for us, and that it will end happily ever after. In either case, let's temporarily consider our lives as an unfolding drama. And further let us assume that we are the heroines and the authors of our own story.

If we can be both the star of the show and the author/director, then our stage has no limits; our story can unfold in any number of ways. We can be powerful, creative, and we can have impact. We can change. We can heal. We can become whole. In order to truly take on these roles, there will be some challenging work to do, as there is for every leading lady, every playwright or author, every director. Much of what we have been considering in these last chapters has been designed to clear the way for becoming the author and the heroine. When we ended our last section with permissions, we began to open ourselves to the idea that we can be and do anything—or almost anything. Certainly we can take some control over our lives and begin to write the remaining chapters of our story in line with our best author's instincts. We don't have to write a tragic story, even if it feels as if we are in one right now. If we think of ourselves as authors, rather than as helpless characters at the mercy of some unknown creator, we will remember that any story can turn around. We've seen it over and over and maybe wondered at the person who managed to put her life together when it initially seemed so off track.

As we begin to take charge of writing our story, we don't have to aim for the happily-ever-after ending that fairy tales so simply prom-ised us. But we also don't need to buy into the Greek tragedy version of how things are. When we discover that we have some basic per-missions—permission to be, to think, to grow—and when we add to those some of the unique permissions that we want and need, then we are set to write the story.

But our story starts, inevitably, in the middle of mother's story. She's already well into her life before we present ourselves on the scene. Let's peek back in time to the story that was in progress when we entered the world. Depending on your age and life circum-stances, your mother may have been a high-powered business woman, lawyer or CEO, giving birth to you in the early "super-woman" years; or she might have been a hippie when she gave birth to you, writing her story in the sixties, involved in drugs, antiwar protest, communes, "love-ins," and the like. Or you might have been born, in those same years, to a mother whose husband was fighting an unpopular war in Vietnam. If you are older, your mother may have been a World War II wife, her husband overseas and not knowing of your birth as he fought and lived or died in a war that was intimately part of your mother's story, and the background for yours. If you are in your eighties, your mother may have been a woman experiencing the changes that the twentieth century brought, a woman surely bound in sex-role stereotypes that hadn't even begun to be recognized, let alone overthrown.

These are just a few rough drafts of stories that might well be familiar to some, and only a microscopic view of the possible stories that were in progress when we were born, no matter how many years ago. Poor or rich, war or peace, this country or that, a father who . . . a mother who. . . . And there were socioeconomic factors, religion, health, illness, styles, customs, heritage, race and politics. These are some of the pieces that are put together to create a story.

What was your mother's story? Have you ever stopped to imagine your mother's life as a little girl, as a woman, as a mother, as your mother? What must it have meant for this woman to bring a daughter into the world in the middle of her own unique life, in the midst of her story that was no doubt full—like yours—of pain and joy, limits and possibilities, hopes and fears?

Clarissa is a forty-five-year-old psychoanalyst. She experienced her own mother as having been cruel to her, and as she gained a professional standpoint she used to confront her mother: "You have a choice. You've always had a choice. You don't have to be cold and cruel. Why were you so cold to me?" Clarissa felt victimized by her mother's cruelty and had chosen to give her own daughter a soft and loving view of life. When her mother got older, she moved back to her hometown in England. Clarissa went to visit her once before she died.

Clarissa had never been there before and she discovered something that changed her view of her mother's cruelty. "I went back to England to my mother's home on the North Sea, and, looking out, it was bleak and harsh and cruel—and that was the look on my mother's face. I know she ingested that sea. I can't understand what she must have gone through in that environment. It's as different from the lushness of New England as she is from me. Maybe she didn't have a choice. Maybe she wasn't really cruel, just harsh like the sea."

Look for a moment at the elements that set the stage for your mother's life and begin to get a picture of the story that you entered as a baby daughter. Your mother became your mother with the same formula that you used to become an adult. *Uniqueness + conditioning = the way she was.* Can you see the spark of your mother's uniqueness as well as the conditioning that molded her? What did she do, express, feel that represented her essential nature, that was above and beyond her conditioning? It won't take much, in most cases, to see that uniqueness in our mothers, even if it is a faint glow of something that stands out beyond her role, her own limitations, her conditioning. To the degree that we feel ourselves conditioned, we can imagine that our mothers were conditioned more heavily and more thoroughly than we. And yet, as we have seen, in the generational advance it is likely that some errors and limitations of conditioning will be corrected. New errors may well be committed, but old, deeply ingrained ones will often change over generations. What are the ways that your mother corrected some of the limitations of her own conditioning? What permissions did she struggle to give you that she hadn't had herself? What injunctions did she continue to give you that she had also gotten? What ways did she hold on to the past and how did she welcome the future and allow you to be different? The answer to these questions will tell us something about the story that was in progress when we were born. No matter what the story-in-progress was, our entrance changed it and soon, in the best and worst cases, we began to take over and write our own story.

THE SCRIPT

We do make the story our own at a certain time, and that time is earlier than we might think. It is not at the age of emancipation that we take over the authorship of our own stories. It is quite typical that children, often under the age of twelve, set the course for much of their lives by decisions that they make at that early age. If we are a part of mother's story in infancy, our life dependent on hers, our happiness revolving around her, by the time we are two we do create our own impact on the story. Even with rigidly controlling parents, a child's responses, interpretations and decisions about her situation indicate her authorship of her own story, at least in part.

Ideally, a child's uniqueness will shine through always, but she will not be forced to decide prematurely about anything ultimate. This is often not the case, however. For many of us, before we know how to write a single word we have begun to create a script for ourselves based on the information that we are receiving from our world. Decisions that we make as children become the basis for a script that will define our lives in deeply rooted and limiting ways. As we grow, we decide what we have to do to get our needs and wants met, and how we'll get along with the people around us. We learn what pleases and how to get what we want by pleasing, or how to pretend that we don't want anything and thus win approval. We listen carefully to the messages we are being given. From all this information, we make enormous decisions early in life. Those decisions fit the experiences we were having at one, two, five or six, but the decisions—made by young children—are sadly lacking in objectivity, perspective and adult thinking skills. They are made out of a view of the world colored completely by our littleness and by how we are being conditioned. Mother's presence infuses all of our experience and thus her hand is clearly seen in most decisions that we make at this young age.

If, for example, every time we asked for something we wanted, we were told, "No, you don't want that," we might decide that we really didn't know what we wanted. If we said, "No," to the offer of more food, and mother made us eat anyway, we might learn to ignore our bodily messages. If our thoughts were discounted, we might decide that we are stupid. If mommy and daddy never touch, we may decide that closeness is not okay. The decisions that children make at very young ages cover every aspect of life and self. Sadly, many of these decisions support the limited conditioning that we are prey to.

How is it that life-altering decisions are readily made at early ages? The child, in order to get by, is forced to analyze and assess life around her and to figure out what to do and how to be. She will, of necessity, make decisions that seem likely to help her grow. For some children the question of how to act revolves around how to act in order to survive at a physical level. "What's the best way to keep from being hit?" is the major concern of an abused child. If she learns that keeping quiet, being good and hiding are strategies to lessen the pain, then she will decide, because she has to, that "I can be safe if I'm invisible." Other children have to make similar decisions, but in healthier households the decisions concern a wider range of options: "What do I need to do to be happy, to get love, to grow? . . ." Early childhood is the exploration of those questions. And the answers that we come up with are the basis for the script that we write. Often a simple one-liner will be the thesis on which we base our whole story:

- "My mother loves me when I'm good."
- "I get noticed when I'm bad."
- "No one pays attention to me when I think—only when I'm cute."

- "My choices always fail. I'd better listen to other people. They know what's best."
- "I'm no good."
- "I'll never make it."
- "I should never have been born."
- "I'll never succeed."
- "Girls are no good."
- "Women are passive."
- "Men are dangerous."
- "Sex is dirty."
- "I can't think."

All of these and many others are decisions that are often made before the age of eight. These decisions, the bases for scripts that define our lives, are what the child does with the messages she is given. Some decisions are made as exact replicas of an injunction given. Decisions made early in life are generally made under duress. Through traumatic events, or families out of balance, many, many children make part or all of their major life decisions when they are too young to truly understand or decide. In the best situations, a child doesn't have to make life or script decisions to feel safe or get by. Decisions about how to be in life will come at age appropriate times, none of them set in stone. But all of us, whether at younger or older ages, make some decisions that create our script. Once the script is in place, it becomes a closed book. There is little room for major alteration and there is little or no consciousness about the defining script. Most women act out much of their lives in line with those early script decisions. It takes an act of will and consciousness, as an adult, to make major script revisions. But doing so is well worth the effort.

⁊⁊ Alice is a thirty-seven-year-old medical student, a late bloomer in the medical community, by all standards. In therapy she attempted to understand her needs, her goals for herself, her possibilities. She discovered along the way that her script allowed her to be a helper. She could remember both her mom and dad saying what a good helper she was and being given positive feedback for that. Her mother assumed that she would be a helper as a wife and mother. That was the preferred path for a woman. Alice had rebelled against that limitation and so had moved, one after the other, into "helping" careers to satisfy her unconscious script decision, "Women are helpers." She came to realize the presence of that decision, but it took longer for her to realize another story line that she had adopted: "Only men are successful." In a painful but illuminating session, Alice remembered coming home at age twelve with a good report card at the same time that her older brother did. Mom had said—and Alice felt those words as if she had heard them yesterday—"With grades like that, Dave, you'll surely be a success." To Alice she had said, "That's nice, dear, and I'm so glad you decided to take the babysitting job Mrs. Smith offered you." When Alice got to the bottom of those messages, she chose to keep the idea of service and helping, because it seemed really to fit her, but she dumped the limitations she had placed on how she could do this, and went off to create her story as a doctor—a successful one.

Alice's limitations were fairly mild, though still painful to her. They were not disastrous or so deeply rooted as to be uncoverable. Unfortunately, when little children in traumatized life situations are forced to make decisions about how to be, these decisions often have tragic consequences. Like the Greek drama mentioned before, there are too many scripts written that end with disaster. Alcoholism and drug abuse, severe depression, lost lives and suicide are often the result of tragic scripts, and the people involved with those unfortunate people have often seen it coming.

🙞 "I still feel guilty about my college roommate. Her childhood was so painful, her self-hatred so great that I feared for her as long as I knew her. Her alcoholism after college didn't surprise me and I encouraged her to go to AA, but somehow it seemed as if even that required more self-love than she had. I felt desperate around her and actually felt relieved when she moved and our friendship faded some. When I heard from her that she was in a relationship, I was so glad and I thought that things would be right for her, being with someone who loved her. She didn't contact me after her relationship ended, and I heard from another friend, only months later, that she had killed herself. I felt angry and guilty. Why did it have to be that way? Could I have done something to help her?"

Probably Jessie couldn't have done any more than she did. The seeds of this young woman's pain were sown deeply and long ago in a difficult childhood. The tragedy of her life was set in motion long before a college roommate felt moved to help. In fact, a script had been written when this woman was just a child, a script that predicted an unfortunate end. Jessie could remember her friend saying, "I always knew I'd never amount to anything. I'm a real nothing!" A script of such saddening proportions is not unusual. These scripts make up a large part of the work of mental health professionals. And yet by the time many of these people come into a mental health setting, there is a grain of hope for changing the script. Somehow, the person is coming to terms with a story that is not right for them, and in the right setting, that story can be rewritten.

But it is not only the tragic stories that need some serious editing. All scripts, because they are unconscious, may need to be looked at and revised. And scripts run the gamut in type and outcome. Some are tragic, others less dramatic but also quite limiting. There are all manner of limiting scripts. Each one puts an inhibition on some or all aspects of being whole. And women's scripts have been uniquely limiting, exhibiting as they do societal injunctions that women not be whole. Some of the classic scripts that women write for themselves might be called by slightly comical names:

Bathing-Beauty Bertha: The story of a woman who always thought she was too fat (skinny, tall, short . . .) to be happy

Mom and Apple Pie: A noble woman puts her love of her children above all else and is a good cook, to boot

Think Like a Man: In this powerful story a woman learns that the only way to get ahead in a man's world is to be like a man, and so she does

Please Help Me: The heartwarming story of a woman who is the victim — of everything

Superwoman: A classic of feminine literature, this is the story of a woman who can do everything, including fly (except take care of her own needs)

So Good: The story of a woman who could please everyone; they referred to her as "the good girl"

But in fact, if you are living out the limitations of a script such as these, it is not so funny. It can be sad and defeating. Alice found out while still quite young that her script limited her. Others may never find out, or come to know it at a very late time in their lives.

❧ Adelle had lived a quiet life as wife and mother. Her family was just as glad to have her be there in that way. She never complained, though in her later life she seemed bored and depressed. When she died, her daughter discovered a trunk full of poetry, fiction and art created by her mother over the many years of her life. No one had known her deep creativity, her wild imagination, her longing to express. No one, Adelle included, had glimpsed her unseen potential.

How will we know if we, like Adelle, are unconsciously inhibiting some important aspect of ourselves? How will we uncover our early decisions so that we may rewrite the script? It is through our present lives that we can come to know whether we are operating from early decisions that limit us now. We can ask some questions that will help us see the limiting edges of our own early decisions:

- *Is my current life fulfilling, challenging, rewarding?*
- *Do I express a wide range of capabilities and styles?*
- *Do I think and feel?*
- *Can I be assertive and receptive?*
- *Do I have a sense of myself as a woman, and as an individual?*
- *Do I feel conscious of how and why I do what I do?*
- *Does the pain and confusion in my life seem overwhelming or insurmountable?*
- *Do I experience myself as having potential or do I feel blocked, stagnant, imprisoned?*

The decisions we make as adults and the way we live our lives are the clue to our scripts and to the early decisions that we made about life. Many of the choices we made were not spontaneous or free, and they are bound by thoughts and feelings that are not within our current awareness. Our present-day choices—especially those that keep us locked into old ways—are likely to reflect decisions that we made as children, when we looked at life through limited vision. Learning to look with a wider lens at our lives and our possibilities will help us to make decisions that are spontaneous and free and appropriate for us as adults.

We go through life making daily decisions: simple ones about what to eat and wear, and more complicated ones about the best way to advance a career or help a family member or friend. A healthy decision is based on current data, values and needs. A scripted one is made without awareness of the thoughts and beliefs that are controlling us. Too often decisions that we make and later regret are controlled by finely tuned unconscious forces that make up our deepest belief system. To become the person we hope to be, it is necessary to explore early decisions as Alice did and to become conscious of ourselves as the author and director of a new drama that we choose.

THE AUTHOR

We all have the power to re-decide and in so doing to *re*write a limiting script. The first step in re-deciding is to bring the original decision into awareness and then to analyze it. We have the right to ask ourselves how we arrived at this point in our lives and where we want to go from here.

As we work on understanding the script that we wrote as children, why we wrote it, and how it limits us now, we will be able to step fully into our responsibility as author. And as an author, we will operate as an adult, calling on our true self as we begin to write and rewrite our story. It is in the rewriting of our stories that we will begin to use the permissions given and those chosen. A surefire way to keep our stories going just the way they have been is to stay unconscious: "I can't help the way I am." "Just my luck." "These are family patterns. I can't override them." If we believe this, then we are fated to live out the scripts and conditioning that were our childhood experience. If, on the other hand, we believe that we can create our lives, we can change, we can uncover old and limiting ways, then we will be able to decondition ourselves and, in so doing, free up the qualities that are uniquely ours. In chapter 1 you circled a list of qualities that reflected your essential self. It is these aspects of yourself that you can write more and more fully into the chapters that remain in your story.

Selena, a twenty-nine-year-old graduate student, worked hard to

understand her script and how it hurt her now. She expressed her dis-
coveries to her sister.

> *Dear Annie,*
>
> *You were always the one that Mother preferred and I under-
> stand why now. You liked to do things that she thought girls
> should do and I preferred to do boyish things like play baseball
> and build models. I tried to please Mother but I never could. I
> think she gave up on me, and I certainly gave up on myself.
> And you always stood by me—even though I know I was often
> nasty and spiteful to you. I haven't seen you for over five years
> because I couldn't face your happiness when I was so miserable.
> Now I want to see you and your family, because I have taken
> the first step to becoming the person that I want to be.*
>
> *I have discovered so many thinking patterns that were untrue
> and even dangerous. I know now that I can lead my life the way
> that I want and not be selfish. I've found many qualities in
> myself that are like Mother, even though she and I never agreed
> on anything. I feel so wonderful to be free of those constricting
> bands that I let keep me from you and the rest of the family. I
> only wish that Mother were here to know that I do appreciate
> her and know she loved me even though I was never the helper
> that you were. I'm looking forward to your birthday and com-
> ing to your house.*
>
> *Love, Selena*

Re-deciding and rewriting mean being responsible *now*. Certainly
we don't need to look at our childhood and take responsibility for
what went on then. Remember, we started our lives involved in our
family and the story that was being created there. But if you are an
adult as you read this, you are free to take responsibility for the

present and the future. Being an adult is more than having attained a certain age. It involves being a thinker and a chooser. It involves being aware and being willing to know ourselves. It may in fact, be comforting to allow ourselves to feel at the mercy of forces beyond ourselves, and it is a common pattern for women to feel that way. If we are helpless, then we are not to blame, we don't need to take risks. Failure and success are not on the line. If we are responsible, however, then in the end the outcome of our lives rests largely on our own shoulders. "Am I willing," you may ask, "to take responsibility for my life, to make choices and face the consequences?" In fact, the answer may as well be yes, because, whether we acknowledge it or not, we are responsible. When we come to the end of our life there will be no place to look but at ourselves and at the choices we made as adults about how to live it.

To be an adult and take the responsibility inherent in that position requires not only thinking and choosing, but understanding as well—understanding our own values, our own set of rights and wrongs, our own purpose in living—for every author must know what the point is of the story that she is writing. Now, lest we get lost in the heaviness of the idea of responsibility, let's look at being an adult a little more fully. All of the old-line messages from mom and others about being an adult probably come under the heading of "shoulds" and they may feel burdensome in the extreme. If we drop those away—though that won't be easy—what we have left is *me!* And that me includes all of the impulses and desires that move me: the loves and hates, the joys and sorrows, the longings, the urges toward this or that, the creativity, the meanings that life offers—all of the me that is unfettered by years of limiting messages.

It is as if the best and clearest of me is allowed to emerge, and to do so in an affirming way. I can be me and make my world around me. And who am I? If we peel away the conditioning, the messages, the scripts, is there any me left? Yes! We must remember our uniqueness.

The me that is left is special, different, worthy, honorable, important.

If you could look in the nursery window of a huge, Earth-sized hospital and see every newborn ever born, all only hours or days old, would any be not okay? Would any not have potential? Each child has potential. Each child is a true self, looking for realization. Each being brought into the world will not be able to reach the same heights, accomplish the same things, and grow in the same way. But each has an expandable potential. And if we have lived into adulthood, then we know that potential still exists, still lies ready to be manifested. Are we living at the edge of our potential? Or have we accepted a mediocre status quo in which we continue to deny many of our greatest possibilities?

Dorothy's Story

"When I went back to school after my first child was born, I studied early childhood development. I had no question about what I wanted to do. I assumed that I would work with children. My mother had, and I had already scripted myself to be a mother. By that I mean not only that I thought mothering would satisfy my every need in life, but I also believed that I probably wasn't capable of anything that required different skills. My mediocre efforts in school in the past had verified my thinking that I couldn't go too far in the world, and I told myself that was all right. Along the way, however, I had to admit that I didn't want to work with kids. I faced the limitations I had placed on myself and began to expand my potential. I moved into the field of psychology, and even here I accepted, unknowingly, the limitations that I put on myself. Each new opportunity that presented itself to me challenged my acceptance of the status quo. And when the opportunity to write this book presented itself, I faced again the potential that existed in me but that I shied away from. I have had to decide and re-decide that I can do anything."

Julie's Story

꿏 "I had complete faith in Dorothy's intelligence and in her ability to do whatever she wanted. I never pushed her in school, because I believed that wasn't good for her. I also was not aware that she was unsure of herself, and perhaps one of the reasons for her uncertainty was my total acceptance of whatever she accomplished without critically judging the finished product. I believe now that she would have been better served if I had been more constructive in helping her sort out good, better and best effort."

WORKBOOK

All of us need to be able to assess our good, better and best efforts, as well as to be able to acknowledge honestly our not-so-good efforts. And the high effort of our lives is our lives and the story that we write. Are we writing it well? Is it our best effort or a not-so-good effort? If we will remember that we are worth being the heroine of a great story, then we can allow ourselves to become the author of that story. To begin conscious authorship requires knowing what is already written: what our mother wrote for us and what we chose, at a young age, for ourselves. In this first exercise, we will join our mother's story-in-progress.

꿏 A Shared Life 꿎

Write a story from your mother's point of view about her life. Have it include the following lines and anything else that is important.

Trust your ability to imagine being her and allow yourself in so doing to suspend your point of view to allow hers to emerge. You may want to write the story from scratch or simply respond to the guidelines set down and add material that is relevant to your (mother's) story.

Mother's Story: I was _____ years old when I had my daughter (your name) _____. She was my _____ child. My life at that time revolved around: _____ (spouse, mother, other kids, social, political realities). I had many thoughts and feelings about the birth of my daughter. These were

_____.

The actual birth circumstances were _____

_____.

When I first gazed at my daughter's face, I _____.

My secret hope and dream for her has been that she _____

_____.

As you finish this story, take over with your own story, following the same guidelines.

My Story: I was born and _____.

I experienced my life with mother as _____

_____.

I believe that my mother felt and thought about me that _____

_____.

As an adult I am _____.

My secret hope and dream for myself is _____

_____.

My secret hope and dream for my mother is that _____

_____.

In the last part of this exercise, imagine that you and your mother are writing a story together.

Our Story: Our story includes many positives and negatives. As a mother/daughter pair, we are/were _____
_____. We are like each other in these ways: _____
_____.
We are different from each other in these ways: _____
_____.
What hurts us with each other is _____
_____.
Our love for each other is shown by _____
_____.

In all of these sections, add whatever is important to you and reread the stories for a view of two individuals and their unique and shared stories.

🙌 An Old Story 🙌

Every story has a plot, characters, good guys and bad guys, and a repeating theme. Let's look at some of the predictable women's scripts we mentioned before and see how their old stories are written.

Bathing-Beauty Bertha

The plot: Woman spends her life dieting and fretting in an effort to become the perfect woman. In the end, she accepts a mediocre level of attainment and secretly doesn't like herself. *The good guys:* other suffering women; men who think she's good-looking (anyway); her therapist, who helps her with self-acceptance; her dog, who doesn't care. *Bad guys:* all attractive men; all thin women; her mother (who should have made her stay skinny); her best friend (whom Bertha secretly envies and competes with). *Repeating themes:* Working hard but never succeeding; being nice; feeling not okay; not daring to look better than mother.

Please Help Me

The plot: "Help Me" is the youngest of four daughters; mother always wanted to "mother" and her rebellious older daughters didn't let her; "Help Me" let mother take care of her all the time. As an adult, "Help Me" wasn't (an adult); she waited for a husband; she was involved in the mental health world (as a patient); she joined many groups. *The bad guys:* everyone who persecuted her (this was probably everyone). *The good guys:* everyone who rescued her (at least for a moment). *Repeating themes:* waiting; feeling victimized; suffering; missing mom.

Take time to write *your* old story. Choose a comical name for your script and write about the plot, the good and bad guys, and the repeating themes. Make sure you keep it light, as this will help you to let go of that old story.

But, as the author, it is your right to make this the best story possible, and so you may need to change the old story in order to write one that is best for you. Now take a look at the story you have just written and identify one or more crucial themes that have been destructive to you and then change them!

Part 1: Write down the core belief or decision or attitude that you wrote into your original script that no longer serves you. See how Bertha and "Help Me" rewrite their old stories and then do your own!

Bertha: "I am not okay as I am. I always have to work to be good enough (and secretly I know that I can't succeed)."

Help Me: "I am a child. I need help to get by. Only Mother can take care of me."

Part 2: Remember, if you can (or imagine), a time in childhood when you made this decision or took on this belief. Write down the circumstances (external) and the response you had (internal).

Bertha: "In third grade, Bobby Severs called me 'Fatty.' I don't know if I really was, but I had a crush on him and I remember saying to myself, *Someday I won't be a fatty and then you'll like me.*"

Help Me: "Mom saw me on a jungle gym and rushed over saying, 'I'll help you.' I didn't think I needed help, but I let her help me. I accepted that I must have needed help and I was too scared after that to climb the jungle gym."

Part 3: Think about the quality or belief or permission that you would need in order to cancel or balance that early experience.

Bertha: "I need self-acceptance and a feeling of power. I would like to have been able to call Bobby 'Four Eyes' and laugh."

Help Me: "I needed a sense of my own boundaries and my ability to think and do for myself. My life might have been different if I'd just told Mom, 'I can do it myself!'"

Part 4: Make a choice to change that early decision in a way that will free you to be your best self.

Bertha: "I can accept myself just the way I am, with all my strengths and limitations. I am acceptable and lovable to others."

Help Me: "I am capable and I can create my life the way I choose. I don't need to be little to get what I want."

Spend time with your re-decision now, and in the next weeks and months. Remember, too: Write it down in several prominent places and check often to see if you are operating out of the old or the new message.

The Present

CHAPTER FIVE

More Than a Daughter, More Than a Mother

How do you know that the fruit is ripe?
Simply because it leaves the branch.

—André Gide

Being an Ex-Child

The past has bound us in so many ways. We can see its powerful effects on our lives daily. And yet, the past is no more. There is only the present. And in the present we are the fruit that has fallen from the tree. We are adult women. We are no longer just daughters. A woman who considers herself first and foremost to be a daughter will be an unfulfilled person. In fact, to the degree that we define ourselves, internally and externally, as primarily a daughter or a child or a girl, it is to this degree that we allow our conditioning to continue to limit us in the face of opportunities to grow. To face the present in a growing way, both mothers and daughters need to discover how they are *more* than mothers and daughters.

Daughters leave home for many reasons. And it is in the leaving that we first make a strong stance for our identity outside of the role

111

of daughter. It is at this same time that mothers are faced with finding a new way of relating to their "ex-child." The ease or success of this process of expanding identifications beyond the parent/child role is determined by many factors. Have we, as children, been allowed to explore the separation process? Have we, as mothers, seen ourselves throughout our child-rearing years as more than a mother?

When a daughter leaves home as an adult, to take whatever step is next for her in life, the childhood relationship between mother and daughter will have its affect. Leaving home, contrary to the secret hope of so many women, will not solve the problems that were not solved while mother and daughter were under the same roof. The problems will change in how they are represented and perhaps, in the extreme, the mother/daughter pair will never again deal with each other, but the same problems, issues and conditions that affected our lives with mother will lurk inside of us as internal dynamics and will show themselves in all our relationships.

When a daughter leaves home, she will do so under a variety of conditions. Some leave feeling unfinished, forced out prematurely by mothers who have overvalued independence. Some will leave angry, in an effort to solve the problems they have had in the family. Others leave by default: There's nothing left to do but leave. Some leave with eager anticipation of their new life supported by the mothers they leave behind.

What is it like for a young woman to take a step that is quite radical for her: the step of leaving her life as a child to begin her life as an adult? Earlier in the century there were traditional family patterns that were considered the only way to behave. A daughter stayed with her mother and father until she was married; then her husband was considered to be responsible for her. She was not to be out in the world on her own but to have someone there to take care of her. Her role was to raise children, keep a good house and take care of her husband. When those trends changed, the role of grown daughters became more uncertain. While in theory women have society's permission to be adults, in practice they are not taught very much about that. Girls are generally raised in ways that support their "littleness," while boys are expected to be adults and raised in ways that support their "bigness." If women are to truly leave their childhoods behind—not just play a game until they can fit back into the child mold with a mate, or as caretaker to an elderly mother, or as an assistant this or that to someone else's adult—then much will have to be learned. Later in this chapter, we will go into what needs to be learned more thoroughly. But the first step in being an ex-child is to make the transition gently and thoroughly from childhood into adulthood. In order to do this with ease and a sense of competency, a positive internal parent will have to be developed that will help the young adult woman in growing up in the world.

It will come as no surprise to the reader that we talk to ourselves. And these conversations are not just foolish ramblings in our head. Our ability to dialogue internally is our ability to rely on various aspects of ourselves, to draw on many resources, to consider and choose from the available possibilities the best ones. This is *very* adult. And the various participants in any internal conversation make up the "voices" that we hear and speak through in our lives. The voice that is important for our purposes now is the "internal parent."

This internal mother is made up of all the messages that were received from mother, as well as many of the decisions we made about ourselves and our place in life. This internal mother can be there as part of our personality and will be supportive and instructive when needed. In the best cases, the internal parental voice offers a discriminating view of the world, advice and a perspective that balances the impulsive nature of the child within. It contains the wisdom of all that we have been taught. It is nurturing. If a positive internal parent is there when we need it, we develop an awareness of ourselves as adults ready to be out in the world. We lose our identification with being a child and move into an identification as an adult. This does not happen all at once, as we walk out our mother's door. It takes place over a period of many years, and we may slip back into periods of feeling child-identified throughout our lives. The internal parent acts as a guide and support in these changing experiences.

Dear Mom,

I carry you with me, like a wise old woman who I can talk to about anything. I still get glimpses of the angry you, critical of me for this or that, but after all these years I mostly carry you in your wisdom and I have come to rely on that soft, wrinkled face that I see to offer me support and love in times of trial. Thank you for having planted the seeds of that caring for myself in me. I wish you were really here to share with.

Love, Deb

Deb is an example of someone who developed her positive mother voice and used it to her benefit in the world. Her job was made easier in some ways because her mother had died and Deb and her mother had been close and loving at the time of her death. Deb recalls going for a job interview several weeks after her mother died and feeling, to her surprise, as if she were actually having a conversation with her mother before she went. When we can create or rely on a *positive* supportive voice, we have an ally within that will balance the fears and needs of the "child" voice, the part of us that still feels little and frightened or confused. Without that positive parental voice, the "child" will often be out in the world alone, pretending to be an adult and feeling terrified that she will be unable to sustain the masquerade anymore. Deb's conversation on the subway on the way to her interview went like this:

Little Deb (described by Deb as a six-year-old): "I'm scared I can't do this interview. I'm too little. I don't know enough for this job."

Parent Deb (described as "like my mother would have been if she'd been perfect"): "They'll love you, dear. Your work in the museum is perfect for what they want. And if you don't get the job, it'll be okay anyway."

Deb got the support that anyone would want and need in a stressful time. She got it from herself, from that internal parental voice that was "like my mother would have been if she'd been perfect."

Most women don't find themselves as lucky as Deb. For many women this internalized parental voice will represent another aspect of mother's voice: her criticism, injunctions, denials of their uniqueness, and that voice, heard in their ears like mother's ghost, will control and limit them, as if they had never grown.

Renee says in therapy: "I feel like having my brain taken out. I hear myself commenting on everything I do, and I sound just like my mother—at her worst. It never stops, except when I finally fall asleep. You'd think I was a total failure, the way I talk to myself. I never have anything good to say."

In most cases we listen to an internal parental voice that is both nurturing and critical. As surely as we had to cope with mother's ever-present inclusion in our life when we were children, we will continue to carry her around as adults, in one form or another. Only now we have the opportunity to create the kind of voice we want to hear. We can re-parent ourselves. And as we take on that role of re-parenting, we will be able to respond to all that we need and feel in a way that even the best mother couldn't. After all, she didn't know us like we know ourselves. In order to do this, we must monitor those conversations that we have all the time and find out what the present "parent" voice is like. Who's talking? Which voice (in me) sounds like my mother (or father)? What is the critical voice like? What is it trying to do? Is there a nurturing, care-taking component to the parent voice?

As we have seen, almost every mother had good intentions for her daughter, and we may assume that this is also true for the voices we carry inside. Even the most negative, self-deprecating voice has, at its core, a positive intention: to help, to sort out a big and scary world, to live correctly. Our exercises at the end of this chapter will help to identify the internal parental voice and to build a positive, nurturing one. As we do this, we will be a step closer to being an "ex-child," to being more than a daughter. When we can begin to nurture and take care of ourselves, to re-parent ourselves, to guide and discern for ourselves, we will be taking over the job that mother did for so many years. In so doing we will give ourselves the chance to be an adult and we will give mother the chance to be more than a mother.

MOTHERS ARE ADULTS

For mother the task of letting her daughter go is very different from the daughter's task. Mother is already an adult and, hopefully, feels that way. But she may have precious little permission to be more than a mother. Letting go, for mother, involves faith in her own ability to be without her daughter and faith in her daughter's ability to be out in the world. Once a daughter takes the big step of leaving, mother will need to learn to accept new ways of behaving and thinking from her daughter. Mothers often have to face lifestyles that are in conflict with what seems right to them. Women are doing things that have been totally unacceptable until recently. Today, sexual identity, the choice of parenting styles, religious beliefs and value—as well as careers, etc.—are all potentially so different from mother's world as to feel foreign and dangerous to her. And yet a daughter must leave her mother's home sooner or later, and she must live in the world of today—not in her mother's world. Every generation has to let go of valued ways of thinking, and for each it is hard. These changing behaviors are threatening to mothers who have to choose either to accept the change or lose their daughters.

Ellen lived with her mother in an apartment that was not really large enough for the whole family. After finishing high school, she stayed home, found work, and gave a large amount of her salary to her mother and continued in her role as docile daughter. But she wanted to move out, as many of her friends had. Every time she mentioned moving out, Ellen's mother told her that she shouldn't move out unless she was getting married. Finally, Ellen found an apartment that she could afford. She moved out one night and told her mother she was moving. Her mother refused to speak to her, but Ellen went ahead with no help from anyone in her family. She was sad and angry, but she thought that the only way she would grow up was to leave home.

Her mother continued to refuse to speak to Ellen but she would leave Bible quotes under her daughter's apartment door talking of a dutiful daughter or a sinful daughter. Ellen continued to give money to the family when she could and to stay away. It took a long time for her mother to see that her efforts were not going to bring Ellen home or make her be the way she thought Ellen should be. Ellen had been independent in thought long before she was in action. She had truly been ready to be on her own in spite of her mother's objection.

Ellen was a gentle daughter in her leaving, respecting in a mature and compassionate way her own needs and her mother's. Other daughters will leave much more forcefully, often flaunting their opposing lifestyles to their mothers in a desperate need to prove to themselves, perhaps more than to their mothers, that they are separate people.

≈ Janna came to a mother/daughter workshop with her reluctant mother. Beverly came expecting to get "more of the same" from her twenty-three-year-old daughter—to whom she was clinging, for her own needs and out of fear that her daughter was in danger in a world that Beverly had experienced as dangerous. She expected the workshop to be a tirade by young women of the wrongs that their mothers had inflicted upon them. As their story unfolded, it was revealed that Janna had left young to pursue a vastly different life course than her mother had hoped for her and that she had constantly kept her mother abreast of every activity she was involved in, including her sexual conduct, her drug experiences, her political views. In fact, it seemed that Janna tended to exaggerate all of the outrageous aspects of her life and underplay the calm, normal aspects. Beverly knew more about Janna's sexual experiences than she did about her job as a childcare worker!

It was no wonder that Beverly clung so to her daughter. She not only had to let go of her fondest hopes and dreams for her only child, but she had to face aspects of her daughter's life that were terrifying and confusing to her, and her daughter gave her very little sense that she was operating as an adult. Beverly finally asked Janna not to tell her so much. Beverly still had to struggle with letting go, but she was able to do so more readily when she began to get a balanced picture of her daughter's life.

But even this was only a small step for Beverly, because she, like so many women, identified herself almost totally as a mother. She actually had a lovely life of her own, but she downplayed the importance of this, having created a script for herself that her life only had meaning as she successfully mothered. Even her willingness to listen to stories that tormented her was part of the script. She had to be there for her daughter, no matter what. And Janna, in turn, was giving mother a role to continue with: the worried mother. Their relationship shifted markedly when Beverly let go of having to mother her daughter and when Janna began to see her mother as a person.

When, as mothers, we see our children leaving home, we too go through a transition, as our daughters do. The daughter is faced with moving from a child to an adult role, and the mother is faced with moving from a parent to an adult role. Both are headed out of their roles as mother/daughter and into new roles as adults! While the daughter may need to rely on an internal parent to help guide the way, the mother may need to dig deep, back into her own sense of herself beyond her role as mother, back into her own sense of uniqueness, back into her own youth, to a time when she may have considered the question "Who am I?" Each mother-turned-adult must answer that question in such a way that it will offer her a fulfilling life in the many years that she will live without her children.

Too many women try to hold on to the mother role, displacing those mothering instincts on to grown children, grandchildren, mates or even unsuspecting acquaintances. A woman may become the perennial mother, virtually holding her breath while waiting for another opportunity to mother. Or she may become the destroyed mother, herself a victim of her lost job. She may be lost and hopeless, face depression or anger, certainly confusion at facing a life that has robbed her, as surely as if her children had died, of that which she was born to do. These are sad and regrettable outcomes of the original noble decision to mother. But that choice to mother really occupies only a fraction of our long life and can be one that supports a portion of our uniqueness in a way that no other choice could. It is never the only thing that a woman is. For the woman who has over-identified herself in this role, her daughter's leaving will be particularly painful. She may cling, manipulate, coerce, cajole, buy, threaten, or otherwise try to control her daughter into staying with her, one way or another. As mothers, we may try to control the distance that our daughters live from us, the careers they choose, the people they associate with, and the values they hold. Any place that we feel we have control will be a place where we still feel connected and where we still feel we have a job to do. Even trauma and tragedy in our daughter's life may be secretly welcomed as a way to stay in our role as mother.

And yet, intrinsically, a woman who is clinging to her role as mother knows that she is living in old clothes. She will yearn, from somewhere inside, to find out about herself as a person, to reclaim her autonomy, her uniqueness. And this is the task that faces each woman when her children leave: to find out who she is when she is more than a mother. One mother, as she discovered this about herself, wrote this letter to her daughter and expressed, better than we can, the struggle and the invitation that exists in becoming more than a mother:

Thank you for being you. You were a delight as a baby and young child. You gave me much pleasure as you gently matured to a young woman. It was hard to let go—a child is a part of you. There is pain in the letting-go process. I was often disappointed and frightened by the directions you were going, but you always had high standards and I was always proud of your ultimate goals. You have now matured to become a fine woman. I feel great pride as I see you in the role of mother. As the years go on, you and your children take on the role of spanning the bridge to eternity. I now have permission to continue to grow and develop as my own self. By my children taking on the responsibility to live their own fulfilled lives, I am given the freedom to develop my own identity. Who knows to what heights I will soar?

Seeing Each Other

If daughters manage to become "ex-children," to think and feel like adults, separate and autonomous, they have taken a huge step. So, too, when mothers can become "mother graduates" and can experience themselves as adults beyond the mothering role, they have taken an important step in their lives. Each of these tasks is difficult in itself, and even more difficult because to fully do either requires allowing the other person to do her part. For me to be an "ex-child," I must see my mother as a "mother graduate." For me to be a "mother graduate," I must see my daughter as an "ex-child."

While women may think and feel that they have moved easily or fully into the "ex-child" (adult) role, it is quite common to still see the woman who gave birth to us only as "mother." We often hear women speak as if their mothers had no respect for them, when underneath they are themselves unsure of their role as adults or/are unable to let their mothers be adults.

- "I'll never be a grown-up in my mother's eyes until I have a baby." (Read: I wonder if I'll really feel grown up when I have a baby?)
- "My mother still thinks of me as incompetent because I don't do things her way." (Read: I still feel incompetent, but mother seems perfect.)
- Whenever Mother is in my house, she is critical. I feel like I'm five around her." (Read: I can't please my internal critical parent.)
- I wish that I could find a partner that my mother approved of and that I liked. She finds something wrong with everyone that I begin to care about." (Read: I don't trust myself!)
- I don't have a relationship to my mother, because she can't relate to my lifestyle." (Read: I don't have a relationship to my mother because I can't relate to her lifestyle.)

These women think that they have grown up, but still treat mother like mother, allowing themselves to be "little" in some aspect of their lives and not allowing mother to graduate from the role. The desire and need to please mother and to feel approved of by her go back to little-girl days. As long as we still operate in that vein, we have not allowed ourselves to become adult. Exploring who we are today is an ongoing process that involves changes in thinking, behaving and feeling. It means that as an adult woman it is not necessary to please mother or have approval from her. It means that we have the power and responsibility to create our lives. Finally, we need to feel and relate to mother from an adult place and not from the one-down position of a child. In order to do this, we need not only to be adults, but also to see mother as a person *other* than as a mother.

Dorothy's Story

"Whenever my mother came to visit, the whole family worked to make the house look nice, but somehow I thought that she always noticed the one thing that wasn't clean. I used to think, *There she goes again—there's no pleasing her.* This went on in all my homes for years. It was particularly amusing (in retrospect) when I lived in a log cabin in Maine, cleaning and cleaning. One day, I gave up trying to please Mother like a good little girl and started treating her visit as I would that of a good friend, which only required a modicum of cleaning!"

Dorothy got to the point where she could let mother be a friend. In so doing, she allowed mother to be a "mother graduate." And doing this requires many things: Feeling and thinking as an adult, taking care of our child needs internally (with our own nurturing parent), seeing mother as an adult and not through little-girl eyes, accepting mother as she is, not as we want her to be or remember her from our childhood. This last aspect of the task is one of the hardest. But it is essential for our own adulthood that we become able to see mother as an adult. This is not easy but is certainly worth the effort!

In our present society the sentimentalized and idealized views of mother are changing to a more realistic perspective and this will help both mothers *and* daughters. For many years, mothers have been thought of as selfless, devoted, adoring, nurturing paragons of virtue. When a mother failed to live up to this ideal, not only did she feel guilty but also her daughters felt cheated. Mothers were to be there for their children's every want and need. If this were not done, then the result would be psychological harm that could not be erased. With the advent of an increasing divorce rate, single mothers and the need for two-income families, mothers went through the painful process of trying to be all things to the family: breadwinner, nurturer, cook, laundress and housekeeper, as well as playmate, advisor and confidante. And children *expected* this.

Gradually, the realization that this is an impossible task has helped women who are mothers to look at themselves not as a martyred mother but as a person who has a job to do and must get help along the way. As this happens, daughters become able to see their mothers in the same way—as a person who has a job to do, and not as a fantasy image of the all-perfect mother (or as a resented, less-than-perfect version). Mothers are beginning to teach their daughters how to be independent, how to manage their lives without a constant caretaker watching over them, and in turn daughters are seeing their mothers as people with lives outside their role of mother. It is a great gift that this is happening. For every young child who begins to catch glimpses of her mother in a life of her own, there will be a girl who has an easier time growing into womanhood. And for each woman who finds a way to see her mother as an adult, there will be a woman who herself is truly an adult.

Mothers have the same task to do. They must let their daughters become "ex-children." They must see their daughters as adult women, accepting them the way they are and not the way they want their daughters to be. This is most difficult for the mothers who, having identified themselves completely in the motherhood role, need their daughters to stay "little" to play their part. These mothers will have a particularly hard time supporting their daughter's adulthood. And yet, even a mother who has moved significantly into her own life may find it hard to let go. Mothers must learn, all along the way, to see their daughters as more than a child. Growing girls can be a source of delight and also a source of fear to a mother. In the dance of separation that we have mentioned, mother is continually faced with having to let go.

Shirley, at about fourteen years of age, told her mother: "I know I will never be the daughter that you want or behave the way you think a daughter should behave, so why don't you have another baby?"

Here is a strong teenage girl well on her way to autonomy. She lets her mother know, in no uncertain terms, that she won't be her little girl forever. Shirley's mother got the message early.

Some mothers take much longer to see their daughters as separate and different. There are many scenarios that create this. If mother was the oldest daughter and responsible for *her* mother, she may expect her oldest daughter to be the same. If the youngest daughter comes several years after the other children, she may be the baby for years and years. If one daughter died in infancy, the next may be kept little and weak for much too long a time. If mother's mother died early, mother may cling to her daughters excessively. The stories are endless. One mother was heard to say to her twenty-two-year-old daughter, who was searching for a job and desperately attempting to be on her own, "You'll always be my baby." Even though she overtly supported her daughter's movement into adulthood, somewhere inside she had a hard time letting go. Most mothers do.

Julie's Story

❧ "I look back on the time I first realized that Dorothy, my youngest child, was a responsible, capable adult. I was attending a workshop run by a forceful, dynamic young woman. I listened eagerly to everything she had to say. When she mentioned her age, I realized that she was the same age as my daughter. Right at that minute, in a clear vision, I saw that my daughter had just as much to teach me, was wonderfully active in the world and very capable. In spite of her obvious career success, I had, until that moment, thought of her as a child. If only I could listen to her as I was listening to that speaker, I would stop seeing a teenager or little girl and start seeing an adult. I left that workshop determined to do so, and this began our relationship as two adults."

When a mother allows her daughter to be an adult and really sees her that way, much of the one-down, protective, matronizing attitude that she may have carried for years will drop away, and a mother will begin to feel free herself—because she can let her daughter go. To do this is as great an effort as is giving birth. Each labor requires that we let go of something deep within us. In birth we let go of the child within our womb—a struggle that is painful and rewarding. In letting our daughters be adults, we let go again: of our deep desire to hold, to protect and to keep little the child that we bore.

A mother learns to love her daughter and then must learn to let her go, and the daughter's role is complementary. She must give up that first fierce attachment to face life alone. For both mother and daughter the fears that this intense bond will never again be found may keep them tied to the past. And should both be brave enough to step into the unknown of the new relationship that awaits them, there will be a period of waiting and even mourning for what is lost while the child and parent leave each other to come back as two adults. There is no way to know, before it happens, that the love and power of the mother/daughter bond is even stronger and deeper when two women once mother and child give up those roles and see each other as two fully responsible adults. That is a constant, ever-growing process.

> In a group, Lisa said: "I do not need my daughters at this time and they do not need me, but we want each other. We share our thoughts and activities and we look for comfort from each other. I, as the mother, find wonderful comfort in the words my daughters say to me when I have a problem to face. We are friends in the most profound meaning of the word."

WORKBOOK

Growing up is not easy. Nor is change. It seems that at any resting place where we find comfort, we are faced, sooner than we would wish, with a demand to change, to move on, to take a next step. And yet this is also the spice of life, the challenge and the excitement of being on our "growing edge." For mothers and daughters, that edge will be different. Daughters will stretch into adulthood, autonomy, and a separate independent life. There will be a shift from importance placed on family of origin to present family (however that is defined). A thorough assessment of our inventory will take place as we face adult life and need to know what tools we have to manage that life. We will look more and more inside ourselves for answers, guidance and advice, and will rely less and less on a dependent stance that had served us as a child.

Mothers may feel even more wrenched from a stable life as their children leave, as their daughters become adults. Most of the years of a mother's life, perhaps *all* of her adult years, have been devoted to mothering; looking to what is next may be difficult and frightening, as well as exciting. If we have kept our hand in a life apart from mothering, becoming "mother graduates" will be easier. If not, we may have to do a fast shuffle to find out about life beyond the role of mother.

The first two exercises in this section are for a mother or a daughter who is ready to experiment with becoming "more than a mother, more than a daughter." Feel free to try them both, however, since there may well be something to learn for you in each.

❧ Daughter's Exercise: "Wise Old Woman" ❧

This is a fantasy exercise. Read the instructions first and then, in a quiet space, refer to them again, allowing your imagination to follow the directions and to create a story for yourself. (An effective alternative is to read the exercise slowly into a tape recorder and play it back for yourself, or have another person read it to you while you experience it.)

Imagine that you are at the foot of a mountain in a beautiful, grassy field. As you gain a sense of your surroundings by smelling the flowers, touching the grass, hearing the birds, become aware of feeling that you want guidance in your life. You may think about specific areas in which you would like support and advice, or tune in simply to wishing that you had an ally, a guide or a teacher who could be there for you in times of need.

After a moment of letting this thought sink in, look up at the mountain, at its height and splendor, and realize that there is a wise being awaiting you at the top of the mountain and that she is that ally and guide that you long for. In the next few moments, allow yourself to travel up the mountain, enjoying the hike, stopping to look back over the vista, encountering and overcoming any obstacles. Take your time on this journey up the mountain.

When you reach the summit you will find a beautiful and sacred space in which to sit and await the entrance of the wise old woman. When she appears, notice what she looks like, how she speaks and moves, what your feelings are as she comes to you. You will find that she is compassionate and wise and completely devoted to you. She is like an ideal mother. When you are with her, carry on a conversation. You will be able to talk to her, ask her questions and hear her answers. Ask her about general or specific concerns that you may have. While her answers may be concrete or abstract, she will surely speak to you of important things and will always speak to you nonjudgmentally and with great love. When you are ready to leave, make an agreement with this wise woman that you will call upon her frequently. As you leave, she will give you as a gift a symbol that has deep personal relevance for you.

When you are finished with the fantasy, take some notes; especially about the wise being and any important information she gave you. Begin to call on her image and speak with her in quiet times when you can allow yourself to hear that supportive voice that you need. If you find yourself in dialogue with a critical, demeaning voice, or if you experience yourself being negative toward yourself, call on this wise being, who will always speak kindly to and about you.

☙ Mother's Exercise: "Who Will I Be?" ❧

In this exercise you will have an opportunity to reconnect with or renew dreams and inspirations about your own life. As you do this, allow yourself to focus attention back to yourself and the uniqueness and importance of your life. Fill in the following sentences, elaborating as fully as you like:

- When I was a child my secret dream for myself was _____

  _____.

- The skills and strengths that I had were _____

  _____.

- When I was young I thought about being a (career) _____

  _____.

- I always wanted _____.

- In order to live my life as I have, I gave up _____

  _____.

- If I had it to do all over I might _____

  _____.

- What's important for me now in my life is _____

  _____.

- If I had unlimited time and resources, I would _____

  _____.

- A secret fantasy that I have for myself now is _____

  _____.

- In order to honor myself fully in my life, I will _____

  _____.

As you review what you have written, consider how you want to live your life; what is important and exciting to you. Consider many alternatives that could enhance your life as a "mother graduate." Allow yourself to fill in the picture of yourself as an adult woman with a life beyond the role of mother.

౩ That Other Woman ౩

Both mother and daughter may have trouble seeing each other as real people, apart from their roles in relationship to each other. As if this other woman—your mother or daughter—were a job applicant whom you knew only in a business sense, write a letter of recommendation about her that includes her strengths and weaknesses. Do this in a clear, thinking way, leaving out emotions but allowing yourself to express the most respectful opinions you have about this other woman.

When Brenda was asked to do this exercise, she was shocked by her answer. She spent some time really getting into the part and imagining that this was not her daughter. In real life she had a deep conflict over her daughter Linda's lifestyle choices and had tremendous fear that her daughter was not "turning out okay." Their relationship had been quite bitter since Linda had told her mother that she was a lesbian. In her answer, almost every aspect of her daughter that worried Brenda became an asset. She writes: "Linda Jones is a competent young woman who has forcefully entered the work arena with high expectations for herself. Her creativity and commitment to her own beliefs will stand her in good stead in any field that she pursues. She is autonomous and a self-thinker, not easily swayed by commonly accepted attitudes and ideas. The quality of perseverance, which is a great gift in this candidate, may sometimes appear as stubbornness. However, when confronted she is willing to use her clear discernment to assess her own limitations. While I may not personally agree with Linda's views on varying subjects, I see her as a capable and resourceful woman who will make a fine addition to any organization."

CHAPTER SIX

Mother in My Life

JUDICIOUS MOTHERS WILL ALWAYS KEEP IN MIND,
THAT THEY ARE THE FIRST BOOK READ, AND THE LAST
PUT ASIDE, IN EVERY CHILD'S LIBRARY.

—C. Lenox Remond

HOOK, LINE AND SINKER

One of the crucial ways to support our ability to be more than a mother or daughter is to weed out the old things that we carry around from our lives with our mothers. This is true whether you are a daughter looking to go into your adulthood or a mother looking into your future. All women are full of their mothers' ghosts. This is our conditioning. We see it everywhere. We are "hooked" in ways known and unknown to us. Like the fish that has swallowed the bait, those hooks capture us as surely and irrevocably as the worms attract the fish. The outcome is often as bad! What are the hooks in your life that go back to your relationship to mother? Can you see them in your relationship with your children? mate? sense of self? How is mother still here in your life, every day? How do you get hooked?

๛ Della is a fifty-four-year-old woman in training for a career as a
ᐇ therapist. She answers the above question: "I didn't know how
to relate intimately with my children but cast myself in the roles
Mother had modeled for me: perfectionist, super mother, quite controlling in certain areas (food, clothing, church). I also modeled not
being able to express physical warmth or give positive feedback. These
behaviors extended to my husband also. Here I took on a similar role to
my mother, seeing my worth mainly through my husband and the children. I was the model homemaker and primary parent, supporting my
husband's work and representing him in the community—but with a
lot of resentment. Mother's denial of her sexuality became my pattern
as well; also, denial of any problems and needing the world to think that
the marriage and family were perfect. Even though I've given up most
of that, I'm still hooked in subtler ways. I tend to experience my therapist in the same way I experienced my mother. I try to please her and
feel like I can't, and I still try to be perfect, even though not as a
homemaker."

Della kept her mother in her life in limiting ways for most of her
fifty-four years, and only through her budding consciousness after a
painful divorce, separation from her mother, alienation from her
children, and a change of career did she come to see and change her
patterns and undo her hooks. The conditioning that we received
becomes part of the script we write. Della wrote herself into a role
just like her mother's, without ever knowing it.

If you still carry around unfinished or unclear business from your
relationship with your mother, if you carry script decisions that you
made at her knee, or if you carry around her voice as an internal negative parental voice, then mother is still in your life, and it won't take
much for you to find the hooks that result from this. Even if she is far
away, no longer living, or if you and she are friends in the present, the

effects of your life with her will be with you in your relationship and in your life.

Remember the list of areas where mother's ghost is likely to be prevalent: with spouses or mates, with children, with bosses or authority figures, with good friends, in job situations, in your self-concept. As long as this is true you will be the victim of hooks that throw you uncontrollably into old feeling, thinking and behaving patterns. And these hooks will be the living remnant of the negative aspect of your relationship to mother. You can see a hook when a hand goes out to slap just as one was slapped, a threat is made just as one was received, a lesson acted on, just as it was taught—all without benefit of examination in the light of current knowledge. Some of these responses are harmless. Some are not. Many do not have the charge or intent that was invested in the same or similar action from childhood, but all are un-thought out and may be a way of being that does not reflect your own ideas and beliefs. Hooks may manifest themselves in a sudden and frightening way or they may be so predictable as to be boring.

The examples are endless and painful. Even a mother with an intense desire not to hurt her children, and a choice not to do so, may find that this is not enough to overcome the unknown and uncontrollable anger that she experiences when she is hooked into an old childhood feeling of her own.

Sharon, age forty-one, came into therapy for this reason. "I have two daughters who are normal, healthy little girls and I love them very much, but once I really scared them and myself because I became so angry with them. I hit Marcie. I rushed to her and hugged her and told her how sorry I was, but she was too frightened to really hear me. Then I remembered a time when my mother came home from the hospital after my little brother was born and my Aunt Joan was taking care of us. We, my older sister and I, refused to eat some of the cereal that she had fixed, just as Marcie had been doing when I hit her. Aunt Joan made us sit there for hours and we both refused to eat. Then she took my sister and spanked her and spanked her. I went to her and screamed to stop it, stop it. She hit me with the back of her hand so hard that I fell down. We told mother, and she said we probably deserved it. I guess I never forgot that, even though I haven't thought about it in years. I had never believed I could do such a thing to my own daughters, but now I am terrified that I might again. How can I get rid of that awful feeling I had and make sure it never happens again?"

It is only through a conscious and concerted effort that it is possible to find the origins of these hooks. Mother's ghost may lie dormant for years and never seem to influence us, and then without warning something will come up that triggers such a strong reaction that we may act in ways opposed to everything we believe, as Sharon did.

Sometimes hooks are everywhere. We may find that a remark or glance or action will trigger an old, familiar childhood reaction and the mechanism that we used as a child to strike back at the hurt or to avoid the hurt will start to take over. When this happens, thinking and acting are so colored by the past that our present behavior is not a response to what is happening at the moment but a response to something that happened years ago. It can be a frightening and confusing experience for the one who is hooked—and for the recipients of the old reaction.

Julie's Story

"Recently I had an experience with a friend that I dearly love. As we were driving together, she said to me in a friendly but directive tone of voice, 'Oh, go this way. Take a left.' A feeling came over me that was enormous. Luckily, I knew enough not to respond from that feeling, for I could have yelled at her as if she had really done something awful. I was so surprised by my reaction of hurt and anger that I left Karen for a few minutes to try to analyze what I was thinking and feeling. I sat quietly and let my mind go back to when I had had this petulant, angry feeling before. I pictured myself as an adolescent wanting to prove to everyone in my family that I knew what I was doing in the world. My mother called me 'Miss KIA' (know-it-all). I could hear myself with Karen sounding just as I must have when I was fifteen 'I can do it. Don't tell me how.' This was an old feeling coming from having been discounted by my mother. After becoming aware that my reaction was based on some early memory, I could go back to Karen and be with her without rancor or petulance."

Hooks like these are caused by intense feelings in childhood that were disowned or not allowed. Julie couldn't express her anger at being called "Miss KIA" and so she buried that feeling. Sharon couldn't get support for her feeling of hurt and betrayal and she buried that. Each stayed buried until the right moment, when two adult women fell backward in time to old, little and intense feelings.

The ever-present, predictable hooks are perhaps even more injurious to the one who is hooked than to those who may feel the fallout from it.

Dorothy's Story

"For all my efforts to be a good mother, I have a hook that plagues me and probably hurts my children. I'm still not certain of the origins, though I know the feeling I have is little. Whenever my children are disappointed I feel a welling up of tears and pain that is far out of proportion to their disappointment. When my oldest child at age five announced quite neutrally that he hadn't been invited to so-and-so's birthday, I felt that pain and a surge of anger at the offend-ing child. Ten years later, I have cleared up some of that, but still inside I ache at their 'rejections' as I know I must have ached at my own as a child. I've had to monitor my efforts to 'rescue' them quite emphati-cally, as I know this isn't what they need."

While Dorothy's is fairly mild, these ongoing hooks can be the source of the most brutal parenting errors as well as of the most per-vasive self-limitations. It can be assumed that most cases of child abuse—physical and emotional—stem from just this source. It is clearly known that an abused child is far more likely to be an abusive adult, even if her intention is not to be. Work to heal that terrible family experience revolves around "reprogramming" the hook; that is, finding an alternative response to the experience of the hook. When you feel the rage welling up in you that will lead you to hit your child, call your support person, go into your room for five min-utes, leave the house. As the hook is separated from the abusive behavior, an opportunity exists for that wounded person (the abuser) to find and heal the source of the hook that is so devastating. And, from there, a chance exists to heal the hurt in the child who is the recipient of a dangerous generational hook.

So it goes, as well, with alcoholism, drug addiction, and other forms of physical and psychological self-abuse. In a predictable and dangerous way, individuals respond to hooks with life-threatening and self-destructive behaviors, and again the way out is to undo that hook: first from the destructive behavior, and then at its roots.

What needs to be done when these sudden emotional responses take over our actions and we lose control? Well, the old adage of "counting to ten" before you do or say anything is still good advice. It does not solve the underlying problem, but it may prevent the creation of new problems. This is the basis of the behavior-change strategies just mentioned. When we can stop long enough to control the impulsive reaction, we can also begin to look at its roots. The more dangerous, uncontrollable or inappropriate the response you have when hooked, the more urgent it is that you explore it. In order to understand your own hooks, you might ask yourself some questions.

🐝 *When have I felt like this before, especially in my childhood?*

🐝 *What is really going on for me?*

🐝 *Who was this feeling originally directed at?*

🐝 *What do I want right now?*

🐝 *What do I need?*

🐝 *What behavior would be aligned with my values and beliefs?*

🐝 *How can I reconnect with those values and beliefs and operate from them, instead of from this hook?*

🐝 *Do I need help to stop this behavior? to explore these roots?*

Many of us will need help to cut out the core of these hooks that are buried so deeply. We may need the patience of friends and family, we may need support groups, we may need professional help, and certainly we need to remember to stay in touch with our loving internal parent, who can see that we are hooked—maybe lost, in this instance but who knows that we are still a good person. The hooks lie deep and our job is to soften up the hold they have on us.

BUT IT'S HER FAULT

One of the greatest hooks going is blame, and blaming mothers is an especially popular sport. As therapists, we see it all the time: in our clients, in our colleagues, in psychological theories and groups, and sometimes in ourselves. It's easy to assume that this most primary figure is at fault. Society has often taken that stance and mothers, as much as anyone else, have supported it—especially by their guilt. Books galore are written to tell mothers how to do it right. Therapists galore have been created to fix up the mess mother made. There is a huge and powerful myth that there is a right way to be a mother and that every mother will fail in her attempt to do it right. As long as we blame others, especially our mothers, we allow our hooks to stay buried firm and deep within our psyches.

But mom is not the only one to be blamed and kids aren't the only ones who do the blaming. Blame is as pervasive in our culture as apple pie. Mother may use blame as a way to avoid feeling guilty about her choices: "The children acted so badly today that I just couldn't . . . [do what my dear husband asked, write a bestselling novel, feel happy or whatever]." Our parents may have used blame to justify their experiences and behaviors. If we saw them blame the trains, the weather, the government, each other and the kids for their own dissatisfaction in life, then we never learned about responsibility, about choice and consequences.

Daughters will particularly blame mothers as they see this important other as their teacher, model, protector, savior. Blaming in childhood is a way to respond to pressures within the family or community that ask us to be different than we are. It is originally a self-protective response. It allows us to defend our sense of okay-ness by placing blame for "problems" outside ourselves. It is a valid and useful response for young children, who struggle so intensely to maintain their growing sense of self. The blame is often appropriate, since children truly can be victims. In fact, it is a far healthier stance for a child to blame her parents than to blame herself. For a child victim who cannot blame the abuser, the problems are much more deep-seated than for one who can. A child who blames may be doing so to create a stronger sense of herself as good and worthwhile.

One way or another, we all learn the blaming game. That blaming game begins to be a problem and an excuse as we reach the teenage years. At this time, we begin to have choices about how to respond and who to be—unlike the younger child, who was fairly limited in her possibilities. If I can blame you because I did not finish my homework I will feel better. I still need to defend my sense of okay-ness and maybe I do that by blaming, rather than by taking responsi-bility. When blaming is a pattern in a young person, it may well point back to earlier roots and feelings of inadequacy that are difficult to cope with. When this pattern continues into adulthood and we expe-rience ourselves as victims (therefore blaming others), the problem is increased drastically.

❧ Cynthia became pregnant when she was twenty and chose to keep her child and give up college. She married the father of the child, who also quit school and went to work to support them. Cynthia came to a mothers' group and under a veneer of acceptance for her situation was a deep-seated blame that kept her in a resentful and helpless position. She finally allowed her feelings to emerge. "I should have known I'd never make it in the world. My mother could have been a singer except for us kids, and just when I might have gone on and become an artist, bang, I have a kid. It's impossible even to paint at home. She sees the paints and has a fit. I threw them all out. I guess I'm stuck with diapers and *Sesame Street*. Nothing ever really works out for me."

Cynthia learned blame from her mother, who in one way or another gave Cynthia the message that she had caused her mother's failure as a singer. It didn't take much for Cynthia to place that same blame on her daughter.

Unfortunately, daughters and mothers blame each other regularly. It is a common theme in childhood; it continues and often increases in adulthood. Listen to some of the comments women have made about their mothers or daughters:

"My mother always fed me starchy foods, gave me candy when I cried, and generally stuffed me. I can't break the habit and lose weight. It's too ingrained."

"My mother was so scared of everything. She was too darned over-protective. I can't risk anything today because of the fear she instilled in me."

"If you had let me eat normally, Mom, like the other kids—Oreos and white bread—I could have learned a moderate diet. But I still feel so deprived. I'm still compensating for the 'health food diets' you always had us on. Now, since I'm free of your demands, I just stuff myself with all the things I couldn't have as a kid."

"My mother never watched over me. She let me do anything at all. I'd climb the highest slide and she never said 'No.' I'm still scared thinking of some of the things I did. I certainly don't take risks like that anymore. In fact, I'm pretty cautious."

These aren't made up. Opposite parenting, same reaction. Remember the saying "You can't win!" Mothers must have invented that one. But it's not much better for daughters:

"My daughter lives so close to home and checks in on me all the time. I appreciate it, but I feel like an invalid. I can't reach out and create a new life for myself with her hovering over me so."

"Katie lives in Europe. How am I expected to get on with my life, being so cut off from her? I spend more time fretting about her than I would if she lived next door."

For an adult, blame is a way of avoiding having to look inward at one's self. The cries that life has been unfair, I deserve better, I've been cheated, it's not my fault are all ways of blaming, not taking responsibility, and giving away our own power. While there are certainly forces that define and limit us, we always have choices about how we respond. This tendency to give our power away is the source of the victim stance in life, a stance particularly well known to women. There are true victims—children, victims of crime and abuse, of political, social and natural oppressions—and there are victim roles. If we feel:

- helpless
- little
- out of control
- at the mercy of life, events, or other people
- powerless
- excessively frightened
- incapable of creating change
- ultimately unlucky
- fated negatively
- controlled by an unjust world (God, life, karma)
- we are damaged beyond repair
- that we were too hurt to heal
- that our conditioning irrevocably defines us
- that mother destroyed us

. . . well, then, we are operating in greater or lesser degree out of the victim role. And that role is nonproductive and defeating.

Being in the victim role is attempting to accomplish the same thing as the blaming child did, keeping us safe from the danger of responsibility. It just doesn't work as an adult. We will attract two kinds of people to us in that role. The first will be rescuers, who will try to bail us out. They will be our friends, lovers, therapists, clergy, family, or maybe it will be mother taking care of us in covert or overt ways for years after we have reached adulthood. We will need them, appreciate what they do, secretly feel that it is not enough, and finally we will resent them. How could we not resent the ones who take our power, even though we give it freely? The other people we will attract will be persecutors, for a victim without a persecutor is no victim at all. These people may be abstract figures—government, authorities, laws, society, men, women—but they will also be personal, such as the banker, the policeman, the teacher, our friends, lovers, therapists, family, and again maybe mother, who may fall into the role of the unloving persecutor driving the wounded victim further and further into helplessness and despair.

Patty was in long-term group therapy and almost everyone would be likely to agree that she "drove them crazy." Each one of them tried over and over to help her and be supportive, even when she took too much group time, came late, asked for time outside the group, and called late at night. Patty presented herself as a "whiner," complaining and begging. When someone would confront her on her victim stance, she would defend it, proving through her stories the "real impossibility" of getting her life together. The leaders of the group despaired of having her there. There seemed to be no help for her and, over time, group members moved more and more into persecutor roles, blaming and criticizing Patty.

One day she came to the group bruised. Her boyfriend had hit her. Everyone changed their tune and leaped in again to rescue her. She was accepted as a victim and got some of the empathy that she desperately needed. But it took only a few weeks for the group to revert to its persecutor stance, since Patty wouldn't do anything to help herself. She wouldn't leave her boyfriend, wouldn't go to the police and wouldn't call the women's center. The therapist finally asked her to leave the group and go into private therapy. She left feeling victimized even by the group.

Many women have a share of victim in them and it is a big task to get through that role. In large part, our training may have supported us in feeling like victims. Society certainly leans in that direction.

Patty came from a long line of victimized women. It was not until therapy with a counselor who did not play either rescuer or persecutor, that she began to find a place to experience herself that was not the victim. Patty was successful in this effort. Many women are not.

To move out of the victim stance requires taking responsibility for our lives and ourselves in ways that may be frightening and at times overwhelming. It is a big, incomprehensible world. To feel the victim of it is not surprising, but to think of ourselves as the cocreators in our own world is a powerful, affirming and limitless response. It is movement toward this position that heals the identification with the victim role.

Taking responsibility for our lives is the first step toward becoming a cocreator. We talked, earlier, about being the author of our own story. That is what taking responsibility in a conscious way leads to. We write in our strengths, our uniqueness, and give ourselves the permissions we need. Let's delve a little more deeply into what it means to take responsibility and how to do so.

A quick way to think of this highly charged term "responsibility" is as "response-ability"—the ability to respond! Response ability sounds a lot more appealing than the "responsibility" that mother and others foisted on us: the messages about how we should be. Responsibility as a term from childhood more often than not is also associated with failure and the experience of inadequacy. After all, most of us didn't quite reach the heights of responsibility that were expected of us. Consider the ability to respond, however. What more could we truly expect of ourselves or others than a clear response?

Patty, who had been so identified with her victim stance, worked long and hard in therapy and in her life to change that. One day, as she looked back over the changes she had made, she shouted in amazement: "I will never create another situation in my life that gives away my power!"

We don't assume that abused women create their victimization. It is simply not true in the larger world. Society and societal prejudices allow and create that. But individual women time and time again discover that they do allow others to victimize them in major and minor ways. We started with our mothers, being little in relationship to her bigness, being victim to her persecutor or rescuer. We may let her still be those ways to us, and certainly we may let others. How and why do we do that? Why? Because it is safer to give our power away at some level. That way, we can stay little. Failure is not our responsibility. We may suffer, but it's someone else's fault! To risk failure and suffering, as well as success and happiness, with no one else to blame is frightening. And it is the major task of an adult.

We stay in victim roles in many ways: (1) by pretending that we don't have any power, (2) by denying our uniqueness and our strengths, (3) by allowing situations to exist that aren't good for us, and (4) by creating our lives in relationship to the least of who we are, rather than the most.

But the real question is: How do we move into a position of responsibility in a conscious way? Among the answers: (1) by owning our power, strength and uniqueness, (2) by supporting the best in ourselves in feeling and action, (3) by risking success and failure in choosing our path, and (4) by being true to ourselves in the deepest way we know.

I STILL FEEL LITTLE

An important aspect of being true to ourselves is knowing all about who we are. Somewhere inside, almost every adult feels, thinks or believes that she (or he) is still little, and if this is true for us, we must come to know that "little" part and work to integrate her into our lives in a healthy, nondestructive way.

A lot has been written over the years about the so-called "impostor" complex, and what we see behind this idea is a very simple and old idea: that we do, in many ways, feel like children. And why not? If we were little in our bodies as a child—in a big world, with big parents—we then are still little in a huge world, with huge authorities and huge problems, and with complexities and questions unanswerable to even the most mature adult. The "impostor" is the adult face we use to cover the experience of feeling like a child. It is our attempt to act big when we feel little. It is not likely that we will get rid of the "little" feelings that we have, nor is it desirable. Seeing through a child's eyes will bring us freshness, spontaneity, empathy and intimacy, but only when those child eyes have been freed of their fear, confusion and self-doubt.

There is an important place for the child part of us. It shouldn't be exhibited in our workplace or in our job as parents. We don't particularly want to present our child face to authority figures or to others with whom we need to be adult. But in caring, mutually supportive, adult relationships, and in an internal self-nurturing way (remember Deb's dialogue on the subway) the child can find a healthy place to be in the world, free to express childlike qualities of playfulness as well as childlike needs for nurturance. Still, being little when we don't want to be, when it doesn't serve us, when it is an old, limiting pattern is a problem that needs to change. How often women find themselves breaking down into tears or confusion, or doubt or acquiescence or rage, in places where they needn't and in situations where they swore, to themselves, that they would stay adult.

Sandra is the mother of two young kids. She fought long and hard in her life and considered herself tough. She had to be to overcome the prejudice against her, her own fears, and the poverty she grew up in. In most places in her life she acted like the mature woman that she was. But sure enough, when she would have a confrontation with the school principal, she would break down and feel little, help-less and wrong. "Even when they accused my son of doing something that I knew he hadn't, I couldn't stand up to the principal. I got weak and weepy when he attacked me for raising my kids to be irrespon-sible. I wanted to shout back, or better yet stay calm, but I felt little and I hated it."

That little part of us can really get in our way, decreasing our potency, keeping us from possibilities that would enhance our lives. What is that part all about? The child voice that gets crystallized and is acted upon over and over is likely to refer back to the time when we began to write our script. As we made choices about the world, and our place in it, we subtly identified ourselves with our child feelings. What we lose touch with as we battle internally between child feelings and adult reasoning, is a sense of our true self, that uniqueness at the core of our being that really is who we are. Our true self existed before we were hurt and limited, before we bravely put on an adult mask, and it has stayed with us throughout our many years silently waiting behind our images and presentations of ourselves. We all catch glimpses of this truth about ourselves in times of quiet, of calm, in inspirational settings, or when we are experiencing deep feelings. At these moments we may know ourselves truly. But most of us live, pri-marily, out of a false sense of ourselves. We live out of the impostor place, a "false adult" that hides our lurking feeling of being a child.

And that child within us is still trying to get her needs met in the world in the same way that she tried as a child. She is still searching for dependency from a supportive mother figure, she is still afraid of rejec-tion, hurt, loss of love. She is still competing, in whatever ways she did as a child, for the things she needs. The false adult develops very young in us and continues to grow as a way to compensate for the child expe-rience, as a way to cope in the world. We act big and feel little.

What we need is to move into the "true self" space, from where we can see the child and take care of her needs. The true self is the essence of our uniqueness. It gives space to all the aspects of the free child, all the while supporting the real adult that is a mature, capable aspect of our being. The true self draws on the skills of the positive internal parent, creating a healthy inner process for the healing of the child. And, in that process of healing the not-okay child, we may need to raise this child again—right, this time.

Sandra wanted to know her self. For her, this involved creating not only a positive parent to help soothe her hurt child, but also developing a strong adult self that could take attacks without crumbling. Every advance she made in this way helped to heal the hurt of her internal child, and freed Sandra from her conditioning. Her true self began to shine through to create a more mature and effective adult woman.

The work Sandra did that many of us will need to do involves knowing the little-girl part, meeting her needs, helping her to heal, and living out the experience of true self. To get to know this child part you need to find out what activates her. Do you get thrown into childlike feelings and thoughts around men, authority figures, stress, money issues, pressure to perform? And what does that child part of you need in those scary situations? When identified with the child, do you need to feel loved and supported, or do you need to escape, to find an explanation, to have time to gather yourself together? As you come to know these things about the child part of you, you'll have a good chance of being able to predict danger situations for the child and set the stage, in advance, for helping that part of you get through a difficult time.

When Sandra realized that she was always hooked at her son's school, she spent some time coming to understand the child needs. Two things stood out for her. The child needed to understand the possible outcomes of this seemingly dangerous situation and she needed to feel supported in handling it. Sandra did a little checking to find out just what kind of power the school principal had and she became aware that it was much less than she had imagined. She also asked a friend to come along with her the next time she had to go to the school. These strategies took a lot of pressure off the child and Sandra was able to operate much more clearly out of her adult.

The child part of you is a remnant from your past, heavily influenced by your relationship to mother. Like all hooks, you may find her operating anywhere. But you will likely find her operating when you are with your mother, even when you may have cleared her out of most other parts of your life. If this part is activated with mother, there may be several steps to take. If you were pushed from the nest early (or it felt so, to you), your child may still be clinging to mother to find the help that you needed to make it as an adult. If there were gaps in your relationship to her, or traumas, or confusions, the child part is likely to be activated in an effort to fix those problems. But the child will try to fix them in the same way that she did (and failed in) as a child. And she will forever feel abused again, hurt again, unloved again, needy again, competitive again, judged again. If you are over twenty-one, then in all likelihood it is too late for the child part of you to have most of her needs met with mother—you're on your own. You will need a lot of creative, adult thinking and planning to help you find the support systems you need so that your child part can get what she needs. Nevertheless, until you can present an adult to your mother, you're going to be hooked.

Dorothy's Story

❧ "When I was visiting with my family, I became quite ill. In typical fashion I made arrangements to see a doctor, sent the kids to a movie, and drove to the office. The doctor, in a rather alarming way, diagnosed my condition to be one that was serious and potentially life threatening. I asked him reasonable questions; got the information I needed and went to join my family at the movie. I told my husband about the diagnosis and we discussed it, realizing that perhaps this doctor was not right, since he seemed to be missing certain key pieces of information. When I went back to my mother's home and told her about the diagnosis, I burst into tears, as if I were surely going to die. Having felt like a thirty-year-old throughout the day, I felt scared and five the minute I saw my mother."

Julie's Story

&ᴈ "When I awoke from the anesthetic after an operation, I wished more than anything for my own mother, dead for over twenty years. I remember the way she babied me when I was sick as a little girl. I wanted that. I knew, in advance, that I would feel this way and I made sure to get lots of people to give me support. I had my husband by my side before and after surgery, I had my daughters calling me regularly, and I had friends with me all the time. I even let the doctor know about the scared part and he was able to give me some very reassuring information before the operation. I think recovery would have been much more difficult if I had tried to 'keep a stiff upper lip' and act always like an adult. I surely didn't feel like one."

It didn't work for Dorothy to be little with her mother at that time. She hadn't chosen it. She didn't even know she was having those "little" feelings. The child had taken over. It is just that power to take over that makes it so crucial to work consciously with the child part of ourselves. And one of the most important ways to work with the child is to find places where it is okay to be that child. Julie, on the other hand, had looked at options for getting that support that she knew her child would need. She had set the stage in advance for having a great deal of comfort and support.

It will work in a healthy mother/daughter relationship to be able to take your child home to mother—and, vice versa, for mother to take her child home to you. In fact, a great gift in that relationship is to be able to mother each other, trading the little and big places. For many that time doesn't ever come, or comes only on a mother's deathbed, when by default the roles are reversed. For most of us, our feelings of littleness are so unconscious that we can't go beyond them. We must first be adults together before we can go on to be able to be little with each other. And in any good adult relationship, there are times to be children together, to play and laugh and be carefree, and there are times to be a parent to each other's child, to hold, to help, to nurture. Adult relationships that are free of old hooks offer an opportunity for intimacy such as this, and the mother and daughter one, because of the depth of its connection, may be one of the most profound adult relationships—when it is free.

Dear Julie,

My mother passed away suddenly last Friday. She was at her sister's and had a heart attack. The last few months were a peaceful, sharing time for us. I had learned in my work with you how I perpetuated the symbiotic relationship, always feeling little and rebelling against it. I finally took a stand on my feelings and felt myself grow up. When Mother retired this summer, I was able to help her through her fears. I let her know that I would be there for her, and I was. She got scared and confused about buying a bathing suit, of all things! She thought she was too old. We went together and got one that looked great. I miss her now more than I ever did in all the years we were apart. I miss her, but I am not depressed. We found out how to love each other.

WORKBOOK

How do we unhook hooks? or even recognize them? We know they operate and that they limit us. We have heard ourselves say, over and over, "I won't do that anymore." "I'm going to be this way from now on!" "How did I let myself lose my temper so?" "Why can't I stay rational in these situations?" The one-liners we offer ourselves (usually critical) in an effort to alleviate our hooks don't help all that much. A hook is a hook, and until we unhook it we'll repeat those unchosen patterns over and over.

What is of even more concern is that the hooks that we know about in ourselves are more superficial than the ones we have not even recognized yet. The more dangerous ones are those that we can't even see. Our defenses and responsibilities in some situations so closely parallel our childhood experience that we have no other perspective from which to view that experience. The woman who feels hurt over and over again because her daughter doesn't love her may never see all the ways her daughter does love her and how she does show her love. She is caught in an old hook that demands that love be shown a certain way. If we want to know about the hooks we can't yet see, we'll have to be very observant: When do I feel hurt, little, blaming, unloved, "righteously" upset? Is there a pattern that I can discern? Might there be a hook in these experiences buried so deep as to be unrecognizable?

Our continued self-awareness will help us uncover hooks throughout our lives, and each time we see one we'll have the opportunity to change it! In the following exercise we will work on doing just that.

🙊 Hurt and Hooked 🙊

In this exercise, take time to assess your automatic responses: those behaviors, thoughts or feelings that you do without thinking. Let yourself recall the times when you regretted what you had said, when you lost your temper, when your response seemed out of control or out of proportion, when you found yourself saying things you didn't mean, or when you noticed you were acting just like you had when you were a child, or just like *someone else* had acted toward you when you were a child. These experiences will help uncover the hooks and they will range from the mundane to the melancholy to the malicious! Explore them all and write a list of these unchosen responses.

"I always cut off the end of my ham, even though I remember afterwards that my pan is big enough!"

"Every Valentine's Day I feel unloved because my husband doesn't bring me flowers. He hates Valentine's Day and calls it a card-company ruse. He brings me flowers quite often, but I still feel hurt on that one day."

"I hate it when those kids leave the top off the toothpaste. I can't stand their mess or them when they don't pay attention to what I want."

Finally, ask yourself the following questions, or those that are relevant, about each hook:

- What am I feeling when I am hooked in this way? angry? sad? scared?
- When have I felt like this before, especially in my childhood?
- Who is this feeling originally directed at?
- Is mother involved in this?
- What do I want when I am having this experience?
- What do I need? (What is truly important for me?)

- What can I do to take care of the feelings associated with this hook?
- How can I unhook the feelings that I am having from the behaviors that aren't appropriate?
- What behavior would be aligned with my values and beliefs?
- Do I need help to stop this behavior? to explore these roots?

The sad-on-Valentine's-Day lady found out about herself that she had felt this same sad way at all holidays in her family, fearing that her mother would give her twin sister a better present. "Unloved" was the experience that echoed throughout her relationship with her mother. What was really going on for this woman was that holidays make her feel little. What she wants, in those moments is the biggest, best gift that money could buy. What she really needs is reassurance for her child part and some adult thinking about that particular day. To handle the feelings, she needs to take in the love and happiness that her current life offers her. To stop the hook, or at least the behavior, she talked with her husband the day before Valentine's Day and got some strong reassurance for her child that she was loved. She also gave herself some adult thinking time. When she asked the last question on the list, in an effort to create more appropriate behavior, she came up with an answer that not only took care of her kid, but also expressed some of her uniqueness at the same time. The sad-on-Valentine's-Day lady became happy when she sent flowers to her husband at work with a note saying, "Bring these home tonight!"

❧ The Blaming Game ❧

Enjoy this lighthearted version of a usually "heavy" game and see if it helps free you from the blaming trap.

Welcome now, to everybody's favorite game show: "The Blaming Game!" Contestants, here are the rules to our game. Write down all the people from your past and present that you have blamed, could blame, should blame, would like to blame or who deserve to be blamed for something they did (or didn't do) to you. And note the terrible effect they had on you. You have only a few minutes, so write fast, using the following format:

I blame _____ for _____.
It made me _____.

"I blame my mother for working so much. It made me insecure.

I blame my sister for being so smart. It made me feel inadequate.

I blame my dog for chewing up the rug. He ruined my date with Mr. X!"

Go to it!

Now that you are done, we will move to the hard part of our game. The winner will be the person who can stay with this process for every person on her list! It's time to play the exciting second phase of our game: "Taking Responsibility!" Rewrite each of the preceding statements as follows: I take responsibility for

_____.

I _____.

Key words here are "pretending," "denying," "allowing," "creating," so it might look like this:

"I take responsibility for feeling insecure. I allow this to continue as if I were still a little girl!

I take responsibility for feeling inadequate at times. I pretend that I can't do many things that I know I can!

I take responsibility for my ruined date with Mr. X. I denied my feelings about the jerk in the first place!"

All right, on your marks, get set, take responsibility.

If you managed to do this with each person on your list, you are a winner. You win freedom from blame, maturity, autonomy and a chance at the grand prize: empowerment! To go for the grand prize, take one last step. Following your last statements, rewrite each as an affirmation and plan about your unfolding empowered self. Use the following format: I can be who I want to be "by _____." Key phrases are: owning (power, strength, etc.), supporting the best within, risking, being true to myself.

"I can be who I want to be by supporting my mature self!

I can be who I want to be by risking success in showing what I know how to do.

I can be who I want to be by being true to my deepest sense of who I am (in dating and everywhere else)!"

Go for it!

You are now a grand-prize winner. Your empowerment can never be taken away from you! Congratulations!

❧ Take Care of This Child ❧

We hope that you have come to a clear sense of the citizens within you that operate in and out of consciousness, helping and hindering you in your growth. There is the "child." She feels more than thinks. She reacts out of past hurts and has the same fears, needs and beliefs that she did when you were actually a child. There is also a "negative internal parent," whose job is to protect the child from a world perceived as dangerous. This parent voice is critical, demanding, condemning and limiting. Its effort to protect is lost in its demeaning and disempowering behavior. There is also the "positive internal parent," a wise old woman who loves the child deeply and compassionately and sees her clearly. Her job is also to protect and to guide in a supportive, nurturing way. The true self that you are can draw on any of these and can learn to harmonize them. Your first need is to take care of the hurt child within you.

In this exercise, you'll take some time to get to know each "voice," each player, and then plan some strategies that will bring greater harmony to your inner world. Write a paragraph about each "part" of you. Make sure to keep them from overlapping. Guidelines: The kid is little and comes from your past. The negative internal parent is critical and a lot like the "bad" side of your mother and other "big" people from your childhood. The positive internal parent is the perfect parent and wise being. Your true self is you: in essence, your uniqueness and your potential. Describe each player.

When you have written about each part of you and about your true self, think and write about the following:

- Who gets the most airtime in my life (whom do I identify with most or feel like most)?
- How does the child respond to the negative parent?
- Is my positive parent actively available?
- Do I feel in touch with my true self in my life?
- What does the child need in order to heal?
- In what situations does she come up in my life?
- What behavior does she exhibit in those situations?
- What would help her make it through those situations better?

As you explore this dynamic in yourself, it may help to think about how Sandra, or "sad on Valentine's Day," worked with her hurt child. Do this work and you'll be on your way to having a healthier child within and, therefore, a healthier you.

CHAPTER SEVEN

Letting Go of the Past

WE ARE NOT FREE TO USE TODAY,
OR TO PROMISE TOMORROW, BECAUSE WE ARE
ALREADY MORTGAGED TO YESTERDAY.

—*Ralph Waldo Emerson*

THE SACRED WOUND

Dear Mom,

What did I do? Was I a bad baby? Did you want to get pregnant? Was I ugly? I don't remember ever being told that I was cute. Being cute is little girlish. I don't remember ever feeling like a little girl. Why?

When did you start disliking me? I don't remember exactly when I didn't like you anymore—but I can't remember ever liking you. Did you ever hug me as a kid? I don't remember you ever looking at me in a kind way. I would give anything to know why you didn't love me. I can't get myself together as a whole person if I don't get some answers or at least some peace of mind. I just want to be able to sort

157

things out. I want to recognize my feelings and be able to sort them out and try to do away with the bad ones—they hurt too much. I want to say, "Well she didn't like me. So what?" or "That was her problem. It doesn't mean there's something wrong with me."

I wish you could come back just to love me for a while. I wish I could talk to you.

Your daughter, Zoe

This woman is wounded. Deeply, painfully, tragically. She suffered this wound at her mother's hands. Whether consciously or unconsciously, her mother let her way of life inflict a deep wound on her daughter. Zoe's wound is the source of her unconscious infliction of wounds onto her own children. The wound may be passed on for generations, without the question ever being answered, "Why didn't you love me?" But for this daughter it is too late to have an answer from mother. Her mother is long gone. And as long as Zoe waits for a magical answer to appear, she will stay wounded.

Zoe needs to ask different questions now. As much as Zoe longs for an answer to the questions she asks of her mother, these answers will not heal her. The child in Zoe needs to hear not why mother didn't love her, but that mother did love her in the best way she knew how. And the adult in Zoe needs to ask new questions: "What can I do with this hurt?" "How can I use this pain to help me?" "What meaning is there for me in this wound?"

We have plumbed the depths of hooks, conditioning, negative internal messages and limiting scripts, and at each turn we have tried to undo a piece of the injury or limitation that hinders us. And if we have been lucky, we may be freer of our own wound now than we were a week or a month or a year ago. And while "time heals all wounds," consciousness and choice will help the healing process move along more quickly and more meaningfully.

The wound from our childhood can be thought of in many ways. To come to know your own wound, just take a moment to scan yourself—physically, emotionally, psychologically, spiritually. Do you have a sense of being wounded? Can you feel its origins in your past? The wound may be thought of in different ways. It may be the total of your limiting conditioning, or it may revolve around your belief about yourself—your negative self-concept.

For some the wound will be more specific: a loss, an injury or disability, a source of grief in childhood. A traumatic experience of any kind or a traumatic life may be the source of pain. The relationship to mother will in many cases be the source of wounds, either partially or entirely. She may have hurt us by her actions or lack of actions, by her way of behaving or her absence, by her infliction of pain or her lack of protection of us from pain inflicted by others. In some way she will be a part of that wound by her very role. She bore us and we turned to her to be taken care of.

Now that we are adults, it is our responsibility to heal that wound.

We must first assess whether our woundedness is being perpetuated in our present life or whether it is simply the old wound still unhealed. If we are being wounded over and over, then healing will be almost impossible. Take a moment to assess the life you are now leading and how it may continue to wound you.

❧ *Am I still being hurt in my present life by forces outside of me, as I was as a child?*

❧ *Is my life such that I am injured, again and again, in the same core way?*

❧ *Am I in an abusive relationship that mirrors the one I was in with my parents?*

❧ *Am I in a job that offers me no challenge and keeps me little and unsuccessful, just as I was kept little and unsuccessful in childhood?*

❧ *Am I caught in self-destructive behaviors that replicate the pain of my childhood?*

If we find ourselves as adults in situations that wound us still, then we must bravely rethink our choices and consider our options for re-choosing. We must continue to work to undo old scripts and messages and to choose our lives in relationship to new values.

Honoring yourself enough to create a harmless life for yourself will be a major step in your healing. It is a huge piece of our work to heal the old, inner hurts, and it is even more difficult, perhaps, to change our lives in order to heal those wounds. If you are reading this and know that your life situation—self-imposed, imposed by others or by circumstances—limits, suffocates and wounds you in a significant way, then you owe it to yourself to find out what ways there are to "right" your life—internally, externally, or both. And if help is needed to do this, give that to yourself.

For many of us, life is no longer inflicting wounds on us in the same limiting way it may have as children. Surely we all have our ups and downs, but this normal flow of life does not wound us: It is the way of life. For most of us, the wounds that still hurt us are old. Pain and injury, self-doubt and uncertainty, fear, sadness, anger, and confusion from our childhoods fester like an unhealed cut, causing us to feel and act in debilitating ways. And because this is true, we must finally heal that old wound.

꧁꧂ Rhoda was an incest victim and she had, by her own thinking, done most of what she needed to do about her rage, feelings of impotence and need to forgive her father. In fact, when she came into therapy several years after her work on the incest experience, the incest was not what she came to deal with. She needed to straighten out her feelings in relationship to her lover. She carried around "an edgy, angry, confused feeling" toward her mate.

Rhoda quickly got in touch with a new level of rage at her mother, who had not protected her. She could reasonably see how her mother had been unable to protect because of her own limitations and fear, but the rage remained and Rhoda came to realize that she looked to her lover to heal that wound, that lack of trust of her mother. And she felt similarly toward her lover as she had toward her mother—wanting and needing her, not trusting and being angry with her. Rhoda had a great deal to do if she was going to really heal this wound.

Leslie, on the other hand, had a normal childhood filled with material well-being and reasonable parents. She felt a lack, however, that tended to slow her down, pull her back, cause her to hesitate in all areas of her life. Her therapy revealed that her parents had been dutiful but not present. Her father played a typical absentee role and her mother had been emotionally unavailable. Leslie had felt lost in her family, and when she became ill as a child she was all the more lost. She turned to her mother over and over, hoping to find the deep nurturing and reassurance that she needed, especially in the face of her illness. Mother always gave her the prescribed dosage of medicine and comfort but never more, never enough for Leslie's frightened self. Though she healed physically, her psychological wound was deeper than she alone could heal. She had, over the years of her childhood, hidden herself more and more behind fear and invisibility. And as an adult she was still afraid and hidden.

What is needed by these and so many other women to heal the wound that may have been caused in so many different ways? A simplified formula for truly healing the wounds from our childhood might look like this:

1. Assess your present life for indications of the wound,
2. Discover its origins in childhood and in relationship to mother,

3. Determine what you need to be healed (that is possible to achieve),
4. Orient your thinking in relationship to present time,
5. Separate clear, present, centered thinking from old, unclear feeling,
6. Discover the value of your wound and how holding on to it helps you, and
7. Put the wound in a meaningful context.

When Rhoda worked with this formula, she discovered that:

1. In her present life, her relationship with her lover was as limited and painful as was her ability to relax and trust.
2. The origins of this were in her relationship to her mother. Not only had the early symbiotic stages been fraught with uncertainty—since her mother had been hospitalized several times for nervous breakdowns—but in her later years, Rhoda's mother had not protected her from the violent sexual abuse of her father.
3. Rhoda felt strongly that she needed to trust herself and her lover and that she needed, at a practical level, to allow herself to be nurtured by her lover and friends. She needed also to develop a self-nurturing stance. What was largely in the way of allowing nurturing was Rhoda's thinking that she was not okay. Rhoda had made huge (and understandable) assumptions about herself, based on her childhood experience; she had assumed that something was wrong with her, that she was unlovable and undeserving.
4. As Rhoda began to think about herself in the present, she realized that she was well liked and respected, that she was strong and capable, that she was giving, and that others wanted also to give to her. All present indications, including a deep feeling inside Rhoda that had long been buried, indicated that she

was lovable and deserving—although she had internalized the message that she was not.

5. Rhoda disciplined herself to stay with that thinking about herself. She believed it was true, but felt dragged into old feelings of unlovableness and unworthiness. She worked with an affirmation that supported her positive thinking and limited her negative feeling about herself. Gradually, as the preponderance of her thinking was supported, a new set of feelings about herself came into her experience.

The work thus far was powerful for Rhoda. Her relationships and self-image improved. But she still felt a nagging sense of her wound, within herself and as a real obstacle to her relationship to her mother. For Rhoda, the next step (6) came quite accidentally. She describes this experience:

> I saw a dog as I was coming here today that had only three legs. I brushed past him as I usually do with the bums and homeless and injured. There are so many. But I stopped in my tracks and felt a powerful surge of caring and of recognition. I felt, for the first time, connected to the pain in the world—not hiding from it, denying it or being overwhelmed by it, just knowing it and accepting it. I felt differently toward every person I saw after that. I think in that moment I became truly human.

Rhoda, by being open to her own wounds, found a place to feel the pain of others and came closer to being connected in a meaningful way to the world. She discovered that her *wound had value*. She had learned about pain and suffering and recovery from pain. This was her strength. Her wound took on new meaning.

As hard as it is to believe, every wound may be considered sacred.

It guides us, as a beacon to our own growth, our own strength, our own uniqueness. Part of who we truly are is our own version of pain, our reaction to it, our interpretation of it and our healing from it. While it is convenient to think of a wound as the problem, the reason why "I can't do or be this or that," an obstacle to growth, it may be enlightening and relieving to realize that it is a part of our growth. The sail on a sailboat is an obstacle to the wind. It blocks the free flow of the wind. Yet because of blocking the wind, it moves the sailboat. Without that obstacle the sailboat could not move. And so, too, for each woman who has a wound. It will help define, in an expanded way, who you are and can be.

A quick word to balance this idea. One cannot excuse abuse or allow themselves or others to harm. Using this thought—that each wound has a sacred aspect, as permission to create (or allow to be created) pain and hurt—is wrong. We must operate out of our sense of rightness, always. And at the same time we have the power to create and allow for meaning to emerge for pain that does and has existed.

Rhoda went on in her life to put her *wound in context* (7). She was able to take it out of the purely personal and put it into a social, political, and psychological context in which she saw her whole family as being wounded. No one was the bad guy anymore. Each was a suffering human. Her own healing involved work with her lover and a concerted effort to be in relationship to her mother. She came, in time, to feel able to forgive her mother and to create a meaningful relationship with her. She also put the value of her wound to work in the world as a lobbyist for children's rights. This story ended happily. Will you let yours?

"Sacred" is defined as "worthy of veneration or reverence." In order to let go of the past in a deep way, the injury that is part of that past must be healed. To be truly healed it must be understood. To be understood it must have personal relevance and meaning. We may cope with our wound, overcome it, ignore it, go around it, get on in spite of it, or deny it. And we may also own it, come to know it, find its meaning for us in our lives, draw strength from it and find that, as part of our unique self, this wound is worthy of veneration and reverence.

To do this healing, we must first allow the pain to be there. Denial and avoidance—common efforts to deal with pain—simply drive the wound further underground, creating infection. When we can accept that we were hurt, we can grieve. Grieving for the lost life, the lost love, the mother that was not there, for the child who has suffered, is so important. Grieving, as we have come to know, is a self-healing process. To fully grieve for a lost loved one will take the griever into self-healing. So, too, with our own grief for the lost and hurt childhood. It is okay to feel that pain. And then to own it. If we have not fully accepted this pain, we may be playing a waiting game. Are we waiting for mother to make it right? Are we waiting for some magic that will make it all change?

Leslie, whose mother had been only superficially available to her as a child, had spent years of her adulthood trying to make contact with her mother in a way that she unconsciously hoped would be healing. She would go back to Iowa full of the news of her successes and be met with the same minimal response from her mother. She would go home ill or brokenhearted and fare no better. She paid little serious attention to her own hopes for a family, looking back always to mother in a never-ending search for healing. It didn't work. The pain is in the past, the inflictors of pain are gone, and mother can't help, even if she tries and wants to. So we must own our pain. After Leslie had turned her attention solidly to herself, she let in her pain and her responsibility for it as an adult. In a lighthearted moment, she said of it: "This is mine, like my blond hair, green eyes, small feet, freckles, fat ankles, creativity, bad memory and sense of humor. This wound is mine!"

Our pain, or wound, is part of who we are, for better and for worse. We already know the worse! We have lived through the pain. So how about the better? Ask yourself the questions that Zoe and Leslie needed to:

☙ *What can I do with this hurt?*

☙ *How can I use this pain to help me?*

☙ *What meaning is there for me in this wound?*

When we can take on the awesome task of healing this sacred wound, we will be well on our way to a fuller, richer life. We will know ourselves in a deeper and more honest way. We will see the world more clearly.

WE ARE BOUND TOGETHER

How we deal with our mothers and daughters will be part and parcel of our healing of old wounds. It may be that this relationship is the hardest to heal. It may be the last bastion where the wound festers. We may hide our dependency behind pseudo-images of maturity, separation and friendship, but behind these masks may lurk the unfinished feelings that do not allow us to be free.

Truly letting go requires the complete and appropriate separation that we have talked about. And separation is difficult for most of us—especially so if we still feel wounded, hooked, unfinished in our relationship to mother or daughter. When this is so, many unconscious strategies for staying hooked to each other surface. We keep up old patterns often in a new disguise in an effort to avoid the fear and the pain of separation or confrontation or loss. Each way that we stay bound—not bonded, but bound—to each other is hurtful and limiting. Each keeps the wound alive and hinders the healing process. Behind each masquerade is a relationship that is based in large part on old, unresolved feelings. High on the list of these old feelings are dependence, resentment and guilt—the ties that bind.

Let's look at the costumes that mothers and daughters wear in some of these masquerades. Each play enacted below is a variation of the many ways that mothers and daughters have lost themselves in their relationship to each other. Each is the story of guilt, resentment and dependence, of wounds unhealed. Each is the story of a relationship that is not free to be full, present and open.

Mother/Daughter Forever. In this masquerade mother and daughter play out an unhealthy dependency, one toward the other or both for each other through their battle cry of "We are so close!" Their relationships to others suffer as they give primacy to the mother/daughter in their lives. They feel glad and proud of their closeness (unlike their friends, "who have so many problems"). They use their codependence to avoid adulthood, intimacy with others, fear of losing each other. They may go so far as to always be in crisis, illness, or need, each taking turns in order to make their efforts to stay so "close" seem reasonable.

Close in Name Only. In this scenario, mother and daughter see or call each other frequently, maybe every day. They think that they are very connected to each other but most contacts result in recriminations and hurt feelings. There are lots of "If you had only . . . then . . ." Both are willing to play the role that they are assigned: one as adult mother, one as child daughter. Many of the same patterns that were seen during adolescence are repeated. Resentment by both, that the other does not truly see or hear her, runs rampant. A covert dependency based on both mother's and daughter's inability to graduate from their roles lies below the surface of this awkward relationship.

Cold and Distant. In this play, mother and daughter both appear autonomous and adult. They probably live far from each other. Family situations that require mother and daughter to be together may be the only time they see or speak to each other. There are lots of reasons why they see each other so rarely: It may be that mother or daughter is too involved in a career or that they live too far apart or that their lifestyles may be different. One or both may play this game, and will probably act as if it is just fine the way it is. Underneath there is resentment for hurts from the past, a longing to reconnect, and guilt at the cold distance that is placed by one or both women.

Let's Be Pals. In this situation, the daughter and mother appear to be close and warm toward each other, but they always manage to share the wrong things. In their "acting" like adults with each other, they disregard their differences and the needs each has, attempting to make the other a perfect companion. While they will frequently be together and share at an equal level, both will find a way to push their own agenda and hurt or reject the other. This is a no-win situation based on hidden dependence, resentment and fear of autonomy.

Let Me Help. This game is usually played by mother in an effort to stay close to her daughter and expiate her guilt. Whether she takes a motherly or pseudo-adult role with her daughter, she offers her this, that and the other thing as a way to support, aid and help her daughter. Usually she offers the things that are not what the daughter wants or needs. Certainly they are not the things the daughter asks for. The daughter is stuck accepting, and thus staying little and obligated—or rejecting and then feeling guilty herself. Mother's pain and guilt in knowing that she has hurt her daughter motivates her to try to fix this, often in the same ways she tried to fix it for her daughter when she was young. Daughter's guilt and fear of independence may keep her playing the helpless game long after she's ready to go off on her own. The daughter's version involves staying to take care of an aging or infirm mother. The mask is one of love, compassion and gratitude for all that mother gave. Hidden is the resentment and guilt at wanting to be free of the burden, as well as an unwillingness to meet one's own needs.

What can be done about the underlying feelings of guilt, resentment and dependency that taint so many relationships? As we peel away the games that cover these feelings and allow ourselves to explore and heal the deeper hurts, we may free ourselves of these wounds and come to a truly adult relationship with our mothers or daughters.

Guilt is a fairly simple process to uncover. Guilt may be considered in two ways. There is "existential" guilt and there is "neurotic" guilt. Existential guilt comes from having dishonored one's deepest belief. This is the guilt we feel for having wronged someone, or having hurt someone in spite of our better sense about right and wrong. Existential guilt has a purpose. It is an internal gyroscope that helps us right a course of action, correct a failure, learn a better way. It is not self-condemning but self-educating. It does not have about it the feeling of badness that is associated with normal, or "neurotic," guilt. It does have, however, a need to correct. If I feel existential guilt about something, I must make amends, apologies or corrections and I must learn from that mistake. When we have corrected and learned the lesson inherent in that mistake, the guilt is gone. Guilt, in this way, is simply a reminder from our true self of who we truly are and can be.

Neurotic guilt, however, is a hook. It is often, at its roots, anger turned inward. When I am angry with my daughter for not cleaning her room, I may turn this into guilt about not being a good mother. When I am angry that my mother is so demanding, I may turn this into guilt that I have not done more for her. Guilt that hangs on, nags at us, supports our worst feeling about ourselves, doesn't go away even though we might change, is neurotic guilt. It is the basis for most guilt in mother/daughter relationships. The catch with guilt of this kind is that it's a no-win situation. You can't apologize and make amends, because you really don't want to. If I say to my daughter, "I'm sorry I'm such a bad mother. Let me clean your room for you," my guilt will not be lifted and my anger will be doubled. This guilt cannot be cured or relieved. It has no lesson to teach. It's mainly a cover-up for anger or demands or needs that have been unexpressed. I can feel free of that feeling I call guilt when I tell the truth: "I want you to clean your room. I'm angry that you don't" or "I feel burdened by having to do so much for you. I want to share the responsibility with others." If we tell the truth, guilt will fall away. If we make amends for our true errors, we will have learned a valuable lesson. In either case, guilt need not hang on and define a relationship.

Resentment is not very different from guilt, though we may find it more bearable at first. It may feel slightly better because the bad feeling we have is aimed at someone else and not at ourselves. Sometimes, however, a whole life pattern is based on resentments. There are mothers and daughters who haven't spoken to one another in years because of some resentment or many.

A disease that is allowed to go untreated develops side effects that make the illness worse, and the side effects of collecting resentments is like an insidious and pervasive disease. Resentments, when they build up, are haunting, hurting and devouring of our life energy, our ability to be free. They grow and then seem to occupy all the available space that might be spent in better ways. They are used as a weapon and sharpened and rearranged so they can be their most effective barb. They can be added to until there is an arsenal of old resentments that could become a fortress against any intrusion of love and acceptance. Like toxic waste, getting rid of them can seem an impossible task.

Resentments point back to deeper wounds and, when we hold on to them, those wounds are allowed to grow. Why do resentments flourish in so many lives? Most often, because dealing with them means being honest, expressing our feelings and asserting our needs. Freeing oneself of resentments means giving up blame. Living without resentments means being responsible for ourselves.

🕸 Roe tells of almost losing her daughter over a meaningless resentment. "I gave my daughter a beautiful gift of some antique dishes that she wanted. I put them in her dining room in a box with a note inside the box telling her that these had been in the family for over a hundred years. I waited and waited for her to mention them. After two weeks had passed and there was still no mention, I was furious. I became convinced that she was ungrateful and didn't love me anymore, so I stopped calling her and was curt on the phone when she called; our once good relationship became strained. I began to think she was growing to be just like my mother, who never appreciated anything I did for her and never liked me as much as she did my brother. I was ready to end the relationship. I considered cutting her out of my will.

Then one day Rosy called and said, 'Mother, I just found the box with the dishes and they are so wonderful. I thank you so much.' I coldly asked her why she had waited so long to thank me and she explained that she had just found that her husband had put them under a shelf in her closet and she'd never known they were there. I realized then that I had built up this resentment with my daughter by expecting her to treat me as I thought my mother had, and, as a result, I almost lost the closeness with her that I value so much. Next time, I'll speak up and not wait weeks and weeks. What pain I put myself through because I was using old thinking patterns."

Roe fell into a downward spiral of old and bad feelings, all because she didn't ask, didn't express her need to know, to be appreciated. In fact, the buildup of resentments in Roe allowed her to behave in ways that she never would have otherwise. We can turn ourselves into monsters if the arsenal of resentments builds up enough. And the simple cure? Speak the truth, take the risk of saying what you think, feel and want. A clear "No" from someone to a request you make will leave you with far less resentment than the imagined rejection built up in your mind when someone doesn't respond to you in the way you wished they would.

Guilt fosters pseudo-closeness in mothers and daughters ("Let Me Help"). Resentments create an unbridgeable gap ("Close in Name Only," "Cold and Distant"). Dependency creates two half-people trying to be whole through the other person ("Mother/Daughter Forever," "Let's Be Pals"). Over and over again in our work with women, we see the issue of dependency thwarting both mother and daughter. Moving out is symbolic of leaving, but all too often it is only a gesture. Dependency can run a woman whether she lives with her mother or lives a thousand miles away. And if her mother is dead, she can transfer that dependency to another available object. Dependency is simply being so caught in the roles of mother or daughter that we need the other person to play their role for our sake. After all, what is Romeo without Juliet, what is peanut butter without jelly, and what is a mother without a daughter (and vice versa)? As long as either party refuses to graduate, an issue of dependency will linger.

On the golf greens, Betty and her daughter Joan could be seen daily. They had played for years together and preferred each other's company to anyone else's. They tended to refuse invitations from other golfers, including their husbands. In fact, Joan and Betty did almost everything together and loved it that way. When Joan's husband got a job offer in another state, it was a tragedy for Joan. She even refused to go, until it became clear that their future and their children's depended on this move.

Phone calls and frequent visits allayed the pain slightly, but Joan was quite depressed in her new home. Her marriage suffered. She had no one to turn to for her ongoing support. She missed her mother dreadfully. Betty felt similarly, but did better as she was more able to turn to her husband and longtime friends to fill in the gap left by her daughter's absence. In therapy Joan began to face her dependency. She was alerted to the terrible limitations she had placed on herself. When her mother became ill and Joan began to think about death, she faced the unrealistic situation that she had helped create.

Letting go of dependency means growing up. It means facing our wound and getting on with our lives. It means letting go of our roles and letting go of that important "other." It requires of us that we fill in the picture of who we are so that we are whole—in and of ourselves. Both mother and daughter may have fearful and inadequate feelings and unmet needs, which are buried in the dependent relationship. As long as dependency is maintained, neither party needs to look honestly at those feelings underneath; neither needs to express her own truth at this deeper level.

We may see ourselves as helpless in the face of our guilt, resentments and dependency. The baggage from our past is large and heavy. Thinking of the growth process and deciding to change old established ways of being may seem a huge task, even though we may be well aware that the old patterns are destructive and hurtful. Yet we are always in the process of becoming. Change and growth are inevitable. We are now given the opportunity to think about ways to disentangle ourselves from the ties that bind. The umbilical cord was cut once and we survived, and now the mythological but stronger cord needs to be cut again.

LETTING GO

Cutting the psychological umbilical cord requires letting go at a deep and profound level. Yet letting go of the old is a difficult process:

We are bound, hooked, stuck in the many ways mentioned through-out this book, and in many more unmentioned. There are good, old, survival-based reasons for these hooks and so it is no easy matter just to drop them. Giving up or letting go is similar to a death. We lose something old and familiar, something that we think we are: a part of us, a way of being, an old feeling. No matter how painful the present is, it is known, and letting go requires dropping into the unknown—into uncertainty, into the risk of whatever lies ahead. Sometimes this path seems too difficult and we hold tightly to what is, trying desper-ately, though perhaps unconsciously, to maintain the status quo.

Mothers and daughters are often torn between leaving the status quo and moving on, between new horizons and old living patterns, between the known and the unknown. When a woman lets go—of her past, her role (as mother or daughter), her old limiting feelings and hooks, she faces the opportunity to become whole. When a mother and daughter pair let go together, the old drops away and suddenly they face new possibilities in their relationship. Choosing to let go is new and risky. And it may feel far more frightening than it will actually be. Perhaps it is the only way, however, to get on with our lives, face the new in ourselves and in our relationship, and jour-ney toward wholeness.

Should we choose to hold on to the known, struggling to keep close to the security that the status quo offers us, change will be demanded of us anyway. The spring will follow the winter and go into summer, which, too, will gracefully give up her hold to the autumn. If we hold on to the loss of summer, we will be unable to enjoy winter, though it will come just as surely. So, too, with the past: Holding on to the old will hold us back from being fully in the pres-ent. We are destined to move on in our lives, to let go of each thing that we hold on to. Finally, we even have to let go of our hold on life.

The question is not whether to go along with this inevitable process, for we have no choice, but how to go along gracefully, consciously, taking the most of life even through its changes. When we fight against the moving river, our energy will be drained. We will fall into old ways of being, feeling, behaving that no longer work, if they ever did. We will not swim forward supported by the flow of the water. The metaphor of the moving river serves us in all walks of life, as individuals, as women, as mothers and daughters. Our task, as we turn and face the future, is to stop holding on to the past and to allow the current to carry us forward.

Meredith, aged twenty-six, and her mother, Jane, came to a workshop together, at Meredith's request. Her agenda was to "get my mother to stop holding me back." Meredith complained over and over that her mother would not let her go. "I have to explain myself to my mother all the time. I have to tell her where I go and what I do." In spite of Jane's protestations to the contrary, Meredith persisted in her belief that she was blocked from going further by her mother's holding on.

In order to demonstrate what was happening, we took a long rope and told Meredith to hold on to one end and her mother to hold the other. Jane was instructed not to let go for any reason. At the same time that she pulled the rope, trying to wrench it away from her mother, Meredith shouted, "Let me go, let me go! Why won't you let me go?" She was giving all the power in the relationship to her mother and refused to hear her mother's words, "Go, do what you please. You are not a child anymore." A long while after the group had seen the punch line, Meredith began to laugh and said, "I can let go of the rope, can't I? I don't have to wait for mother to!" Meredith let go, freeing herself from a prison she had created. With a huge feeling of relief, she realized that she had been the one afraid to let go.

Letting go is the final piece of the puzzle of the past. It is the last step we take before we face the future, free to be ourselves. For no matter how much work we do to heal the past, be unhooked, and change the issues and hurts that limit us, we will never be able to fully rewrite our history. And so, at a certain point, we need to let go. This requires acceptance of the pain, the wound, the imperfection of our being and acceptance of our past and mother. It requires accepting the challenge of taking responsibility for our lives, and it means creating meaning for ourselves about who we are and what our goals for the future are. If we let go, we give up our choice to be a victim, our ability to blame, and our identification with the feeling of being little. We step into adulthood and with that into the reality that faces each adult.

WORKBOOK

We have considered that hurt from our childhood is more than just a trauma, a problem, or a limitation. It is perhaps—like the sail on the sailboat—a crucial part of our growth and our journey. We can certainly wish that it had been different in our own lives, that we had been spared some of the pain that still hurts us.

But we now know that each wound has the opportunity to teach us something that will help us to grow. If we allow it and choose it, our own wound can become a valued teacher. Rhoda saw the wounded dog and drew an analogy that helped her see her wound as sacred. Her woundedness and her coming to terms with that wound had changed her and helped her to see and feel in a new way. How can you learn from your own "sacred wound"?

READER/CUSTOMER CARE SURVEY

We care about your opinions. Please take a moment to fill out this Reader Survey card and mail it back to us.
As a special "thank you" we'll send you exciting news about interesting books and a valuable **Gift Certificate.**

Please PRINT using ALL CAPS

Name
First   MI.   Last Name

Address

City   ST   Zip

Phone # (   )   —   Fax # (   )   —

Email

(1) Gender:
_____ Female   _____ Male

(2) Age:
_____ 12 or under   _____ 40-59
_____ 13-19   _____ 60+
_____ 20-39

(3) Marital Status
_____ Married
_____ Single
_____ Divorced/Widowed

(4) Did you receive this book as a gift?
_____ Yes   _____ No

(5) How many Health Communications books have you bought or read?
_____ 1   _____ 2-4   _____ 5+

(6) How did you find out about this book?
Please fill in ONE.
1) _____ Recommendation
2) _____ Store Display
3) _____ Bestseller List
4) _____ Online
5) _____ Advertisement
6) _____ Catalog/Mailing
7) _____ Interview/Review (TV, Radio, Print)

(7) Where do you usually buy books?
Please fill in your top TWO choices.
1) _____ Bookstore
2) _____ Religious Bookstore
3) _____ Online
4) _____ Book Club/Mail Order
5) _____ Price Club (Costco, Sam's Club, etc.)
6) _____ Retail Store (Target, Wal-Mart, etc.)

(9) What subjects do you enjoy reading about most? Rank only *FIVE.* *Use 1 for your favorite, 2 for second favorite, etc.*

	1	2	3	4	5
1) Parenting/Family	○	○	○	○	○
2) Relationships	○	○	○	○	○
3) Recovery/Addictions	○	○	○	○	○
4) Health/Nutrition	○	○	○	○	○
5) Christianity	○	○	○	○	○
6) Spirituality/Inspiration	○	○	○	○	○
7) Business Self-Help	○	○	○	○	○
8) Teen Issues	○	○	○	○	○
9) Sports	○	○	○	○	○

(14) What attracts you most to a book?
(Please rank 1-4 in order of preference.)

	1	2	3	4
1) Title	○	○	○	○
2) Cover Design	○	○	○	○
3) Author	○	○	○	○
4) Content	○	○	○	○

TAPE IN MIDDLE; DO NOT STAPLE

BUSINESS REPLY MAIL
FIRST-CLASS MAIL PERMIT NO 45 DEERFIELD BEACH, FL

POSTAGE WILL BE PAID BY ADDRESSEE

HEALTH COMMUNICATIONS, INC.
3201 SW 15TH STREET
DEERFIELD BEACH FL 33442-9875

FOLD HERE

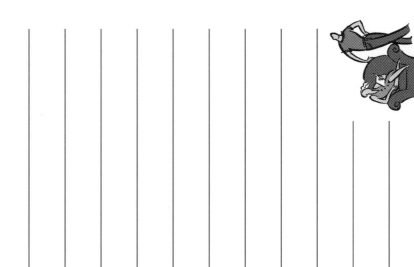

Comments:

&ε Obstacles as Stepping-Stones &ε

In this exercise you will have a chance to see where your hurts and pains and limitations are leading you in your life. In a quiet place, letting go of your conscious thinking and moving into a steady and peaceful rhythm of breathing, allow an image to come to you that represents you in your ideal life. See this ideal life at the end of a long path. Become aware that you have always been on that path, moving toward that ideal. As you move along the path you will sooner or later encounter an obstacle that makes movement difficult. This obstacle is the "sacred wound" that you carry from your childhood. What is your image of this obstacle as it blocks your path? If you feel inclined, draw your image. And now, looking at the whole of your life as this path, take a moment to be aware of all the obstacles that have existed. See them, symbolically and actually, as the pains and injuries from your childhood. In considering the wound you carry or the obstacles of your life, what can you see about how these obstacles are like stepping-stones for you in your life? Where are they leading you? What strengths, skills, and qualities are you learning about as you surmount these obstacles?

Take time to write down your answers. When you get in touch with what you have gained in relationship to the obstacles and wounds of your life, appreciate your growth and your struggle, and if it seems right to you, appreciate the wound itself, see if perhaps it is worthy of veneration and reverence. Finally, imagine this path that you are on and see how you can overcome those obstacles that are in your way now. Take time to enjoy the metaphor of your life as a path.

ॐ "Oh, what a tangled web we weave when first we practice to deceive!" ॐ

No one sets out to tell lies. We begin to bend the truth, hide the truth or deny the truth when our lives force us to. We do it to protect others or ourselves from outcomes that seem dangerous. In the mother/daughter relationship the stage is set by the time we are adults to lie to each other in subtle or overt ways. Often the lies wouldn't even be considered lies but "tact." More than likely, they are just cover-ups: of our feelings, thoughts, needs, opinions, hopes and beliefs. And often these deep truths are buried—as we have seen—behind resentment, guilt and dependency.

Write your own version of the way you and your mother/daughter masquerade. Does your status quo match the ones we talked about?

- Mother/Daughter Forever
- Let's Be Pals
- Cold and Distant
- Close in Name Only
- Let Me Help

If it does, take some notes on how you two operate in similar ways. If your way of operating with each other doesn't fit one of these scenarios, write about yours. What are the ways you behave with each other? Are they honest and congruent, or is your routine a masquerade for deeper feelings that are unspoken? If your mother or daughter is not alive, think of this same exercise in relation to significant others in your life. When you have done this, answer the following questions:

- What do I want that I don't ask for?
- How do I feel that I don't admit?
- What beliefs and values do I hold that I do not honor in this relationship?
- If I were honest with myself, what would I do differently?

- How can I change in a way that will honor the potential of this relationship?

Goodbye/Hello

Saying goodbye is not easy, especially when we are deeply attached to that which we are leaving. We are perhaps more deeply attached to our own past, our personal history, even our pain than we are to most things. But there is a time to say goodbye so that we can say hello to the future.

In this exercise we want to find a way to symbolically let go of the past, to say goodbye. There are a number of options and you may well create new ones that work expressly for you. Find or create some symbols of your past—photos, mementos—or pictures you draw now; or even do a written page on your past. Try to have several different things that represent various aspects of your past, such as, you as a child with your mother, a symbol of your wound or limitations, something that represents your feeling of "littleness," and anything that speaks to you about aspects of the past that you need to say goodbye to.

When you have these assembled, find a significant and suitable way to say goodbye. This could be as dramatic as burning the picture that symbolized your not-okay feelings or as mellow as speaking the words to a photo or childhood doll. It is important to make a strong affirmative statement as your goodbye, one that supports your growth toward wholeness.

> "It's time for me to say goodbye to my role as a child, because I am fully adult now."
>
> *Goodbye, childhood wound. I am ready to move into my own strength.*
>
> *Goodbye, Mother, I am ready to let you go as a mother and welcome you as an adult.*

Carefully choose your words. Put them in *positive* terms. Make sure the statement points toward your growth and expansion and not toward your limitations. Write these statements down and keep them handy.

CHAPTER EIGHT

Who Am I?

To BE NOBODY-BUT-MYSELF —
IN A WORLD THAT IS DOING ITS BEST, NIGHT & DAY,
TO MAKE YOU EVERYBODY ELSE —
MEANS TO FIGHT THE HARDEST BATTLE
WHICH ANY HUMAN BEING CAN FIGHT,
AND NEVER STOP FIGHTING.

—*e. e. cummings*

LAYERS UPON LAYERS

We have spent a lot of time exploring who we are. As we ask that question one more time, let us look at some of the layers that form us. A small child comes into the world as a newborn (or really earlier as an embryo) and as a self. The true self we have referred to is our essential being and our inherent uniqueness. This true self has not been wounded or conditioned.

We carry within us both genetic traits and the essence of our future personalities. The loud, expressive baby with a new and

181

frightened mother will have heavy conditioning from the start. A daughter who is better "fitted" to her mother will receive her conditioning more gradually and gently. Adapting and learning to fit into the world into which we are born soon covers the free and natural self that appeared at birth. By the mere fact of being little in a big world, of being unsocialized in a social world, of being impulsive and instinctive in a controlled world we come to a sense of ourselves as little and not completely okay. We build an experience, from early on, of both a negative self and a positive self.

The negative self is built on: all our feelings of inadequacy; our fears; the traumas that hurt and limit us; the distortions that we internalize about ourselves; our unfettered impulses; our self-centered demands; our ever-present feelings and desires; and aspects of our uniqueness that were not acceptable in the family. All of these are bound together in this not-okay self. In the process of growing and building a limited sense of who we are, that precious uniqueness, the true self that is our birthright, is covered up to one degree or another in every person. The negative self, starting at a young age, silently slips in as our beginning definition of who we are.

As we grow and begin to evolve a personality that will represent us, we add on to that negative self a layer that covers up the negative, not-okay self-image. We begin to gain skills in the world, we learn how to be, we get in touch with our strengths, we notice some of our uniqueness as it shines through—and we begin to fake it in different ways, in an effort to make it in the world! The process of socialization that our parents, particularly our mothers, are obligated to enforce upon us clearly points out to us what is all right, acceptable, socially correct, and what is not all right and must be hidden. To one degree or another, each of us creates a mask or positive self that will stand us in good stead in the world. At least it will help in better ways than the negative self. That positive self is a combination of elements of our uniqueness, the skills we have learned in the world, and the compensations we create to cover our negative self. The positive self works for us in some very important ways, and it limits us. It represents some of our true self and it denies some of it.

The diagram on page 184 indicates the layers of ourselves: true self, negative self, positive self. In order to be a whole person, we need to operate from our true self, for that is the core of our being, and it is from there that we will be able to draw on the wealth of possibilities that we are. Just as we have covered up our true self out of our needs to stay safe in the world, we must uncover our true self out of our needs to grow and be whole. To uncover this core of our being requires getting to know the layers that cover us.

THE POSITIVE SELF

The positive self is the first layer that we encounter in our search for the true self. As adult women we are more than likely to present the positive self to the world. We say to the world, "This is who I am, all these good things. I fit into this world!" And if we have been fortunate in our lives, that positive self will be pretty good. We will have learned to survive and fit in, to be skilled in certain ways, and to be appropriate. Our positive self will be crystallized around the need to "make it" in the world. Every healthy way of being that we have learned will be put to use here, as well as every learned message about "good" behavior. The cry of the positive self is: "I can make it!" And this is what we show to the world.

The positive self is like a resume. We write about all the good, impressive, interesting and acceptable things we have accomplished, and we don't mention the rest. Why should we? We want to sell ourselves to an employer. So, too, with life. We want—in fact, we feel and think that it is crucial—to sell ourselves, to someone, for something. We may think we have to sell ourselves to a man, or to a career, or to our family or friends, or to society—in each case putting out our "good" side in order to be "bought." This is what we learned in child-hood; it became quite clear that all of what we were was not okay. To better get by, we split ourselves early into our good self/bad self, put-ting forth the good, hiding the bad. As much as we are able, we want to be the good self, to look good to the world, to be seen and loved for our goodness, to "make it" because we are good.

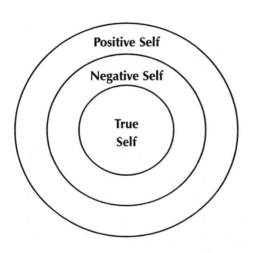

The true self is our essential, true and unconditioned being, our uniqueness and our individuality.

The negative self is our not-okay self-image. It is all the ways we think and feel that we are not enough.

The positive self is the compro-mise position that we show to the world. It is our coping mechanism, our "best face."

When we can't find authentic or spontaneous ways to build our positive self and when we see the demands that the world places on us, we are likely to move into fake-it-to-make-it mode (the imposter). In this mode we add on to our natural way of being those ways of being that look as if they will work in the world. When the socializ-ing that we receive demands of us that we be a certain way that is not authentic, we will struggle to behave that way. We will fake it, because it seems essential to get by. This starts at a young age.

 Reba learned young to fake it and it hurt her. "From the time that I was little, I pretended to be other than I was. I'm sixty-four now, but no one knows that. When I was six, my mother told me to tell the dance teacher that I was five! To make it in the world, I finally figured out, you had to be young. My mother never aged past fifty! But it wasn't enough to be young; you had to be precocious to get by. I built my life around looking young and acting precocious. When I hit fifty, I practically died. *Who am I really*, I wondered? I clearly wasn't young and precocious anymore."

Whatever injunctions we received, whatever we picked up about the way to be in the world, whatever was labeled as acceptable, is built up into the positive self. This self has taken many people to fame and wealth, to great deeds and superior accomplishments. It has *never* taken anyone into lasting happiness, however. It is only a layer of who we are, and much of what we do from that place will feel, secretly inside, like a sham. We may feel we are living a lie, or living on the edge, ready to fall (into the negative self). It may seem that discovery of our negative self waits around the corner or that the next challenge will destroy us. Our positive self, with which we so firmly identify, is built on a mighty weak foundation: our deeper sense of not-okay-ness, our negative self. Since this positive self is based on so much repression and denial, it will hold together for only so long, and then it crashes.

Star was the author of several books on healing. She was well-known and well-loved. By all standards, she was a success. A nagging sense of doubt grew within her as she became more and more well-known and, at the same time, her ever-present sense of giving and loving began to slip away at times. She would find herself suddenly enraged at her children or disgusted by one of her students. She began having violent dreams and feeling and acting in "nasty" ways toward her friends and family. She became quite frightened. "My world is falling apart. Everything I have worked for and built, all my dreams, everything I am seems at risk. What is happening to me? I think I'm going crazy."

When Star discovered a place in herself that "felt like all darkness," she began to open to her own depths. To turn and face that place was a painfully difficult task. "What if I am this darkness? I've run from it all my life. I can't face finding out how awful I really am." At the moment that she faced this question, Star had to let go of the "image" of her all-perfect positive self and come face to face with her "negative self." This bright and shining Star in the world had to face her shadow. Her effort to be that positive self could only sustain her for so long, before her negative self leaked through and demanded attention.

When Star was willing to see her negative self, she discovered anger, hurt, unfulfilled needs. She found her "little" self and her wound, long unhealed and buried. She began to see that her positive self had been a compensation for all her own hurt. From a young age, she had become a helper, a giver, a guide for her own mother and siblings, as well as her friends. She did this only because her earlier efforts to be healed and given to and guided had failed. She had tried before her "training" took effect, to be the recipient of all these good things but had found no success. Since she couldn't take care of her own needs, she took care of others' needs. Even her choice to change her name to Star when she was in her twenties was part of her building of a positive self. Star held tightly to this positive self. She had gone far enough to wipe out most of her experience of the negative self within. She had done so because she knew no other way to make it in the world.

If our positive self has helped us survive and get by, even at the cost we pay of denying some part of ourselves, we will be afraid to allow or even to acknowledge the negative self. But scratch the surface of most adults and there will be, not too far buried, a negative self. It is common to hear a one-liner like "If you really knew who I was, you wouldn't like me!" We have decided along the way that we are only okay—lovable, capable, worthy—because of our positive self. It seems frightening and dangerous to let our "dark" side out. We think that we would be a bad person—angry, dangerous, stupid or whatever—if we were to give up the masquerade and let this deeper layer be exposed. And certainly we are convinced that others would think badly of us, if they only knew.

While we boldly present our positive self to the world, we tenaciously hold on to its boundaries in our inner world, always trying to keep that not-okay feeling at bay. But each of us finds herself slipping more or less frequently into that deep and painful inner experience of the negative self and when we do, we must face or avoid it. To play the game of avoiding this dark side is our natural first response: We may run from it by adding more and more skills and accomplishments to our positive self, by creating more and more in our lives to keep us occupied and unable to look inward, or by denying more and more emphatically the feelings and needs that come from the negative self.

Inevitably, however, women who struggle with self-knowledge will face this inner negativity. It may happen through conscious effort or through the gradual disintegration of the positive self, as in Star's case, or through an abrupt and painful crisis that shatters the illusion that we have been living. What is particularly difficult as we face internally the knowledge that we have this negative self is that we may be totally unaware that we also have our true self. If we turn inside and see only our negative self, then we must fight to keep the negative self hidden. After all, if there is no true self, than the negative self must be who we truly are, and that perhaps is the most frightening thought that an individual has to face: that she is truly, and deeply, not okay.

THE NEGATIVE SELF

Women who want to come to know themselves in a deep and full way will find a way to face and integrate the negative self. We must go back through that negative (wounded) self to reclaim our true self, and that is the goal of the journey. We cannot be whole and autonomous by presenting just a positive self. That mask, or presenting face, will serve us in many ways but it will also deny a great deal of who we are: our hurt, our need, our littleness (the inner child), our "darkness," many of our impulses, our desires and our creativity. In so covering that negative self, we cover also our true self.

No one will be surprised to hear these words about the negative self, because we all feel its presence inside, underneath, hidden or perhaps expressed too often—to our regret or confusion. Who, after all, has not felt the darkness within? All literature, mythology, psychology and religion address this darkness in one form or another. Just as we looked at the bad mother and good mother within our mothers, we must look at ourselves within this universal polarity of light and dark, good and bad, positive and negative. The negative self, as we are exploring it, is the accumulation of experiences, ideas, self-concepts that are negative. It is not simply negative or "bad" aspects of ourselves, but *negated* aspects of ourselves.

If being smart was bad for a girl in her family, then her own hidden intelligence will be part of her negative self, as well as her anger and hurt at being denied. She will bury her anger, because it doesn't work in her family. She will bury her thinking because it doesn't work. Both are threats to her sense of well-being. The development of the negative self is based in our experiences, in childhood, of a world that does not "work" quite right for us, in which we are not protected or supported in being ourselves in a healthy and expansive way. That we must be socialized for our own protection, as well as for the best interests of society at large, sets the stage for the creation of a negative self. In as simple and appropriate an act as denying a child's impulse to run in the street, she is being taught to repress and control certain aspects of herself. When all the idiosyncratic, distorted or limited ways that are peculiar to our upbringing are added to our "socialization," we build a very complete sense of who we are that is not acceptable.

While the cry of the positive self is "I can make it!", the hidden cry of the negative self is "I can't make it." While the positive self proclaims to the world, "This is who I am, all these good things!", the negative self proclaims internally, "This is who I am, all these bad things! I don't fit into this world." If given free rein, this negative self would do things in our lives that we would never allow from the vantage point of the positive self. It would succumb to littleness, to victimization, to despair, rage, violence or hopelessness. It would overthrow the constraints of the positive self to express its unique and negated qualities in an unrestrained, impulsive way. When this side is repressed for many years, as it is in so many of us, it will erupt, as Star's negative self did, in minor or major expressions of itself. Like the pressure cooker that is overheating, the negative self, when it is contained, cramped and stifled, will build up a fury that is much exaggerated in its efforts to be released. If we are lucky, we will be able to take that lid off the pressure cooker before it explodes. As we turn inside to find out who we really are, we will have the opportunity to consciously and safely bring this dark side to light.

Julie's Story

"When I changed careers from a school teacher to a therapist, I began a process of conscious work on myself that revealed to me the negative self that I had hidden. In our family there was a 'joke' that I was the perfect mother. We all bought that story. I bought it because it was how I had built up my positive self. This role was a large part of how I made it in the world. I truly am loving and concerned for my family, but built on this was the compensation for my own fears about whether I could really do a good job as a mother. Not only was I invested in being a good mother, but also I had denied many of my other aspects. (Remember my quitting college for the wedding!)

"As I unraveled the mystery of my own being, I discovered some darker sides of me that I had never faced. I did not just love; I was also angry and critical. I felt needy and sometimes rejected by my family. I was horrified at first that I was not so wonderful as I thought. As I looked further, however, I was relieved to find that I was, after all, only human. When I could give up being the perfect mother, my family could see more of me. Their experiences of my 'less-than-perfect self' validated their own experiences of being less than perfect.

"This process was most apparent with my daughter. Dorothy had pulled away from me when she had her first child. She told me not to talk about raising children with her. I felt hurt and rejected, but discovered later, as we both revealed our darker sides, that she was overwhelmed by the image of me as a perfect mother. She knew full well that she was not, and so how could she deal with me, until we both acknowledged that I, of course, was not either. I am far more available as a real ally now, and I am also able to be helped by others, since I am no longer perfect."

Both Star and Julie discovered and owned their negative selves and, in the long run that discovery led to an increased sense of well-being and authenticity. Star began to share her needs and fears with others close to her and found that she could be supported and cared for as a friend. The years of being up on a pedestal were over. She discovered, as well, that she could do her healing work in a much deeper fashion, having come to terms with her own negative self. Julie discovered that in her perfect-mother self she had negated other important aspects of herself. The positive self had not only protected her from her "bad" feelings, but it had denied her many other strengths. It is a scary job opening up to that negative self within. Even with the promise of greater self-knowledge, it requires an act of faith to open that Pandora's box.

In some especially painful cases the negative self will be all that is ever presented, and this is scarier still. The positive self we have built is a great asset, even as we choose to move deeper within ourselves. We have a place to return to, a sense of ourselves that is okay, if not complete. We have skills for managing that have and will continue to serve us well. We know how to be in our society in ways that work, at least reasonably well. For the person who has not developed a sufficient positive self, life will always look bleak; in the worst scenarios she will be mentally unstable, antisocial, unable to care for herself at even a survival level. For that person, there was perhaps so little support or guiding input in life that a positive self could not be built and the only cry known is "I can't make it." For the many who had so little given to them, whose positive self is weak or nonexistent, life is terribly hard.

Dorothy's Story

"I came to know about the darkness of human life through one of my first clients. Theresa had been badly hurt as a child. She had been regularly beaten, spent most of her hours hiding in the basement or in and out of hospitals with injuries she received. When she came to therapy as a twenty-five-year-old, she was depressed, confused, and not certain that there was any point in living. She had never had a good feeling about herself that she was aware of, and even her primary behavior as an adult was self-abusive. She cut herself and ran headlong into walls and trees.

"I was too naive as a therapist to know that I probably couldn't handle this case, and I was too taken with this lovely, wounded person to even consider that option. I cared for her deeply and painfully from the day I met her. As she talked to me, always in a quiet voice, of her pain, past and present, I could feel mine. When she described running her head into a wall, I could feel in me where I hated myself. When she considered that she was perhaps not worth the efforts that it took to stay alive, I could feel everyone's doubts about themselves. When she told me one day that she would leave our session and walk in front of a car, I knew about darkness."

Theresa's task was greater than most. She had nothing to fall back on that knew how to "make it." She had only the vaguest ability even to fake it, and so get by. But, in her rawness, she was not so far away from her true self. When she fell through the pain into a deep space within, the small, faint voice of her true self could be heard. When she thought suicide was the only answer, she reached deep within and found a taste of true self.

Dorothy's Story

❧ "I couldn't let Theresa walk out of my office ready to kill herself. I had been a therapist for less than a year. I was as deeply scared as I had ever been. I knew I, alone, couldn't save her. Was there a place in her that would save her? I asked her where she could go for help, where she could find a reason to go on. In the quietest of whispers, as she held on to the rosary that was her ever-present companion, she called on her prayers. It felt miraculous, her reaching toward something so profound in the face of such great despair. More miraculous still, she was answered in her prayers and she began to feel a sense of relief and acceptance that grew in that session and over the next months. When she left my office with a look of serenity, I knew that she had begun to find herself. And as I had come to know with Theresa the world of darkness, I came also to know, with her, the home of the true self."

TRUE SELF

What could sustain a child like Theresa through such a tormented life? What does she hold on to? Where does she find, within herself, a place that can make meaning out of her pain, that can find a sense of acceptance of herself and her life? How does she overcome her terrible limiting conditioning and go on in her life to find success and happiness? There is no outward and visible sign that each of us is a self—a true and essential being, inherently fine and right—but evidence points that way. The spiritual and philosophical traditions throughout the ages have posited a similar idea. Psychology and even science, of late, have begun to formulate ideas that correlate with this. And people, women and men everywhere, discover this for themselves daily.

Perhaps as you did the first exercise in this book, you began to get a feel for the *you* that supersedes all the answers to that question "Who am I?" Or perhaps you have found that still, small voice within in the course of your own life. In calm and quiet ways or in joyful exuberant ways we may come to know our true self. Walking in the woods, sitting with a child, creating, meditating, praying, laughing, making love, seeing the first flower of spring, doing for another, taking in or giving out love are all moments that may reflect our true self. At these times we feel a "rightness" about ourselves, a certainty that who we are is good, that we belong. We experience our individuality not as isolation, but as an expression of our uniqueness. We may also experience our connection to all things: the commonality of our being as well as its uniqueness. We are free from the painful, isolating experience of duality, of the "me against them" frame. These moments have no doubts, no question or criticism, no internal checking or even dialogue. We have found, for a time, the source of serenity in our own being.

As adult women who have chosen to explore ourselves and grow into our potential, we have the unique opportunity to come to know ourselves in a deeper and more conscious way than we may have before. And yet how do we do this? How do we even identify what that true self is amidst the myriad of other parts or voices, messages or conditioning, little and big aspects of ourselves. The first guideline is that our self is not any of these. If we peel away layer after layer, voice after voice, we come closer and closer to that self. With our first look around, we may think that the adult within us is the true self. But even that, a mature, skillful and highly functioning part of each of us, is not the self. Don't throw it out, though! Just as you must not throw out any of who you are. When we come closer to being our self, everything within us will have a place.

Our job is to orchestrate the many elements of our personality so that we can use each in our best interests. We might consider ourselves to be like an orchestra. When we hear a symphony, we hear the sounds made by the musicians. We may hear the string section, the brass, the percussion. There may be a solo performance here or there. Each piece of music will have a different emphasis on one section or one instrument or one style of music. We hear the whole piece of music, performed in such a way that we are never drawn, inappropriately, to one instrument over another. Every player knows the score, knows how to play her part, and does so. And to understand how this comes to be that so many disparate instruments play in harmony, we need to look to the conductor.

While we never hear the conductor in the piece of music, we know that she is there and that it is through her that such a melodious sound comes forth. Without her there would be chaos in the orchestra. The true self is like that conductor. In fact, at an even deeper level the self may be considered to be the composer as well. We don't see or hear the true self, but we know it by the sound that we make in the world. Do we play a harmonious tune? Is the tune moving and deep, is it light and airy? Is it played well? Or do we find that the tubas play out of turn, that the violins squeak, that the flutist is asleep in her chair? If so, the conductor hasn't enough power. She hasn't been revealed fully to the musicians, so that they will hear and respond to her cues. This was Theresa's arduous task, as it is ours. She was faced with having an ever-so-slight experience of her self. For months in her work, the hold on her self was so tenuous as to be frightening for her concerned therapist and, no doubt, for Theresa. But each week, and each step forward that strengthened that self, brought the music into tune. Our goal, simply stated, is to find the self within, become that self, and harmonize our many aspects from that clear place.

If we set about discovering this true self, there will be no clear-cut path but there will always be pointers: cues and clues to guide us. To follow the orchestra analogy, we would say that resonance would be our cue to the true self. When we experience resonance—an inner congruency, harmonization and sense of rightness—then we are on to something. The self is our source of being and doing; it shows itself through our uniqueness, our individuality. A connoisseur of music will hear a piece by Bach performed and say to herself, *Ah, that sounds like the touch of so-and-so, the famous conductor.* That conductor will have placed her mark on the piece of music, in such a way as to distinguish her presentation from any other. In just such a way we distinguish ourselves from any other through our uniqueness. This is the gift of the self.

Yolanda had competed with her mother all her life. Her mother was an editor. Yolanda struggled to be a writer. Her mother was slim and attractive. Yolanda fought a constant battle with her weight. Her mother married a wealthy man. Yolanda searched for a man endlessly. Her mother was happy, Yolanda was not. Finally, in her late twenties, it appeared that Yolanda was on her way to creating the life she wanted. All the pieces seemed to be falling in place.

At a party with friends, amid congratulations on the publication of her short story in a leading magazine, she said, to everyone and no one, "I hate writing." She shocked herself more than anyone else. Luckily, Yolanda listened to what she had said. She began a process of introspection, through meditation, journal writing, talking with friends and being by herself, and she asked herself the question *Who am I?* As she delved deeper into that question, so many levels fell away. She was not a child, she was not a writer, she was not fashionable, she was not particularly outgoing. She was not interested in money very much. She was not ready to be married. So many things fell away that, at times, she feared that she would find herself empty. But with each falling away, she felt freer, not emptier. Her question began to have neutral answers: "I am a woman. I am a human. I am alive. I am me."

And in that space she felt more like herself than she ever had before. As she let herself be just that "me" that had emerged, empty and naked, she began to explore the qualities of her being that were unique.

As we come to find our true nature, we will begin to formulate our being in the world in an authentic way. Every tree that grows, every flower, starts as a seed, many indistinguishable from the others. And yet each holds, within, the plan for its own unfoldment. The acorn "knows" that it will grow to be an oak. It is not random or serendipitous that every acorn has within it its own "oak-ness." And yet, at the same time, no two acorns, as similar as they are, will be the same. So, too, the self, like the seed of our being, holds within a plan for our own unfolding, a blueprint that will take us to our greatest blossoming. To find this blueprint that will help us find out who we are becoming we do not look outward, we look inward. As we do, we will hunt for those cues and clues that take us closer to our own potential. Yolanda, who had defined herself by her competition with her mother, lost touch with herself in a painful way. She was living an unfulfilling life because she had no personal sense of meaning or value in her life. If we commit to finding and creating a life that is imbued with meaning and if we honor the values that we have in life, we will be committing ourselves to ourselves.

Life will be unbearable without this sense of meaning. Each of us must struggle to create a sense of "why." Why be alive? Why be me? Why is there suffering and unfairness? We will work to uncover the meaning of our lives and the meaning of all life. We will likely never come to easy answers for those questions. The asking may be as important as the answering. As we ask and struggle with answering, we will find a sense of purpose for our lives. We will begin to know our own "oak-ness," and that will help us define and choose the life that we create. Why turn left or right? We couldn't decide without a sense of purpose. Why be a writer rather than a dancer or a dog-catcher rather than an astronaut?

Each must answer the questions that will lead to a unique and deep sense of the meaning and purpose of her life. Women who have taken on the meaning and values that were given to them, in the form of injunctions and dictates from the past, may find along the way that it is not enough, as Yolanda did. We may well discover that it is not enough to have a child, to be a wife, to be a success, to be thin or rich, to be good, to be of service, to be anything that we were taught to be. Until our lives are guided by meaning that is personal and relevant to us, it won't matter what form life takes. Rich or poor, this or that are relevant only as they are filled with meaning.

It has been suggested that suicide is the response to absence of meaning in life. This seems likely. Even great pain, in and of itself, does not lead to the despair from which there is no return. Theresa suffered as much pain, perhaps, as one could bear. Women lose their children, their loved ones, their homes. They are injured, crippled, blinded. They are prisoners or victims. They may be tortured or killed. The quality of life will not finally be decided by those circumstances. Finally, it will be decided by the meaning that is understood about the circumstances.

> Helen's children were killed by a drunk driver. As she plummeted into the depths of despair, she found that she could not give up on life. She couldn't understand the why of this horrible unfairness, this cruelty, but somehow she knew there was meaning for her in her life. Her life did not end or go dry. She let in her great pain and sorrow and allowed that to be a part of her. "Life is to live," she mused. "If we are given a breath, then we must breathe it. It will lead us into the next and the next breath. If there is more, I don't know, but I know to take each breath."

> Claire had felt truly loved and understood only by her twin sister. When her sister died in an airplane crash, Claire discovered that she could feel her sister's love inside her. She experienced, for the first time in her life, a sense of self-love as sweet as the love her sister had had for her. She knew that to let that love for herself grow and flourish was the gift that her sister had given.

We cannot simply create meaning. We must uncover our deepest sense of purpose for ourselves and this will help us define meaning. And meaning will never be stagnant. It will grow and change, it will deepen with each step of our lives. Meaning will be reflected in the qualities that we discover in ourselves.

Theresa, Helen and Claire all found meaning in their lives and in their suffering, yet each woman was different from the other in the qualities of her being. Theresa found in herself quietness and reverence; Helen, persistence and her passion; Claire, self-love. As each of these women came to know themselves, through their tragedies, they became aware of the qualities that were unique to them. In the same manner, Yolanda threw off the burden of her competition with her mother. Each of us must do the same as we come to our autonomy. It is not enough to be even a fully functioning, separate, adult individual. We must also be "me"!

What makes you you? If you could let go of all restraints, what secret you would emerge? As you look back to chapter 1 and the exercise "Will the Real Me Please Step Forward," who is that real you? Do you surprise yourself with the qualities you circled or the people you admired? To come to know more about the quality of your being requires staying in touch with what makes you happy, what feels worthwhile to you, what excites you, what you do that feels right to you. We generally look outside ourselves for guidance about how to be and who to be, but in order to tap into our true selves we must look inside—to who we are and to help define how to be. If we ask the questions "What should I do?", "What are my injunctions?", "What is appropriate to satisfy the 'big' people in my life?", "What can I do and how can I cope?", we will be drawing from a limited well. If we ask the questions "What has meaning to me?", "What expression fits me?", "What do I value?", then our well is not only unlimited, it is also unique to us.

Values tend to be the cornerstone of life. Values come, in truth, from our self. They are not defined by the injunctions or morals that our parents or our society lay down for us. Our values may coincide or conflict with those that are expressed around us. As we grow into our own integrity, we will become more and more in touch with our values. Women, on the whole, have been given less freedom than men to have their own values. As the bearers and trainers of children, we are supposed to follow society's dictates to create the future generation. When a mother honors her own values—against those of her mother, her mate or her society—she is often slandered and cast out. And yet, in a generally quiet and non-public way, women have often fought to honor those values that were crucial to their own truth, even in the face of persecution. While men stand out as heroes, women are often the unsung movers. Women have created changes everywhere by their commitment to their values. From Florence Nightingale to the advocates of women's rights, to the mothers who have supported their sons' war resistance, to the nuns and missionaries in war-torn countries, to the brave and unknown women who saved children in the Nazi Holocaust, to the present-day women's underground that protects abused children, women have fought for their values from time immemorial.

There are no right values that can be laid down for all to see. There are only true values: those that reflect each person's deepest sense of what's right. Wherever we stand on any given issue—moral, social, political, spiritual or personal—we cannot look outside ourselves for an answer. Our own truth must guide us. Yolanda could not be happy letting her mother's values guide her. She had to find her own. Each of us must do so.

WORKBOOK

It is of course, easier said than done, this journey home to the true self. And to undertake it requires, as all heroic journeys do, travel and travail. We will certainly face both light and dark in this journey. It is ever so tempting to stop in the light, avoid the shadows, hide from the rain and venture forth only in the safety of the daytime. But it is a shallow world, this positive self, and precarious. All we can do is take the first step by allowing ourselves to look honestly at our strengths and weaknesses, our positive and negative self. And setting forth to integrate these elements is a noble task. The mask that we wear for the world will not readily let go its hold on us. It has served us well as a place to hide, a base from which to operate, a crutch in the face of our own weakness. Fortunately, when we do choose to look at our mask we will find that we will not have to give it up. Anything that we have which serves us will be kept and utilized in a more deeply integrated way.

ᘒ Mask and Shadow ᘒ

Take time to consider the positive self/negative self split within you. This exercise will be an opportunity to assess these aspects of yourself and begin to integrate them in a healthy, non-limiting way.

Consider first the positive self that you put forth. Remember the cry of the positive self: "This is who I am, all these positive things. I fit into this world!" Elaborate your version of this mask. List all of the positive things that you proclaim to the world as your proof that you can make it. Include both the authentic strengths that you put forth and the fake-it-to-make-it attitudes, styles, beliefs that you present. Exaggerate your presentation as if you were presenting a resume. Allow some humor to enter in, if it wants to.

When you have written your paragraph, look at what is really going on when you present this mask. What are you trying to prove, cover up and convince others or yourself of? What do you have to hide of yourself in order to keep this mask up? If you dropped this mask, what would be revealed? Write about these questions.

Turn to the shadow side of this mask now, the negative self whose hidden cry is: "I can't make it. I am all these bad things!" What are the elements of your negative self? Elaborate on these. You might think in terms of the one-liner "If they only knew ____

_____ about me, they wouldn't like me." Fill in both real weaknesses/limitations and all the not-okay lines you feed yourself. You can exaggerate again.

Look at what's really going on as you experience yourself in this shadow. What are you really feeling and needing in this place? What have you internalized about yourself that is not accurate? What is a reasonable view of yourself? Write a paragraph about this. See if you can step back from both selves and take a balanced, objective, and compassionate view. What needs to happen for you? What can you do to support your whole self? You won't need to exaggerate here. Just tell the real truth.

ॐ Secret Self ॐ

If the layers that clothed you disappeared, what might happen? Take a moment just to imagine and feel that possibility. Let it be a pleasant idea for you, as if you were dropping away old clothes, knowing that new and beautiful ones would replace them. Write a poem that expresses this secret self that would emerge. Have fun with this. Here are a few first lines for the poem. Choose one, or by all means write your own.

When it all drops away, I _____.
Behind the mask, and deeper still behind the Shadow _____
_____.
My new wardrobe has arrived. I see in it _____
_____.

ॐ Things I Do Value ॐ

Since values are so important in creating an integrated life, and honoring our true self, it is important to articulate our own, and more important still to sort out the values that we truly hold from those that we perhaps have taken on unconsciously. Begin a list of your "Principles for Right Living." Allow everything of importance that you value to be listed.

When your list is complete, go back and check each one to make sure that this is a value you hold. If you have any doubts, ask about the source of this value. Did it originate outside yourself? Does it resonate with you? Is it partially true, but not fully? Make sure that your list is an accurate expression of your current values.

If you want to take this one step further, take time over the week to note how much of each day is spent in ways that support your deepest values, how much is spent in nonvalued ways, how much is spent in conflict with your values. Monitoring your life in relationship to your values will be a difficult and rewarding job. Good luck!

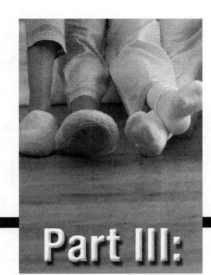

Part III:

The Future

CHAPTER NINE

Acceptance and Forgiveness

To UNDERSTAND IS TO FORGIVE,
EVEN ONESELF.

—Alexander Chase

WHAT DOES THE FUTURE BRING?

We may return for a moment to our theme of life as a book and our very crucial role as the author. If this is so, then we may look at the future as an unwritten page. Surely there are tendencies, themes, conditions already set within the past and present of our lives and these will color the future. But under no circumstances can it be assumed that the past creates the future, as if we were already fated to live out certain things. The future calls on us to move ahead, to go beyond, to transcend the past, and to stretch ourselves to the greatest potential that we have available. To be less than we are capable of being, to give in to the limiting status quo, to accept defeat—these are perhaps the greatest pitfalls that face us. While outer circumstances and all the pain and tragedy that exist

may seem like the disasters that ruin a life, in truth the outer circumstances never define the quality of a person's life, nor the magnitude of her effort. This is the internal truth that wants to be
realized in the face of benign or tragic circumstances: to be all that
one can be! This is not your mother talking nor your religion or your
own conscience nor any of the people or philosophies that have
"shoulded" you into feeling not okay. This is simply the quiet call
from within that pulls you. We each know it in our own way. When
we go for it, it may be grand, public, profound, or it may be quiet,
unnoticed and internal. We each know what going for it feels like in
ourselves.

We may never know the final outcome that we aim for. A life committed to being all that one can be will rarely be defined by a project
or time-limited venture: "I'm going to be a musician, have a baby,
forgive my mother, learn to belly dance." These may be pieces, tiny
parts. Going for it is about the quality of our lives and the integrity
with which we live them. It is about following the dream, doing the
best that we can, honoring our own uniqueness, giving life our best.
It is about finding our own voice. There is no judge outside of ourselves to proclaim our success or failure or to define integrity—or
even to notice us. Finally, this is the task of our true self, to gently
pull us toward greater and greater levels of personal integrity, to give
us that loving nudge that allows us to go for it!

Grace's happiness had gradually diminished, as her early
excitement about life, her career goals, her general enthusiasm
faded into the background of her husband's demanding career, their
marital difficulties, and the pressures of raising a family. She gave of
herself and gave of herself. As she approached her forties, she became
more and more depressed. Her life had no meaning. She began to feel
deeply angry with her family, feeling victimized by their demands and

the lack of love they seemed to exhibit toward her. When her husband left her, Grace began to feel suicidal. A choice point came for her, internally. She knew she would have to do something radically different with her life—or kill herself. She had so long ago lost touch with her true self and given herself away, as it were, that she was not sure there was a place within her that could live a fulfilling life.

Thankfully, for those who loved her and those who would come to know her in future years, she gave herself to the choice to change her life. She listened to the still, small voice within that had hope and meaning and value for her life. She went back to school. She had been a brilliant student in her twenties but had given up academics for her husband. Back in school as a graduate student, she again excelled. She found some of her long-hidden strengths. Her caring, which had drowned in her "obligations" to family, reemerged in her own unique way as a fellow student, as an intern in her counseling program, and finally as a fine family therapist. Some years down the line, Grace attributed her meaningful life to having chosen to listen to that voice within her that urged her on.

Grace's story has no mention of mother. Actually, both her mother and daughter are very prominent in her life, for good and for bad, but in these crucial moments neither her mother nor her daughter was the issue. She, by herself, alone in the world, was the issue. More and more in the last chapters of this book, we are addressing women, not mothers, not daughters. If we are beginning to be ex-children, mother graduates, autonomous adults, then these next steps are less about mother and daughter than about me. And before we turn back to our mothers and daughters we will have to give serious consideration to me and what my future will bring, because it is only in knowing myself that I will be able to go back to mother or daughter as a person able to create a new level of meaning and relationship with her.

Grace managed to find the inner self that could guide her into her future in a meaningful way. This is the task of each woman. Grace could not see the light at the end of the tunnel when she made that choice to go for it, but in faith she took the expanding, rather than the limiting, step. For each of us as women, what is the expanding step? How can we step into the future as our best self?

Julie and Dorothy's Story

"We have both had to find our own voice, our own truth. In the end it has brought us closer together at the same time that it has granted us each more autonomy and separation from each other. At times, the need to go for it has caused one or the other of us to have to leave, to change, to abandon the status quo of our relationship in search of the more compelling pull that we felt individually."

Dorothy: "I left my mother and her whole world to pursue an alternative vision. It left her frightened, confused and probably angry at times, as I traveled in places unknown to her, took risks unheard of to her, made choices inappropriate to her. We reunited as better friends, more as equals, for I had followed my vision, learning much about the world and myself."

Julie: "When I took some drastic steps in changing my career from a teacher to a therapist and when the work I did on myself in this process began to change me, I warned Dorothy that I was changing. She wrote me a letter at that time: 'I felt frightened and threatened when you said I might have a new mother. I could accept my moving on and changing, but I too have my demands on you, and part of me wanted you to stay always the same, safe and secure for me there.'"

Julie and Dorothy: "In the years since we began a professional relationship, we have written two books, offered hundreds of workshops and keynote presentations, done interviews, television and radio shows. We truly discovered a way to be adults together that we cherish to this day. At the same we are not bound in limited ways. We have spent years living far away from each other. Julie has traveled for months at a time to foreign countries, while Dorothy has stayed at home raising children. In the last few years, Julie and her husband, Dorothy's father, have moved to Dorothy's hometown. Now we live practically next door, but still have clear and strong boundaries, separate lives, and lives that come together as well. We follow our own voices, and when they come together it is a joy; when they part, it is not a loss."

SEEING TRULY

At the deepest level our own loss of self-love is bound up in non-acceptance. We tend to fight the past, fight our mothers, fight our weaknesses and hers, as if fighting would make everything better. Surely there are places to fight, but acceptance is a powerful alternative. In order to follow our own voice, to honor our own self, to move into the future in a complete way, we need self-acceptance. In order to have a good relationship with any other person we need to accept them. If we could peel away the layers and come to that self within us, and at the same time peel away the layers of mother/daughter and so see her true self, we would be seeing truly—and from there we would settle into a place in us where demands and resentments, blame and rejection, hooks and wounds would fade.

We have spent a great deal of time looking at what and how we can change. We can change our hooks, our old feelings, our relationship to life, to ourselves, and to our mothers/daughters, all of this without so much as ever expecting anything but ourselves to change. Having focused on the ability to change ourselves, in ways that are healing, we come to the equally large task of learning to accept that which we can't change. Yet, even within ourselves how do we know what to accept and what to try to change?

꿈꿈 Kelly was in an assertiveness training program. The goal was to
꿈꿈 help women learn to advocate for their own rights and needs
in a powerful way. Kelly appeared to be a good student, eagerly taking
in information and practicing the skills she was learning in the group.
However, a month into the course, when an assignment was given to
find something to practice the newfound skills on, Kelly's deeply unresolved feelings about herself emerged. When the group members
came back to report on what they were doing in their lives, the range
of projects was wide—confronting a doctor, applying for a loan, disci-
plining the children, etc.—but Kelly's project was to stop herself from
exhibiting any negativity in her family. She reported, as well, that she
had failed miserably. In spite of her best efforts, she had been unable
to stifle some of her feelings and demands. She was very disappointed
with herself.

Kelly was trying to change what could not be changed: her
humanness. She had an image of herself as a perfect wife and
mother, carried on from her image of her mother as that, and as she
constantly fell short of this perfection, she worked harder and harder
to change. Kelly needed to accept herself, accept her needs, her feelings, and her imperfections. Without this acceptance she will always
live out a try-hard-but-fail script. Even successes that she has will pale
in comparison to her general failure. What else can one be if the
model is *perfection?*

To separate that within us which we must accept from that which
we might change starts with common sense. We must first accept
ourselves as *human beings.* We are not a superior life form. We are
not superheroes. We are not gods. While that sounds obvious, it is not
common to truly accept this belief. As long as we play out "super-
woman" scripts—"Can't fail," "Do everything," "Never rest," "Give
and don't take," and the like—we are acting as if we are not human,

for human beings are filled with needs and requirements as part of being human. Until we take these needs into account and accept ourselves, with these aspects, we are not even accepting that most basic fact: our humanness.

Next on the list of the obvious things we need to accept is our gender. We must accept that we are *women*. This, too, may be easier said than done.

- Are we envious of or competitive with men because they are men?
- Do we feel ripped off by men or the culture because of our sex?
- Do we wish to have a son as our first or only child?
- Do we feel sorry for our daughter(s)?
- Do we accept limitations because of our sex?
- Do we feel we have to fight like devils to overcome our sex?

To accept being a woman means that we accept our biology, our physiology, our psychology and our heritage as women. We accept our relationship in the lineage of mothers and daughters. We accept our bodies. We become aware of what it means to be a woman in our culture, for better or for worse. We accept what is unique about being female, whatever that might be!

🍂 "I guess the truth is that I've never accepted myself, as a woman. I've spent years in competitive karate—a black belt and highly ranked competitor. It's never enough. I feel something lacking even with lesser-ranked men. My body, which is strong and lean, always seems inadequate to me. I think, finally, that I look in the mirror and expect (hope) to see a man's muscles."

Accepting our humanness and our femaleness may be even easier than accepting our "littleness." But feeling little, needy, vulnerable, afraid, wanting comfort, aid, support, asking for help, being unable to accomplish this or that, seeing the world as big, not understanding, making mistakes . . . these are human. And they define the bulk of our "little" experience. With all else, we must finally acknowledge the child feelings within and accept these as a positive part of our being: a source for spontaneity, creativity, lightheartedness, intimacy, sharing, belonging and accepting. If we try to do away with our child part because she has needs, we will lose the best of her as well.

> "I finally had to quit the support group I was in. Everyone got so mushy—feelings everywhere, hugging, caring, crying. I could really feel how nice it would be to feel so supported, but at the same time I can't afford to be weak. What's the point of feeding that infantile need? My life depends upon being strong. I'm not going to blow it by giving in to childish needs."

When I deny all that is little, vulnerable, sensitive, I will have to shut down a huge part of who I am, and when I accept my little aspects, I can start to find out how to live and love and be fully human. That's the punch line of acceptance. It is not until we accept ourselves that we can really, deeply change. Before that acceptance, our efforts at change are really efforts at compensation, making up for this or that weakness, hiding or making up for aspects of ourselves that we do not accept. This is not healing, it is a cover-up. It is not transcending, it is denying. It is not change, it is fraud. Truly, we cannot transcend that which we do not own, we cannot change that which we do not acknowledge, we cannot heal that which we don't accept. And so, as we come to this point of growth, when we are ready to move on in our relationship to our mothers/daughters and ready to let go of the past, ready to come to know our uniqueness, we will need to give ourselves the gift of self-acceptance. We need to be willing to say in a deep and profound way: "I'm okay the way I am! I love myself!"

❧   "After years of self-doubt, I look at myself now as a whole person. I feel a smile about myself, for I know that I am human, no more and no less. It's a good thing to be."

❧   "I struggled for so long to be perfect. In the process I lost so much of who I was. I was a well-built robot—did everything right, except feel. Now I can cry and it's okay. I can yell and it's okay. I can be joyful and it's okay."

❧   "Peace has begun to overcome me as I practice letting go. Acceptance, equanimity seem to flow from within when I give up trying—and start being."

All that we have said for ourselves applies also to our mothers. As you begin to understand and separate from your mother, you may begin to accept the way she is given the circumstances of her life. Maybe you will be able to see the love and good intention behind her ways of being, maybe you will find empathy for her. As you do these things, you will move deeper toward accepting her, just the way she is. Surely, if the greatest wisdom and compassion were ours, we would see our mothers benevolently, in spite of what has hurt us. We would see ourselves with positive eyes as well. And in each of us a touch of that wisdom and compassion exists. Learning to connect to that will open the doors for acceptance.

Acceptance of mother requires coming to understand her. We must have a sense of her origins, of the conditions that molded her, of her pain and humanness, and of her intentions to do good. Acceptance does not mean approval or agreement. It certainly does not mean assuming that mother was always right, nor is it a justification for what she may have done that hurt us. Acceptance is simply an acknowledgment of what is and what was.

Dorothy's Story

"For a long while I would categorize my mother, especially in the newfound psychological jargon that I was learning. She was this, did this, this is why I, etc. I got lots of support for that from other women who were busy labeling their mothers as well. As long as I was labeling mother—making her bad or good—I kept her at arm's length. I could diagnose her, assess her, analyze her, but I couldn't accept her. The edges of this began to soften over time until, one day, I noticed that I wasn't talking to myself about her. I had no comments to make. I just saw her. In that moment I accepted her, just as she was, wanting or expecting nothing different, needing no explanation or strategy. Just Julie."

Part of the difficulty in accepting mother, for many women, is the inability to let her be human. We may have colored her in our eyes to be the all-good mother. But now that we are adults, we can do away with the fantasy image of a perfect mother. She'll never be that. And when we drop the demand for a perfect mother, it may be easier to drop the demand for a perfect self. If we are unwilling to take her off of the pedestal, we cannot accept her. The real mother, with strengths and weaknesses, does not exist, is not accepted when she is on a pedestal. We may also do the opposite and be equally unable to accept her. We may blame her, cast her out and make her all bad, thus aiding us in the illusion of acceptance of ourselves. "It's her fault. I'm okay. She's not." This may feel soothing for a while, as blame can be, temporarily, but it will deny us the truth. We will be unable to hear the self that calls us to move on. We will be stuck— smug, perhaps, in our limited complacency, but stuck in mud that is thick and deep, for here we do not see mother any more clearly than if we make her all good. She is just an image: a negative image.

To accept your mother finally means to step back, to think of yourself as an ex-child, as responsible for yourself, the author of your story. When you do that, you can look at mother truly. You may choose to look at her as you would any woman, seeing her strengths and weaknesses, her uniqueness or idiosyncrasies, her styles and beliefs. You will know what you agree and disagree with, what you like and don't like, and you will accept her.

Dear Momma,

I have learned to accept, to accept you as a whole person, one who loved me deeply, one who gave love and affection and caring. I accept your struggles, your weakness and the pain I suffered. I don't understand your life and your pain; they were unique to you. It is enough to accept. I love you.

Mothers learning to accept their daughters will have the same task: understanding, feeling in control of their own lives, being able to see their daughters for what they are and not what they wish they were. A mother will know of her daughter's origins, but she will not be able to see her daughter's experience of life. It is common and understandable for mothers to color the picture of their daughters' lives, to see the rosy side and not the dark side, to forget or dismiss or deny the daughter's pain. For this pain hurts us too much. To think we have allowed—or, worse, caused—our own daughter suffering seems at times to be more than we can bear. And yet every daughter did suffer.

Every one of us has our wounds. Every mother has been imperfect.

Without taking the blame, making ourselves bad, or laying the blame on our daughters or anywhere else, we can let ourselves see her. We can listen carefully to her version of life and know that she too has strengths and weaknesses, uniqueness and idiosyncrasies, styles and beliefs. We must give up the images that we have put on her since before her birth. We know how important she is to us, how dearly we love her and want for her the best. Can we let her be herself, and accept just that? When a mother is willing to accept her daughter, she will have to face her daughter's pain, her own pain, and the possibility of coming together again in a way never before experienced.

When both a mother and a daughter can truly see each other, their lives will change. The many masquerades they have played together for so long will begin to fall away and they will have the opportunity to come into a relationship based on authenticity.

FORGIVE US OUR TRESPASSES

To forgive is to give up resentment against someone and to need neither material nor emotional reward for the grievance. The act of forgiveness requires that we take control of our life, that we not be its victim. Forgiveness leads to self-renewal. It is, at the same time, a humbling and empowering experience. We surrender ourselves to what is and was without the fight that demands that life be different, and we empower ourselves by letting go of the past, the excuses, the blame. We stand fully human, in its best sense, when we can forgive.

"How do I forgive, when I was deeply hurt by what my mother did to me? Must I pretend it never happened? Am I simply to give in to her yet another time? Does this all mean she was right to have done what she did?" . . . "How can I forgive my daughter who turned me away when I was in need, all in the name of her own independence? No one has hurt me as much as she."

Forgiveness does not deny that you may actually have been wronged. It does not condone cruel or unfair actions, nor does it mean you are to forget. Forgiveness means simply that you do not benefit by hanging on to the hurt. It means you feel no need, anymore, to punish the perpetrator. Forgiveness does not require you to swallow anger or become a goody-goody, for it is better to acknowledge anger and dislikes than to deny them. Forgiveness, without a doubt, does not mean allowing further pain to be inflicted. It is the clean sheet of paper from which we can further write our story. It means that we can end the old and hurtful thread about this other person and look again at her and at ourself.

We have all been hurt by our mothers and daughters, but to hold on to grievances is to hold on to the worst, most limiting assumptions about this relationship. "If Mother was cold to me, must I assume that she didn't love me?" . . . "If Daughter has forgotten my birthday, must I assume that she doesn't care?" Until we understand the context, the intention, the feelings of the person involved, our negative assumptions cannot be trusted. We are likely to be operating out of hooks in us that leave us unable to see clearly.

🙎 When Maria was sixteen, she was told to leave home by her own mother because of her conflicts with her mother's live-in boyfriend. Filled with resentment and betrayal, Maria left.

Years later, Maria walked down her former street and saw her mother in her second-floor apartment window. The sadness in her mother's face brought Maria to tears. She thought about what her mother's life had been like: She had been married at sixteen when Maria was about to be born. She had left her native land for "a better life" in America. She spoke only broken English. She had three other children, all younger than Maria. Her husband had been killed. Her boyfriend had been the only thing that sustained Sonya and her children. Maria realized that her mother's decision to ask her to go was not based on any bad feelings for Maria, but on desperation and fear. Love flooded over Maria. She forgave her mother.

Maria was hurt. She had a right to be angry. But there was actually nothing she could do to change the situation that hurt her, except to forgive. Her assumption, which was understandable, was that her mother did not love her or did not love her as much as the boyfriend, or something along those lines. Her ability to see more deeply into her mother's life erased that assumption and it was replaced with a new one: the assumption that, perhaps, underlies the ability to forgive: *She did the best she could.*

In most cases, if we delve deeply enough, we will find that our mothers and daughters love and have loved us. If we are open to seeing truly, we may discover in the worst of circumstances that our limited assumption is not accurate. There is likely to be a more expansive, caring one, based on good intentions and limited resources.

Abby and Delores almost lost each other as they operated out of limiting assumptions.

Abby: "I couldn't share my life with my mother. I felt too confused and inadequate. I thought she was so perfect and I so imperfect. She had such high hopes for me and I knew I was a failure."

Delores: "I have felt abandoned and rejected by Abby since she was a teenager. I gave my life for her and it seems as if she dumped me like so much trash. I thought she despised me. I was devastated for years."

Abby: "When I became sick, I felt worse about myself than ever. I thought this was my just reward. Even then, I couldn't reach out to my mother."

Delores: "I heard from her sister that Abby was sick and I was too angry and hurt to care—on the surface. My pride wouldn't let me break our awful silence."

Abby: "When I finally had to face the possibility of my death, I let go of everything. I did call Mom and told her about my illness and about my feelings of inadequacy and failure and why I had hidden from her. I thought she had understood why I wasn't in her life. I guess I believed that she was just as happy to be rid of me."

Delores: "I never knew until that moment how stubborn I was, how hurtful I had been by pressuring Abby to be something I wanted, and even more by holding on to my grudges and not reaching out to her, as if I didn't care. When she told me she might die, I became a changed person. I could suddenly see what was important and what wasn't."

Abby and Delores are not alone in being stubborn, in losing their priorities, in holding on to grudges and limited assumptions, in clinging to their own "rightness." Playing life out as a right-and-wrong proposition leaves everyone in a bitter standoff. Would you rather be free, or right? Abby and Delores found a way to be free, and rightness didn't matter. There was no grievance left to hold on to, just the freedom to reclaim their love.

Forgiveness need not come under such pressure, or at the last minute, or years after death has taken one of us away. If death were around the corner for you or your mother or daughter, would letting go be easier? What would be worth holding on to at that moment? What resentment would seem important? What point would you have to prove? Would you still need to be right?

WORKBOOK

As we turn inward to ourselves, looking toward the future and what it can bring, we need to play with the question "Who can I be?" The struggle for autonomy that is one of the first major tasks of our lives prepares the stage for another important task: becoming the best of which we are capable. This pull within each of us toward our own "greatness" is not a pull toward fame and fortune, nor toward building an indestructible positive self, but it is the inevitable growing of the acorn into the oak that will take us to our own blossoming. It is said that we cannot become that which we cannot imagine, and correspondingly we are pulled toward that which we do imagine. If our images of our self are based on limited assumptions, on old and unconsidered conditioning, on anger directed inside and outside, on a basic nonacceptance, then we will be slowly pulled more and more into that limiting worldview. If, on the other hand, our image honors our true self, it will pull us equally into that expansive worldview.

❧ To Be All That I Can Be ❧

There are many ways we think of ourselves that will be limiting: the image of ourselves that comes from how others expect and want us to be, the image we try to project as we "fake it" in the world, the image we have of our "not-okay" self, the childlike images we have of how we wish we would be. Then there is the model of our potential, our growing edge. This is an honest and evocative image that will magnetize our various aspects around it. Like the score of music that the orchestra sets out to learn to play, this "growing image" can be a support for our movement into true self.

With crayons or markers at hand, take time to think about the different limiting images you hold of yourself. (Examples: what you think others expect of you; the not-okay you; the positive, superficial you; the unrealistic fantasy you; etc.) One at a time, draw them and name them. Funny, lighthearted names will be helpful.

When the assembly is complete, look at them all and acknowledge that these images are not the true you. They represent partial aspects, thoughts and feelings. They are not the best that you can be. Quiet your mind with silence or soothing music for a moment and allow an image to appear that does represent that which you are moving toward, your true self. Draw this. Spend time with all the images, coming to understand them. Double-check your growing image to make sure that it is not contaminated with "shoulds" or other limiting intentions. Place this image in a highly visible spot within your home and notice it daily. Make an affirmation for yourself about your movement in this direction. Enjoy the experience of your own growing!

❧ My Mother Is Human ❧

To come fully to acceptance of our mothers and ourselves means accepting our humanness. We are, after all, only mortal, prey to all the pitfalls of that truth. If only we did not envision perfection, we might be easier on each other and ourselves. In this exercise, we offer an opportunity to fully embrace our mother's humanness and in so doing accept our own. In this exercise, you may read the narrative to yourself, tape record it and play it back, or have a friend read it to you. Listen to the narrative and allow yourself to follow it, slowly and deeply:

Imagine a time before your birth. The world was not yet yours, but it was your mother's. She lived as a young woman in that particular time in history, in a certain place, born of her own mother.

Allow yourself to get an image of this young woman, pregnant with you, wearing the clothes and hairstyle of that day. Simply watch her for a moment as she walks down a street, being herself. Take a deep breath and choose to become, for a time, this woman who will soon become your mother. Feel yourself floating into her body. How does it feel to be weighted with this unknown child? What are your clothes like? Glance in a mirror and notice your looks. And expand your identification with this woman.

Answer the questions that follow, and others that occur to you from the first person, from within your mother, as if you are she. Hear them one at a time and slowly respond to each, out loud if you can, in writing or inside yourself:

- What is my name?
- How old am I?
- Is this my first child or are there others?
- What is my life like for me?
- Where do I live? In a city or the country?
- What country do I live in?
- Is it the country of my origin or am I an immigrant?
- What is the state of the world that I am living in?
- What are the political and social situations?
- What are the economic influences?
- What about the father of this child that I will soon bear?
- Is he with me? What is my relationship to him?
- How is my relationship to my own mother?
- What am I afraid of in my life? What excites me?
- How do I feel about the impending birth of this child?

Taking time to feel yourself being your mother, allow yourself to move into the experience of labor and delivery. What is this like for you? Are you in a hospital? at home? with loved ones? What is labor like? and delivery? How do you feel during this process?

Take some minutes to relive this experience of giving birth to your daughter. When you first come into conscious contact with her as she leaves your body and comes into the world, see her, feel her, hold her. And in this first moment of your bonding, as if all weakness and limitations are erased from your being (as your mother), know how deeply you love and care for this child, your daughter.

Say her name (your name) to her, tell her you love her and wish the best for her. Savor that precious moment that exists before the world and its demands, the personality and its weaknesses begin to infringe on this love. Take a deep breath and allow your consciousness to move out of the mother and into the child and feel this love coming toward you. Feel safe and trusting, held and protected. Savor this moment.

And take another deep breath. Allow your consciousness to leave the child and move into your adult true self, into a clear, expansive compassionate you that can see both this mother and daughter. What is it like to gaze benevolently at these people who will struggle to grow, will stumble, will fall, will hurt each other and themselves? Can you allow them their humanness, can you forgive them both their weaknesses? If you can, make that statement to your mother: "I forgive you." Fill it in with every hurt that you have felt that needs forgiving. And as well make that statement to yourself, the child: "I forgive you for everything you will do that will need forgiving." Finally, enjoy the experience of being the compassionate observer to this scene.

When you are finished, take time to write a letter to your mother, your daughter or yourself expressing what you have found in your efforts at acceptance and forgiveness. Choose to mail or not mail this letter. Let it simply be an expression from your true self.

The following are letters mothers and daughters have written in response to this exercise over the last ten years. They touch only a portion of the caring, acceptance, forgiveness and love that grow between a mother and daughter and within a woman:

Dear Mother,

I know that you loved me very dearly and wanted all things to guide me to a happy and filled life. I understand your fears and anxieties in bringing me into a world at war. The frustrations of a home without the support of loving arms and heart that you wanted. I carried these fears, frustrations and lonely feelings within me. A deep sadness. I can sincerely forgive you and myself and look to a fresh start with joy and acceptance reigning.

Dear Mother,

You did the best you could and so did I. It wasn't easy being your daughter, but I did what I needed to do and look at me now— I'm really a grown-up woman. It's getting better and better, and I'm happier than I ever thought I'd be. I wish you were alive to see this.

Mother,

All my life I have been walking around in a room full of shadows, mourning your lack of loving, doubting myself, knowing I must be horribly guilty. Today I walked out of that room and shut the door. I know that you did what you could, what you had to do, and that is okay with me now. Finally, I know that I am not guilty, that it was not my fault, so now I can stop punishing myself. I know I am someone beautiful, who has a right to be. I think you are, in so many ways, a beauty too and I thank you for the good things in you that you have passed on to me. I want to accept you as you are.

Dear Self,

It's time to forgive yourself for past mistakes and start over, to begin with a new view of yourself. Shut off that inner critic and stop looking for critics outside. Treat yourself kindly with love and caring. Appreciate your gifts, for they are many and worth much. Know that you are and have been loved. Love, Your Self.

Dear Daughter,

I love you and I believe in you and I trust that you can be your-self in this world, your unique self, and not lose your way. You can let go of what you hold on to that stands in your path and not let go of yourself. I forgive you for anything that has hurt me. I know that you did the best you could—always have and always will.

Dear Daughter,

I want you to know how very much I love you. I am proud of the woman you have become. I am so sorry that your childhood was so stormy because of the fight you had to be your own per-son instead of fulfilling my expectations. You are my firstborn and will always be special to me. Continue to grow and be your own person always.

Dear Daughter,

I give you permission to be yourself and take risks and make your own way. I accept you as you are. I think you are a warm, wonderful person who will make your own way in your time. I will make every attempt to let you go as a child but return to me as an adult. I love you very much. You are very dear to me.

CHAPTER TEN

Together, by Choice

EVERY PARTING GIVES A FORETASTE OF DEATH;
EVERY COMING TOGETHER AGAIN A
FORETASTE OF RESURRECTION.

—*Schopenhauer*

THE REUNION

Acceptance and forgiveness are the cornerstones of the new adult-to-adult relationship that exists in potential for women with their mothers and daughters. If you are without your mother or daughter, these same experiences are the cornerstone of your autonomy and ability to be in relationship with important others. If the work you have been doing has moved you closer to feeling acceptance and forgiveness, then your next step may be to re-choose how to be in relationship to each other. The range of healthy and adult experiences is vast and your relationship will be unique. Behind whatever form it takes, there will be a core of love that is deeply ingrained in the history and bondedness of mothers and daughters.

More than two thousand years ago, the power of love that existed between mothers and daughters was eulogized in a myth that became the symbol for reunion and rebirth, for hope and for blossoming:

Demeter was the goddess of the earth and all was bountiful and full. She had a daughter, Persephone, whom she loved with abandon. Persephone was good and loving, and all who came in contact with her saw her beauty and grace. One day she wandered off to look for flowers for her mother. Each flower she saw drew her further from her mother and her companions. Suddenly the earth opened and she was swallowed up, taken by a god of the underworld because he, too, had seen and fallen in love with her.

Demeter was bereft. She searched the lands far and wide. Finally in a rage built on despair, she caused all things on the earth to stop growing. Bleakness settled over all the land. The first winter ensued. The land was barren and the people suffered. Zeus, fearing for his people, summoned Demeter and begged her to return the land to fruitful production. "Only when my daughter is returned will the flowers bloom again and grain and fruits grow to ripen," Demeter replied. Zeus called on the god of the underworld and said he must give up Persephone, but he refused. Zeus at last reached a compromise between the two—the god who loved Persephone and the mother who bore her. The man could have Persephone for four months of the year, and the mother for the rest. The reunion between mother and her now adult daughter was joyous. In exchange for this blessed reunion, Demeter allowed the plants and fruits to begin their growth again. Spring ensued: rebirth and reunion.

How graphically this story portrays the depth of love between mothers and daughters. This is a love that can be missed along the way unless both mother and daughter search for the right solution to being together. We have seen many find each other and see each other anew, with eyes that are not blinded by childhood hurts and problems. That reunion has become a powerful symbol of the mother/daughter love that exists: love that is so deep and strong that nothing could tear it asunder.

This romantic version may touch a chord in us. Many of us have felt so deeply bonded to our mothers and daughters that we, too, would render the earth barren if either were threatened. And mothers have been known to do just such things in protection of their daughters. It is classic, the story of the mother who will lift a car to save her child. We are like mother wolves—at the cave door ready to fight and die to protect our litter.

We have alluded throughout this book to the something that is special and different about this relationship. It is a mystery and an intrigue, and philosophers have considered this bond for centuries. No other relationship has quite the depth of connection, quite the history, quite the continuity. Perhaps, finally, it is the continuity of women that adds such an impact to this already profound relationship: grandmother, mother, daughter, on and on forever, repeated without end. We are continued through our daughters. Eternity is gained, in small measure, through the lineage of mothers and daughters.

The lineage is ever-present, whether we personally continue that bearing of daughters, or whether we simply live within the community of females for whom this lineage never ends, for whom eternity is gained. Because of this ongoing thread that surrounds the relationship, there is a profound pull to move toward that other person. Both consciously and unconsciously we are drawn to and into our mothers and daughters. Women, over and over, say they feel themselves in their mothers and their mothers in them, they see themselves in their daughters and feel themselves living on in their daughters.

Dorothy's Story

"As I sat rocking Sarah when she was just a few days old, I noticed myself feeling as if I were being rocked by my mother. The sensation was unmistakable. I could feel her arms around me and the comfort of the movement. I shuttled back and forth for a moment, rocking and being rocked, mothering and being mothered and finally returned to my position as the mother. This was a profound experience for me, and one that I thought was rather unusual, but I have heard other mothers report similar moments with their daughters, and daughters, as well, with their mothers."

If the bond is so great, then the coming back together, adult to adult, is a most significant experience. The possibility is at hand for a deep and lasting friendship magnified by this mysterious connection. But the coming together must be as adults. Daughters need not be protected in that same way anymore by their mothers. If the bond can only be created through the continuation of the old roles, then the daughter will have to stay a child, the mother will have to stay a parent, and this will interfere with the natural cycle of the relationship. The time is coming, only too soon in this cycle, when the roles will be reversed, when daughter may well play mother to her mother, as the elder woman moves into old age and finally into death. This is the end of the living relationship, but not the end of the impact of mother in one's life.

Julie's Story

"My mother died when I was forty-five. Years after she died, I found myself driving home from work wondering if there would be a letter from Mother. I wanted so much to tell her about the flowers that were growing in my garden, about my grandchildren and about the new work that I had begun.

"Somehow over the years, all the faults in my mother disappeared from my perspective and all I saw was her ready humor, willingness to try new things, and most of all her love for me. I will always miss her and in my heart share my thoughts and dreams with her. Sometimes when I see my granddaughter, Sarah, who is named after my mother, I see my mother as a young girl; and sometimes I look at Dorothy, when she hugs me, becoming my mother."

SHARING AND CARING AND BEING TOGETHER

Demeter and Persephone had the odd arrangement of being with each other full time for part of the year and separated for the rest. It apparently worked for them, but each of us, as we face a reunion with our mother/daughter or as we apply these principles to important others in our lives, will have to define what it means to come together again as adults. The dance that started in childhood will continue in a new style.

Both mother and daughter will equally negotiate the dancing. Give and take and respect and caring will be the guidelines. As daughters, we may be used to following mother's lead or blending into the family system in such a way that we continue to respond unconsciously even after we have grown and created lives of our own. How surprisingly often we see women planning to go "home" for the holidays, dreading it and never considering that they do not have to go. It is often a huge, wrenching apart of family norms to have a daughter who, instead, makes other plans. But she must, at some time, create norms for herself. It is equally surprising to see how often a mother feels no permission to change her norms and create a life that represents herself as a mother graduate. The coming together again will not be defined by old patterns, by obligations, by family structure. It will not be defined by our old roles as parent and child. It must be created, cocreated, by two new, adult people.

☙ Therapy with Connie was marked by holidays. She had been in therapy several months when Thanksgiving rolled around and suddenly everything in her life became despondent. "I'm going home next week. I'll miss our session," she said in a dead voice. "Home?" the therapist queried, for Connie had lived in her own home for at least six years. "To my mother's" (dead voice). Christmas brought more, and worse. Connie hated to go home, wanted to create special holiday traditions with her lover and friends, and yet she had never considered not going "home."

"Why don't you stay here?" the therapist asked innocently. "Oh my God, you've got to be kidding. My mother would die! Gramma, the whole family. It's not done. *Everybody* comes home!" But the seed had been planted and grew in Connie like a wildflower. When Easter came around—"a time for big family reunions"—Connie decided not to go. It couldn't be her mother's way anymore.

Connie had never separated in a healthy way from her mother, but her choice to begin to create a life of her own opened the door. Somewhere there was the possibility for a mutual relationship with her mother.

As surely as if we took a magnifying glass to our conditioning—the internal structure that has defined and often limited us—we must take a magnifying glass to our outer relationship with mother and daughter and see if this is what we choose it to be, want it to be, enjoy it as. Both mother and daughter need to do this. Mothers really can't live in their daughters' worlds, nor can daughters live in their mothers' worlds. Where will we find a place to come together?

What is the way that it will be now? It can't be *just* the mother's way and it can't be *just* the daughter's way. Are we friends now that we are adults? or is it something different? Relatives? Companions? Soul mates? Mother and daughter? Playmates? Mother and grandmother? Two mothers? Acquaintances? Mother graduate and ex-child? Can we define what we are?

Probably not in words or pat phrases, but we will need to understand our boundaries. What works and what doesn't, for each of us? How do we want to spend time or be together? There are some very deeply bonded mothers and daughters who spend little time together, and there are the opposite, of course: next-door neighbor mothers and daughters who haven't found much depth in their relationship. The quality of the relationship, the style, the playgrounds in which we play will need to be discovered. Hear what a few mothers and daughters have said to each other as they begin to create the arena in which their new relationship will unfold.

Daughters

"I love you and admire you and am grateful for all the strength and nurturing you gave me throughout my life. As Daddy's death has pointed out, our days together are numbered. Please now count on me as a friend, a companion, a daughter and perhaps a teacher. I love you so much."

"My mother is my best friend in all senses of the word. I think of her as my age and would rather do things with her than many of my women friends. She is lively, creative and funny. We laugh together and thoroughly enjoy each other. I will certainly miss her when she's gone and hope she lives to be a hundred!"

"It feels good and okay to know what I have when I look at my mother and our relationship. She is neither my confidante nor my friend, but she never chose to be so. She is someone I greatly admire and respect, and we often share parts of our daily lives together. We talk about our families, what we do at work and at home, but never about our anxieties, fears, hopes and dreams. I have someone else to share that with and I don't need her intimacy in that respect any longer. We don't know each other well, but we want good things for each other and we care about each other like two adults closely related."

"I look forward to the day when I will walk in your shoes as a mother, and feel anew the bond that began between us so many years ago."

Mothers

"All at once, I felt a freedom never felt before. I think that we have taken a very important step, together and separately, one that can only lead to a lovelier relationship together."

"I want to stop worrying about what I did right and wrong. I just want to hug you. I love you for keeping the door open so that we can be friends. Friends—that sounds so strange. Will we begin to be friends when you read this?"

"I want to baby and be babied by you. I experience you as both mother and child."

"I am a very fine person and you are, too—loving, generous, sensitive, kind. We need to let each other fully be each other, and then we will both feel loved."

There is no right or wrong way to come together again. What is your hope and desire for this relationship? What would you like to create? What do you really need and deeply want from this special person?

Let's Talk: New Ways of Communicating

Learning specific communication skills makes the job of relating in new ways easier. With the best of intentions, our communications can go awry—simply because we haven't learned suitable ways to talk, listen, express ourselves, argue and communicate at all levels. If it is important for you to create a new way of relating to another person, then learning skills to facilitate that will also be important.

The way we communicate in large part reflects the way we heard communications. And often these were not effective. Without even being aware of it, we may be giving messages that we don't want to give in some of the subtler aspects of our communication. To communicate effectively there are lessons to be learned about language, nonverbal communication and process.

Language

This is more than the words that make up our speech. The use of words conveys meaning at many levels. There are some simple guidelines for the use of words that can make all the difference in the world in the clarity of your communications. The first is the use of the word "I." Using "I" is a clear way to express your thoughts and feelings. If you are angry, sad, disappointed, confused, or have any internal experience that needs to be shared, that "I" is valid and important. But if you move to blame or criticism, you have left your truth and moved into labeling the other.

Two ways to get across the same message will have very different effects: "I feel sad that our plans didn't work out" versus "You always change plans!" "I'm angry that you chose to go with Dad instead of honoring our agreement to have lunch" versus "You ruined my day. You don't care about me!" "I feel hurt that you didn't come to lunch with me" versus "You're mean!"

Everything you feel has a place in an intimate relationship. Everything can be said from within your experience without causing the other to have to defend or protect herself: "I'm scared of losing you. I wish you wouldn't hitchhike" versus "Don't be foolish. What's the matter with you? When are you going to grow up?" "I really love you. I'll miss you if you don't come home" versus "We always come home for the holidays. What could be more important than your family?"

I can say what I mean, what I want, what I feel—and not have the other be made bad, little or not okay in any way. Having one of us be little—in any way—is often the crux of communication difficulties. When we blame or criticize or make pontificating "You" statements, we act big, attempting to make the other little, consciously or unconsciously. We may, on the contrary, initiate the difficult communications by presenting ourselves as little, through the use of passive or victimized language. "I can't" and "I have to" stand out as ways of keeping ourselves feeling little or helpless and making the other big, as rescuer or persecutor. There are some valid uses for "I can't," but they relate to inability rather than choice or preference: "I can't possibly manage the children tonight. I'm too frazzled." "I can't come to dinner next week." "I can't talk to you at work." "I can't get my life together." All of these statements, and many others like them that permeate conversations, are likely to mask a preference or a choice. On the other hand, these statements make clear the preference or choice: "I don't want to deal with the kids tonight. I feel frazzled. Will you take care of them?" "I won't come to dinner next week. I have other plans." "It's difficult for me when you call me at work. I'd prefer to talk when I'm at home." "I feel confused and uncertain about my life. I don't know what's next for me." It takes more responsibility to acknowledge your preference or choice than it does to hang out in "can't." It also allows the other equally to have preferences and choice. Mom has a lot more freedom to accept or refuse the request to baby-sit when I make a preference statement than when I make a helpless one. Her choice is then allowed to be an adult one, rather than a rescuer or persecutor one.

"I have to," "I must," and "I need" leave us in an equally powerless position. We act as though we had no choice, no authorship when we succumbed to a "have to." Try changing the following sentences from "have to," "must," and "need" to "choose to" or "want to," or "choose not to" or "don't want to":

"I have to go on a diet."   "I must write to my mother."
"I need help."   "I have to go see my mother."
"I have to help my daughter."   "I must finish this book."
"I need to be there for her."   "I have to be good."

Add some others of your own.

When we move to a choice or desire (want) statement, we force ourselves to become aware of what we are truly experiencing. When we know that we are free to choose or not to choose, we are responsible. We allow the other to also be responsible and not fall into the one-up/one-down trap.

"Shoulds" also keep communication in a one-up/one-down mode. "Shoulds" in adult relationships put the speaker in a covert parental, authoritarian or morally superior stance. The listener will tend to feel little, and feel guilty and obligated or angry and resistant, to the comment and to the speaker. "Should" statements also defy the first language principle of making "I" statements. They require a labeling of the other: "You should . . . come home . . . write to your mother. . . be good . . . do this . . . feel this . . . try this." All offer a so-called correct position, leaving no room for equal discussion or consideration of opposing viewpoints. "Shoulds" hide a strong preference, hope, desire or belief and couch this point of view in powerful terms, thus hoping to create an uncontested outcome. "You should hold your wedding in the church" really means "I want you to. I think it's spiritually correct to. I hope you do."

"Buts" also create miscommunication or covert communication in many instances. "But" tends to be a discounter. When I start my response with a "but," I have probably discounted or ignored what the other person has said. "I think you'll handle this difficulty very well." "Yes, but I'll never get it figured out in time." "I'm angry that you didn't come on time." "But the traffic was so heavy." I can dismiss compliments, suggestions, the other's feelings or needs with a simple "but." I can also discount what I have to say when I use a "but" instead of an "and." "But" tends to discount what comes before it. "I know you tried, but you really didn't get enough done." "I want to come to dinner, but I'm so busy." "I love you, but you've been so out of touch with me." Which half of the sentence is heard? What is it that really needs to be said? The first words get lost in the power of the "but." How does the sentence change when we use "and"? "I know you tried and you really didn't get enough done [to satisfy me, to accomplish the task . . .]." Suddenly the first part stands out as true and the second half becomes open to further clarification. The speaker is required to take more responsibility for her statement. "I want to come to dinner and I'm so busy [that I won't be able to this week . . . that I won't stay long . . . that I'll have to drop something in order to come]." "I love you and you've been so out of touch with me [that I feel sad, scared, angry, lonely]."

Language offers us many more subtleties than are immediately obvious. This leaves us in the position of needing to be clear in what we say. Taking responsibility, talking about our own experience, being straight in how we present ourselves will facilitate communication, though it may be awkward and difficult at first.

Mother: "You should come home this week. I have to take care of your father and I can't stand not having my daughters here to help. You owe it to your father to be here for him. I know you care, but if you don't come more often, how will he know?"

Daughter: "But it's not my fault I don't come home more often. I can't possibly come home this week. I need to study. You always blame me. You never care about my side of the story. You should ask my sister, not me."

Without ever raising a voice in anger, two caring women have hurt each other and themselves in one small conversation. They both feel defensive, blamed and uncared for. They have not heard each other's real desires or feelings. They will go away from each other unsatisfied, at the least. The same conversation can produce an entirely different outcome.

Mother: "I hope you'll come home this week. I've decided to stay home from work and take care of your father. I really want some help and support from you. I think your father would appreciate your company as well. I know you care about both of us and when you don't come home for long periods, I feel sad about that."

Daughter: "I hear that you are having a hard time. I won't be able to come home this week, though. I want to study for these difficult exams that are coming up. I feel sad that my choice to not come home is hard for you and Dad. I hope you can understand why I'm staying here right now. It would be great if my sister could come this week."

The same physical outcome evolves from this discussion. The daughter will not come home this week. The emotional outcome will be vastly different. Mother will still feel sad and disappointed, but probably not angry, blamed and blaming. Daughter may also feel sad and even conflicted, but she will not feel blamed, coerced or guilty. She will have made one of the many difficult adult decisions that face us every day.

Nonverbal Communication

This is as important, perhaps, as language and is something we know even less about. When we remember the intensity of mixed messages that we received as a child—messages in which the words said one thing and the behavior another—we will know the power of the nonverbal level of our relationships.

Nonverbal communication includes everything from facial expression to body language, to listening skills, to the more abstract concept of presence. Presence is the central element of nonverbal communication. It has to do with being fully there for and with another, not half there. It means giving full attention to the other and attempting to see her clearly. This is more than hearing words. It includes that, but also having empathy for the other's perspective, curiosity about her reality, caring for her being.

Mothers and daughters are uniquely suited for presence with each other: It is a natural part of their past together. A mother and baby daughter have intense presence with each other as they delve deeply into their mutual bonding and exploration. As the boundaries and roles get set, the status quo settles in and presence, which is always alive and new, fades into conditioned patterns of interaction. This reunion offers a perfect place to rekindle the excitement of discovery in something/someone new. This adult woman who used to be only your mother or daughter is a new person to you. Do you know her? What is she like? What does she like? What would it be like to walk a mile in her shoes?

Listening will be a profound way to come to know and be with this other person. Learning to listen sounds easy, but it is not. Listening actively to what is being said means coming to an understanding of all that is meant. At the simplest level, it means asking for confirmation about what you've heard. It means that you don't assume that you know what was meant without checking to be certain. Making assumptions is a terrible pitfall. Second-guessing leaves us playing out old patterns, projecting our truth onto another's. When she is sick, what does she really want? I can't assume that her needs will be the same as mine. What does her birthday mean to her, not to me? Am I willing to ask, to listen to her answer, to consider responding based on her uniqueness?

If we can do that with each other, we will be able to create the new dance that will reflect us both.

❧ When Kate and her daughter Susan came back into a relationship after a stormy separation of several years, they found that they really didn't know each other. Kate invited Susan over for Susan's birthday and made a cake and had lots of presents for her. Susan just wasn't comfortable with the way her mother celebrated her birthday. In Susan's adulthood, she had found new and more meaningful ways to honor her own birthday. She and her mother were fortunate in being able and willing to talk about these things and Kate really heard what was true for her daughter. The following year, they had a quiet celebration, with a picnic and walk in the park that felt much more fulfilling to Susan—and to her mother, who realized that her desire to give something special to her daughter was better met giving her what she really wanted.

Communicating clearly means being present, listening, using clear language and being congruent. All of the correct language doesn't mean anything if body posture, expression, voice tone say something different. Being congruent means telling the truth. Saying, "Of course I'll baby-sit for you on Saturday night" in a flat voice, between clenched teeth, leaves your willingness open to doubt. The listener will not be able to accept either "message" easily because they are in conflict. Anger, sadness, opposition, expressed in body language and denied in words will create a conflict that cannot even be addressed. Are you willing to know what you actually feel and want before you respond verbally? Are you willing to express the various levels of your experience so that a truthful, congruent message is given? "I want to help you out and be there for you and your children, and I am worried that I won't be able to handle your two-year-old. She is so rambunctious these days, I fear that I won't manage well." This may leave us with some issues to work out. How can grandma be with the kids and feel comfortable, how does daughter feel about her mother's opinions regarding her children, can mother and daughter find workable ways to meet each other's needs? Certainly there will be issues. This is a relationship, and mother and daughter will have a chance to build a good one if they will allow themselves to be real with each other. The true self that shines through for each will find a way to relate, if the conditioning, guilt, expectations and old patterns are peeled away. We do love each other. We don't need to fake it to honor that love.

Process

The process that creates any relationship is complicated and involves many factors. This renewed relationship will face many tests. Where it becomes shaky and uncertain will be the arenas in which we have our greatest challenges. Many of these challenges will come to us through conflict situations and any relationship that has depth will have conflict. Much of what creates or maintains conflict, however, needn't be there at all. The simplest level of conflict comes with the simplest word, "No!"

Learning to accept and to say "No," makes your "Yes" ever so much more powerful. This applies to both mothers and daughters heading toward a new adult-to-adult relationship. Whether it is an invitation to dinner or a request for money, the unwilling "Yes" will leave each of you with a feeling of dissatisfaction and will foster conflict. And yet, how difficult it is to say, "No." We attach so much negativity to no's: They seem to reflect more than another's personal preference. "No, I won't baby-sit." "No, I don't want to come to Thanksgiving dinner." "No, I'd prefer another restaurant." "No, I don't feel right about lending you money." These things may not be the easiest to hear; after all, they do conflict with our desire. But each of them is more bearable than the unwilling "Yes," the unclear "Maybe," the unanswered question.

The choice to say "No" or "Yes" is often not easy. How does anyone weigh the pros and cons, the personal needs and preferences versus those of another, deeply loved person, the values at stake, and the intensity of the request? Each of us faces those complexities as part of being an adult and as part of being in a relationship. The important issue is that we learn to make our choices, give our "Yes" or "No" without feeling or thinking that we were coerced, manipulated, guilted, pressured into doing something. Our "Yes" or "No" is our responsibility. When we consider the give-and-take of our relationship, we will notice the balance of "yes" and "no." Are we able and willing to say both? Or are we stuck in being a "yes" woman—compliant, rescuing and dependent—or a "no" woman—rebellious, defended, closed? Either limits us. The real power to choose comes from that deep uniqueness within that holds our values and our preferences. From that self both "yes" and "no" have space to emerge; from that space we have room to hear and accept both "yes" and "no."

The ability to honor our own self will allow us to have both our "yes" and "no." It will also allow us to ask for what we want. Learning to ask for what we want from each other empowers each of us to be honest and caring as well as separate and independent. Whether it is a hug, a favor, a loan, or a request to be alone, asking adds a new dimension to the relationship. If I know that you have the right and the willingness to say, "No," then my request will be free of negative consequences. When we ask for what we want, it means we no longer have to guess about each other. It means we can give up assumptions, as well as give up waiting to have the other read our mind and give us what we want without having to ask. It means that we trust each other to accept and understand who we are. It means we tell the truth.

When we are willing to ask for what we want from our mother or daughter, we will also be able to take the next step of confronting each other and allowing conflict. Confrontation can be gentle and mild or it can be loud and hurtful. Our goal is to learn to allow conflict and confrontation and to skillfully manage it. If we could but stay in touch with our deepest values when conflicts arose, there would be precious little that would be worth fighting over. Abby and Delores discovered this when Abby came close to dying. What could be so important that it could threaten their love? If we keep those deepest values in mind, conflicts about the nitty-gritty aspects of life can be kept in context. And if we see through the content of the conflict to the person behind the conflict, then we will remember our deepest truths. When I can say to myself, "This is my daughter (mother), whom I love deeply," I will be able to take some of the pressure off the actual words or things involved in the conflict, and at the same time I will be able to allow the conflict.

WORKBOOK

If we are in a position to come together again with our mothers or daughters, then we may count ourselves lucky. If we are not, then our own healing will be all the more precious and important. Finally, the coming together again is about coming inside of ourselves to that place where we are able to be whole. And when we move toward that, we will create relationships that support that wholeness and encourage greater and greater levels of growth. The exercises in this chapter will direct themselves toward the coming together again of mothers and daughters as adults and the coming into wholeness that each woman can do.

&c Create Your Mythology &c

Demeter and Persephone symbolized a type of reunion between mother and daughter. Faced with the loss of each other, their love grew and held them strongly connected. Their struggles—Demeter on Earth, Persephone in the underworld—paid off and they could be reunited. Write your own myth about the mother/daughter reunion. It doesn't matter, in this case, if there is an earthly reunion possible, for mythology transcends time and space, life and death. Everyone can write this myth. Be creative and realize that in mythology anything can happen!

Guidelines

1. Create the original scene of the mother/daughter relationship. Don't be stuck in the blissful model of Demeter and Persephone's relationship. Let your original relationship reflect what it really was.

2. Write in a threat, loss, separation, or crisis that reflects the losing of the relationship. This may also reflect what has actually happened in your relationship or may magnify the possibility of loss in some way.

3. Consider the struggle to create a reunion. What part do both mother and daughter play in their efforts to get together again?

4. End your story with a resolution that is fulfilling and symbolically meaningful. It might even be a . . . "happily ever after."

&2 The New Dance &2

If a reunion is forthcoming, a new dance will start. Mom knows the waltz and her daughter jitterbugs! What will they do? What will you do? Take some time to write about how you want to be in relationship to your mother/daughter. What parameters would you create? Where are you firm in your demands ("I won't move back home") and where are you flexible ("I could visit or write letters, maybe even move closer")? Write about this new dance from the abstract ("We will always love each other") to the concrete ("We could go shopping together, go to movies together, but not double date!") If appropriate—and only you will know—share this with your mother/daughter.

&2 Let Me Rephrase That. . . . &2

Take some time to practice communication skills. A little dress rehearsal may go a long way toward learning some new and more effective ways of being with each other. Start off by imagining the worst scenario of an interaction with your mother or daughter. Remember times when these types of communication have happened. What was likely to prompt them? The telephone? certain subjects? stressful situations? intimacy? Just imagine or remember one such difficult, unsatisfying and painful encounter. Then revise it. Rephrase your part of the conversation using some of the communication principles mentioned. You can't rewrite the other person's part, however! It will be particularly effective to write down your own half of the conversation, stated in clearer language. When you are done, think about what it is like to speak more responsibly, more clearly, more congruently and more truthfully.

Helpful Hints

Make "I," not "you," statements.

Use responsible, not passive, language ("choose" rather than "have to," "won't" rather than "can't").

Express preferences, hopes and desires—not "shoulds."

Allow for "ands" instead of "buts."

Create presence: curiosity, caring, understanding of the other.

Listen, deeply and carefully, to the words and to the person behind the words.

Be congruent and tell the truth.

Allow conflict, and remember the deepest values you have.

See the other person always.

Stay connected to your love.

CHAPTER ELEVEN

When Problems Arise

EVERY PATH HAS ITS PUDDLE.

—*English proverb*

EASIER SAID THAN DONE

Throughout the book we have explored the ways to separate from mother, find personal autonomy, and then face the choices we have about how to relate to each other once again. Facing those choices sounds easy on paper but often is very difficult. While we have eulogized the mother/daughter relationship and the depth of love that may be experienced, we know that there are many women who have painful and difficult situations that are not so easily resolved. People, circumstances and conditioning may be so oppressive or confusing as to seem unmanageable.

The model of Demeter and Persephone is symbolic. It symbolizes not only the depth of mother/daughter love but also the travail, the pain, the heartache and the loss. With all that has been said about the possibility of a deeply meaningful adult-mother and adult-daughter relationship, finally each woman must choose—as she chooses in all areas of her life—just what and how she wants (or doesn't want) to be in relationship to this significant other. We do not assume that we must be friends with any other person as readily as we assume we must be friends with our mothers and daughters. And while all of this potential does exist, it is not possible for every mother/daughter relationship to touch these depths, nor even to come close. Before all else, a woman must consider her own autonomy and values in coming to an understanding of how to be in a relationship with her mother or daughter. There are good and valid reasons to choose not to be in an active relationship with your mother or daughter, or to define the relationship in ways that keep it workable for you. The real task for each one of us is to take one step.

This one step is first and foremost for yourself, an honoring of your growth. Second, it is for your relationship to that significant other that you take the step. In the sections that follow, we will, oh so briefly, talk about some of the greater obstacles to growth between mother and daughter.

The Path of Destruction

Anger, hatred, jealousy, fighting, favoritism, competition involve a great degree of energy and emotion and may totally overrun a relationship. Sometimes, as well, these feelings and behaviors hide a great deal of love. When dysfunctional or unhealthy interactions are the basis for contact between mother and daughter, something needs to be done. Screaming, crying, demanding attention, backbiting, cheating, lying, covert behavior, cruelty in all forms are, unfortunately, common in the world. In the extreme, any one of these is dysfunctional. In typical "human" proportion, all of these can be included in a relationship without ruining it. They can be grist for the mill. As we look at some of the extreme experiences that limit the mother/daughter relationship, we will attempt to lessen their power enough to give room for the growth that may want to happen.

There are some women who hate with a deep passion. These women have been deeply hurt and may have little or no motivation to look at a solution to their strong emotion. Hate itself is the result of an unresolved conflict, often long buried. As long as you feel hate in your life, you will also feel, somewhere within, not okay, and unable to be all that you are. Hate is a draining emotion and injures the hater much more than the hated object. Learning to be with someone whom you think you hate requires a deep understanding of why you hate. There may be things that have happened to you that you hate to think about, there may be behavior patterns that you hate to be around, but hating a person robs you of the clarity of reason that is needed to decide how to be.

Erma hated her mother with all her heart, she said. She had been mean, cruel, even abusive. She had neglected and rejected her. Therapy sessions were filled with her anger and hate. She felt that her life would work if she could only be done with her mother; "but she lives so close and the children seem to love her."

When Erma's story began to unfold, it was clear that she had been hurt being raised by her mother, who was cold and fearful, especially when she had small children to care for. In a particularly moving session, Erma felt as though she were a child again. "If you could tell your mother how you feel, without fear, what would you say?" "I hate you! I hate you! I hate you!" burst forth, followed by wrenching sobs. "And if you could tell your mother what you want from her, without fear, what would you say?" "Hug me," she sobbed, "Just hug and hold me. Don't let me go, don't make me go away."

Erma had needed that hug all her life and had built up more and more bad feelings toward her mother. Mother had not known how to be soft or tender, but she had loved Erma and had devoted her life to her in her own limited way. Erma was asked to listen to her children's accounts of their time with Grandma, and to her surprise she discovered that Grandma did hug them, but only occasionally— "and not the way you do, Mom!" said her daughter. Erma's hatred dropped away. She began to see her mother's pain and confusion and her mother's caring. Erma was reserved in her behavior with mother for a long time, testing the waters, so to speak, for the new possibility that existed. In time, she even began to feel love for her mother again. Her therapy terminated shortly after she dared to offer her mother a hug. Mother received it gratefully but awkwardly.

Hate may be the hardest feeling to deal with, and at the same time it is one of the most "hooked." If you feel it, you may want to dig a little deeper before making any decisions from that place.

Dislike has a lot less power to it and can be easily accommodated, in many instances. It is a pretty common theme in mother/daughter relationships. It has none of the intensity of hatred. In fact, it may be quite bland. Styles, values, personalities may all lead to discordant interchange. We may well be too different or opposed in significant ways to be friends.

&2 Cary's relationship to her mother had always been difficult but not terribly painful. As she left home, she never considered it important to have much to do with her mother. Her mother reached out, but wasn't pushy. Cary was fond of saying to her friends that she "had outgrown" her mother. When Cary's mother was diagnosed as having Alzheimer's disease, Cary was shocked and confused. In her unclear assumptions she had thought that it wouldn't matter to her if her mother died. Cary's efforts to reconnect with her mother in her disabled condition were sadly unfulfilling. The caregiving had been taken over by another child, and there were few times when Cary could manage even to communicate with her mother, whose early death left Cary dazed and uncertain. Her easy choice to let her mother go became a heavy burden for Cary for some time afterward.

If we don't easily get along with our mother or daughter, we may be able to define a relationship that doesn't require being friends. Having personality differences does not mean that we can't be polite or kind or loving. The decision to let a significant relationship end is not one to be taken lightly under any circumstances, and, for the mother/daughter one, this may be particularly true. If we can't be friends, pals, buddies, can we be cordial, familial, casual, occasional or caring? We may find, to our surprise—as Cary did—that we *love* this other person while not *liking* her. If this is so, we have an opportunity to define that relationship around values other than friendship. We may care for her, be concerned for her, want her in our family's life, want the best for her, feel grateful to her, and still not want to go shopping with her even once! This will work fine. There is no *right* way to be with this other important person.

Anger, jealousy, competition, fighting, clinging, demanding and the myriad other experiences common to relationships and especially prevalent in this one are generally the result of old business. Inappropriate and destructive behaviors that stem from these sources are likely to throw a relationship into turmoil, blocking any potential for growth.

Much of what we have worked with throughout this book offers cues for releasing those old feelings and controlling the undesirable behaviors. Looking at your conditioning, separating unskillful behaviors from the "hooks" associated with them, taking responsibility, connecting with your deepest values and your love and forgiveness for this other person, taking over authorship of your own story, and moving out of "little" feelings and responses, will help untie these unpleasant knots. Defining your relationship in such a way that the hooks are less present will also help. So will taking a good look at your feelings and your behavior, remembering the power you have to choose how to be in the world.

Some pointers to the roots of these destructive feelings may be helpful in freeing yourself from them. Most "hooked" behaviors stem from unmet and often unconscious wants. Anger, and the fighting that often results from anger, is almost always a want that is not being met. Turn any "I'm angry" sentence into an "I want" sentence and you will likely get to the core of what's going on. Jealousy is also a "want," and it generally has to do with wanting safety and assurance: the safety and assurance of knowing that love or a person or a relationship will not end. Competition, like jealousy, is a need for assurance, in this case an assurance that "I'm okay the way I am." When we compete, we are working from the assumption that I need to do or be more in order to have love or some other desired outcome. Clinging and demanding come about from the same source: a fear that there is not enough (love) or that "I am not enough [to get love]." Operating from an idea of scarcity, that the glass is half empty, that there is not enough and the like, stems from a "needy" and unsafe-feeling child place within. When we act any of these out in the world, it is time to go deeper and begin to take care of the child needs in a conscious way, so that we will be free to act in the world from an adult place that can see the world through positive eyes.

Even with our own power to create our lives, there will be some situations in which there is no safe way to be with this other important person. There are abusive women, cold women, selfish women, indifferent women, unloving women, damaged women—and more. But none of them are essentially that way and life has undoubtedly dealt them blows from which, in significant ways, they failed to recover. There is no need or profit in making them bad, but if this is true for the woman who is your mother or daughter, then you may need to set boundaries for yourself that protect you. Your health and well-being are at stake. What must you do to preserve it? If hostility, cruelty or abuse meets you at every turn in your relationship to this or any person, you will need to consider what to do.

It is very difficult to accept a mother or daughter who treats you badly. In the worst scenario, your mother or daughter may be mentally ill, unable by anyone's standards to change her behavior. In less extreme situations she may be so caught in her own pain, that she has no ability to change or let go. The emotional seesaw that some mother/daughter relationships entail is sometimes too exhausting and hurtful to continue. You may well find at times that the damage that is being done is too severe for you to cope with. When you have honestly examined your own side of the "problem" and made your best effort to come to a place of acceptance of your mother or daughter, you may discover that being together is still damaging to you or to your loved ones. If this is so, you may find that for your own best interests you must leave or curtail the relationship. In these cases, you will need to use a clear, guilt-free thinking process to assess how to be in the situation. Can I, do I want to, maintain a relationship at all? If so, how can I define it so that I am protected? Protection is crucial in "toxic" relationships.

But leaving such a central relationship is painfully difficult, and to make the best of a bad situation requires skill and faith. The skill needed has to do with carefully and thoughtfully assessing the situation and the options:

- 🙶 *Do I have some responsibility that I need to honor?*
- 🙶 *Is the other person in a position to contribute to changing the relationship?*
- 🙶 *Can I create a limited relationship that is safe for me?*

👯 *Will I allow my decision to be reconsidered as time and circumstances bring about change?*

👯 *Finally, if I need to severely limit or end this important relationship, can I do so with integrity and faith in myself?*

👯 Gerry is a thirty-nine-year-old woman who has spent much time trying to improve her relationship with her mother. As the years wore on, she found that the relationship ate away at her more and more, decreasing her self-confidence and causing repercussions in her own life. She finally felt that she couldn't continue to have her mother come visit. It was too painful. She wrote to her mother: "Dear Mother, Our lives have been in conflict as long as I can remember. I feel so criticized by you. There is nothing I can do that seems right to you. You say you do not like my lovers or friends or roommates; you tell me that you are furious that I don't want to have children; you do not respect my job; you hate the way I look; and every time we are together, you tell me over and over again of my failures. The hardest part for me is that you compare me not only to my sister, but all the other cousins and friends that you know. I know if I were less sensitive and could shrug off the hurtful things that you say, I'd be able to be with you now and then, but I'm not. Therefore, I've made the decision that I will not see you for a while, however long that may be. The sad part about this is that I don't believe you'll even know the difference. I can't say that I'll miss you, because most of our contacts have been because of a sense of duty on both our parts. I feel better having made this decision and I don't feel as guilty or angry anymore. If you wish to communicate with me, I will respond. I wish you well."

Gerry has understood many of the issues that hampered her relationship with her mother. She recognized her mother's limitations and stopped trying to be the daughter she thought would please her mother, knowing that she could only fail. Ending the relationship was the only way she knew that would free her to go her own way without feeling guilty for failing her mother or angry because her mother never approved of her. She made a conscious choice, as well, to be willing to reopen communications at some future time and to allow her mother the same option. It is likely that Gerry's choice will serve her well and that she will reach out again at a later time when she and her mother and circumstances have changed. Gerry is better off having made this clear decision than she had been being eaten up with anger, longing, resentment and pain. Luckily, the problems in most relationships are not so severe and can be handled by less drastic measures.

PUDDLES IN THE PATH

With even the greatest love available, circumstances in life may well make the path to a new relationship difficult. Unless the puddle is quicksand, it is worth learning how to get around it or deal with it. The obstacles most mothers and daughters face are the result of the dynamics of the relationship that we have dealt with extensively. The keys to navigating through those obstacles have been laid out.

External circumstances may also create obstacles and these, too, are worth considering. When illness, disability, medical choices, drug or alcohol dependence enter the equation, how much harder the path becomes to travel. A change in a daughter's values and choices for her life, as well as mother's similar changes, may provoke distress and may threaten to undermine the foundations of a good relationship. Money will cause problems as often as it will solve them. Political alliances, eating habits, marriages and divorces, all these will have an impact. The path to a reunion is difficult under ideal circumstances. In the real world it may seem well nigh impossible. Specific added burdens can feel like the straw that breaks the camel's back, but none of these outer circumstances needs to be that straw. Whatever factors enter into the equation, except in the most damaging of situations, are simply part of the dance. Some dances are harder to do than others. But the same guidelines apply.

- *What are my values?*
- *Can I separate these true values from old hooks and feelings?*
- *How can I put these values into operation in a way that is respectful of the other and honoring of my own self?*
- *Given my unique qualities, what solutions might I come up with that will help?*
- *If I feel victimized in relation to these outer circumstances and feel at the mercy of the other person, or life or fate, can I step back and become adult?*
- *How do I put any problem or obstacle in a meaningful context in my life?*
- *How can I understand this one?*

You'll need to give up being perfect in any circumstance that adds complexity and uncertainty to your choices. You'll need to be patient with yourself and with each other. You'll need to set your sights on reasonable goals. You'll need to be creative, flexible and have faith.

For all the puddles that appear in all of the paths, there are several that tend to come into the mother/daughter relationship with some regularity. Answers or solutions to these particular circumstances cannot be laid out. There are no rules about how to face difficulties. There are no right answers about how to handle each dilemma. There is no Doctor Spock for adult life but, with that said and underlined, there may be some commonality in certain situations and there may be some pointers, some guidelines that will help us through.

The Aging of Mother

When mothers age, great stress may be put on the relationship. As well, there is great opportunity. To put a mother in a nursing home or take her into your own home will cause ripples in the calmest sea. Choices will not be easy. Mother's own needs and wants may not even be clear, as she may be forced to give up her hard-won autonomy and move into a "needy" or "little," position in the world. And daughter will be faced with innumerable areas of conflict and uncertainty. "What is best for Mother?" "What is best for me?" "What is best for the other family members involved?"

In these challenging times, our adulthood will be sorely tested. We may well find ourselves being pulled by old feelings of inadequacy or guilt, bullied by other people's needs and ideas, out of touch with our own truths. And yet our adulthood can see us through. We will be able to rely on our skills, our experience, our intuition, our ability to communicate in order to help us find a workable solution. We may also find—if we allow ourselves to—that we have a new opportunity to give back to our mother, to trade roles as nurturer and provider, to support and honor her "littleness" from our own loving adultness. This is not to make her little, force her into helplessness to satisfy our fears about her care. Above all, we must honor each other's intentions and stated needs and wants. Here, too, lies a great opportunity: to face the aging and dying process with integrity and openness. This may be very difficult.

 "My mother was an extraordinarily independent woman. As often as any of us children would ask if she would like to live with us, she said, 'No.' She lived alone, with minor help from others, until her later eighties. When she fell and broke her hip, we got together and took over decision making for her. We decided that she needed to be in a nursing home when she left the hospital. She refused adamantly, but we thought she would adjust. Her recovery went well, and the day came when she was to be moved to the nursing home. She died that night in her bed. Her will had been strong. I will never know what happened, but I feel, in retrospect, that we could have honored her more, trusting her choice. I feel sad that she left this world in conflict with us."

And for each side of a story that we might tell, there will be another that is opposite: the mother who wanted to be left to her own care and who suffered because of that choice, the one who wanted to be taken in and wasn't, the one who wanted a nursing home but was coaxed into her daughter's home. Also there are the ones who chose their independence and were honored in it, the many who needed care and were given just what they needed, the women who talked, struggled, succeeded and learned to love even more deeply in these last years of their living relationship. That is the challenge. Not to find a right solution, as if that would be the end of it, but to continue to grow throughout.

The Changing of Daughter

When daughters change, the need to continue growth is equally pressing. In the letting-go process, mothers are likely to leave a fair amount of room for their daughters to be different, but every mother has a limit. When a daughter changes drastically or suddenly, or without explanation, a mother will be left with a far greater task in holding on to the growing relationship than she had before. The status quo has been thrown upside down, the puzzle pieces into the air. What will come of it? We can stretch into an acceptance of almost anything. We can allow and support so much more than we initially believe we can. Each person reading this may easily imagine what line her daughter (or mother or any other) would have to cross for it to be not-okay, and each of us may think that that line we draw is appropriate. But what happens when our daughters cross it? There is certainly no easily defined right or wrong limit we could put on another person's options. Even ethics are best when they are situational and not ultimate. Would you reject your daughter, or be angry and nonaccepting of her, if she:

&e *changed her religion?*

&e *married a man you didn't like?*

&e *chose not to have children?*

&e *lived with a man outside of marriage?*

&e *consciously chose to be a single mother?*

&e *became a lesbian?*

&e *adopted a baby of another race?*

&e *moved to another country?*

&e *had radically different political views than yours?*

&e *became a nun?*

&e *changed her name?*

&e *became a vegetarian?*

&e *gave her baby up for adoption?*

&e *used drugs?*

&e *broke the law?*

&e *became a stripper?*

Some of us will cringe at all of those possibilities; others will cringe at a few. Wherever we cringe will point to an expectation that we have that might limit us. Of course, we will have hopes and preferences and these will not get in the way of our growing and accepting. It is the deep-seated "If you do this, I will not love you as much" expectations that threaten and harm a relationship. When daughters change—as they will—and especially as they stretch outside of the parameters that we have set for our own lives, will we still love them, accept them and honor them as adults? Being able to answer "Yes" to these questions will guide us through the rough spots of our learning to be with these new and different people who were once our little girls:

> "My daughter married a man of a different religion, radically different from our loose Quaker-style belief system. Her visits were difficult because of the strict dietary and religious requirements that she lived with. I resented her and she, I suspect, resented me as well. I secretly thought that this was another postadolescent rebellion directed personally at me. I imagined that she was not nearly so rigid at home and that she used her religion to torment me. It—or should I say 'I'?—drove a wedge into our reasonably good relationship. I guess it took me about five years to see that she had made a real and meaningful choice for herself and that that choice worked for her. I came to appreciate and accept her beliefs and to support her in being able to be with me and still honor her own religion. I guess I was the one who was rigid."

The Involvement of Family

When families get involved, the progress of a relationship on its path toward a new level of connection may well be hindered. While a mother and daughter may have taken many steps toward their own reunion, the added pressures of other familial relationships may throw a curve ball that sets back the work that has been or could be done.

"I always get along well with my mother when we're together, but when I talk about her with my sister, I remember all the rotten things she did. Then I don't call her for weeks."

"My husband is quite annoyed with my daughter (his step-daughter). He has supported her since she was ten, but now that she's twenty-one, he really wants to stop giving her any money. I always find myself expressing his feelings to her, causing us to have a terrible time whenever we're together. I feel trapped."

"Mother always complains to me about Daddy. I want to support her, but I hate these conversations, so I try to avoid phone calls or I make sure to call when I know Daddy is home."

As we discover how we want to be in our relationship to each other, we will do well to try not to involve the rest of the family. When we play off other family members, we will muddy up whatever clarity we might otherwise achieve. Taking sides with siblings or spouses, trying to get them to change in order to support our choices, paying homage to one relationship by belittling another will never serve us. Nor will comparing different relationships, setting up expectations (good and bad) based on any one relationship within the family, trying to prove anything about ourselves to the family at large. Can we consider the relationship to our mother or daughter as just two people and work from there? It may be difficult, but it will be worth the effort to let other family members have their own experiences, their own relationships, for better or worse, and not let them contaminate our own growing experience.

When Crisis Comes

When a crisis hits, this is perhaps the greatest challenge to a relationship, no matter how solid or weak it is. Crises may bring out the best or the worst in us. They may elicit our true self or our "little" self. They will certainly challenge our feeling of safety and security in the world or in this relationship.

As with every outer circumstance that presents itself, a crisis will demand something of us. It will offer an opportunity to expand how we are: internally as an adult individual, and in this relationship that may suddenly be fraught with confusion or fear or danger. Crises run the gamut from divorce to death, from financial problems to life-threatening problems. One woman's crisis is another woman's norm! And herein, perhaps, is the most valuable key to crisis. How do we think about life and its ups and downs? What do we hold on to enough so that it is a crisis when it is threatened? If our house is our life and the bank forecloses, then this is a crisis. If our house burns down but all the family is saved, then this is a blessing. There is a point of view that would say that nothing is essentially a crisis, just an unfolding of possibilities. A teenager's crisis over the freshman prom looks like a normal process to her mother. The statistics on death seem acceptable and normal as we read about them, but the loss of one of our own is a crisis.

Crisis is defined simply as "a decisive or critical moment," and certainly these will come to everyone. And here we will test our mettle. Will we finally make that decisive stand from our own values, our uniqueness, our true self, or will we be pushed by that critical moment into being less than we truly are? Finally, this may be the only vantage point from which to look at a crisis. We seem not to be able to predict them, less even to control them. But perhaps we have some control over our responses.

   Rebecca faced her life crisis when she discovered that her twenty-year-old daughter was a drug addict. She had had a rough time with her daughter in all her teenage years, and she had practiced "holding her breath" and waiting for one minor crisis after another to pass. This one would not pass and Rebecca floundered, felt helpless, looked for others to blame and then to save her, and finally took a stand.

The stand she took began to pay off. She involved her ex-husband and other family members. She confronted her daughter. She learned what she needed to know. She stopped holding her breath and started to breathe deeply. Her values about her love for her daughter outweighed the fear and difficulty, and she stood firmly through the years of her daughter's recovery and her own discovery of her power and commitment in life. Both mother and daughter were changed and the crisis led each to greater wholeness.

Simple Truths

Whatever you encounter in this rewarding but difficult journey, you will need to choose over and over, to modify your decisions, to expand your ideas, to see more than you have ever seen before. You will take risks. You will succeed—and you will fail, at times. This is education and this is life. Only you will ever be able to take this journey, and there will only be one right way: yours. There is only one teacher, one judge and jury, one peanut gallery, one cheering team: you. Nothing we have said can be true unless it becomes true for you.

Our efforts to understand the essential principles and dynamics of a powerful relationship have led us down many roads and many women have been our guides. They have taught us and asked us to teach them. As we have worked over the years with mothers and daughters in improving, changing, healing and nurturing themselves and their relationship, some guidelines have emerged that may be useful. These are not, by any means, set in stone. As you create your own autonomy, you will create your own set of guidelines. The guidelines we offer may be a jumping-off point for your own growth. There are guidelines for mothers and guidelines for daughters. They have emerged from the experience of hundreds of women. If these guidelines serve, even in part, to ease the transition from parent or child to adult and adult, then they are worth their presence here. Here then is the "short form" of ideas and ways to be and grow with each other.

Guidelines for a Mother Graduate

Advice is a pitfall! Most daughters agree that mother's advice tends to keep them feeling little, especially when it is unsolicited. "Mother knows best" is a hard trend to break, but a good way to do it is to trust your daughter's perceptions and choices. Mothers have also found that the tendency to give advice is based in the old feeling that their daughter is little, thus continuing in them the parent/child trap. On the one hand, daughters may have to push mother away to keep from having to sift through all the advice and their own feelings in relationship to it.

"Don't talk to me at all about my career or my friends or my religion, Mom. I need to do life on my own, and I don't need your advice!"

On the other hand, the daughter may come to depend on mother's advice as an adult as much as she did as a child, and her life is defined by it.

"Mother, I didn't realize till after your sudden death just how much I depended upon your intense affection and protectiveness to see my day through. I feel very insecure knowing that there is no one to help me in some of the decisions life has called on me to make. I long for your ever-present advice and feel hopeless without it."

Never assume. Never assume that your daughter wants the same things from you that you might have wanted from your own mother. Over and over, women try to make up for their own losses or repeat their own positive experiences by foisting them on their daughters.

The intentions may seem good, and generally are not harmful, but they may, as well, be shortsighted. If I offer to take my daughter to dinner whenever she expresses sadness, I may be giving what I got and loved, but there is no way for me to assume that this will make my daughter feel the same way it made me feel. Before you give or do something for your daughter, ask yourself whether this is what she wants. Don't replace "wants" with "needs!" When we assume that we know what our daughter needs, we are again playing "Mother knows best." Then when you've asked yourself if this is what she wants, ask her! Be straight with her! Communicate and don't guess.

❧ Eleanor's daughter Joan asked her to stay with the kids while she was away on a business trip. Eleanor readily agreed. While in her daughter's house, she cleaned and reorganized and painted one of the rooms and fully expected her daughter to come home elated. Joan was furious, felt invaded, disrespected, made "little" by the assumption that she read into this act that she was incapable and by what seemed like her mother's general sense of "I can do it right!" This incident put a great rift in an otherwise good relationship, and it was not until Eleanor realized that she was making some inappropriate assumptions that things began to get on track again.

Rescuing doesn't help! Only a victim needs to be rescued. Mothers who step in and take charge for their daughters tend to promote in their daughters any victimized feelings they may have. A friend and someone who loves me will offer me help, ask what I need, share her own experience, give me an ear to talk to, a shoulder to cry on, but she will not fix anything for me. And for this I will be grateful, as it is a more respectful stance. Respect your daughter's capability. Let her know that you do! And then be there for her in any way that you want to and she wants you to!

ﷺ Leah was a bright college student whose mother loved her dearly. She also rescued her regularly. When she had boyfriend problems, mom said, "Come on home." When she overspent her monthly allowance, mom said, "Have some more." When she found school difficult, mom said, "Take a semester off." When she was depressed, mom said, "I know a good therapist." In therapy Leah looked and talked like a sixteen-year-old, not a twenty-one-year-old. She felt little and inadequate. She felt tied into her mother and resentful of her. She felt unable to make it on her own and could barely face the thought of being an adult, though mom had told her "not to worry." Leah was drowning in her rescuer's grip.

Interference is worse than advice! Mothers may be wiser, more capable and more mature than their young-adult daughters. They may have greater resources, skills and insights into life. They are likely to be able to handle some of what a daughter faces better than the daughter could — but it won't work.

You don't like the man she's dating; you've met his kind before. So what? Let her figure it out. Got some strings you can pull to get her off the hook or get her a better deal — don't bother. Let her do it the hard way! Don't like the way she's raising her kids, think you could do it better? You can't. It's her life. Leave her alone. Certain that she needs a little spiritual guidance? Want to send her those articles on morality? It won't work. She'll run farther away. Growing is learning. Just as we let the two-year-old learn to feed herself, though we could have done it better, we need to let the adult learn about life and do it her way. Trust stands out again as the guiding light!

"When I was in the hospital having my second child, my mother took it upon herself to toilet train my two-year-old. I have never forgiven her. I think she damaged my child and she certainly damaged any faith I had in her."

"I saw my daughter walking down the aisle with a man that I knew was no good for her, but I kept my mouth shut. The marriage did end, but her son is the joy of her life as well as a gift to me. Thank God, I didn't butt in."

Guilt hurts. Duty is a poor substitute for friendship. In most cases, out of guilt, a sense of duty can be extracted from a daughter. She will come to the family gatherings, send birthday gifts, call once a week—if she has to. But all spontaneity, originality and intimacy are lost in a relationship based on guilt. Mothers who instill guilt as a motivating force may well be assuming that daughter will have no real interest in her without the guilt to motivate her. The mother who instills guilt or in other ways gets what she wants covertly (through manipulation, coercion or plotting) is likely to be fairly unhappy and unsure within herself. And she may be cutting off the possibility of a meaningful relationship with her daughter. Telling the truth will work better: Letting your daughter know what you want and feel will allow her to have a genuine response rather than a preprogrammed one.

> At a mother/daughter workshop, one mother in the back of the room brought up over and over again how her daughter refused to live in Chicago, where the whole family was. In many ways she enticed, bribed and tried to "guilt" her daughter into returning. The workshop seemed to have little impact on her and her parting words were, "Maybe she'll come back to Chicago now that she's dealt with some of these issues." The daughter left, more determined than ever to stay away.

"Well, in my day. . . ." This is an unsatisfactory way to start a sentence and mothers do it all the time. When you compare your

daughter's way of life to the way you used to live, out loud or to your-self, you set up a barrier in which you are unable to see her for her, living in her time and place with her uniqueness. You fail to accept her the way she is. You operate under the old assumption that "Mother knows best." Let her be. This one goes back to trust and to acceptance and to a willingness to suspend your views in order to build the relationship!

> 꿍 "I can't stand having Mother at my house. Our eating habits
> 꿍 upset her. She thinks we waste money and she is always ready
> to point it out. Even when she doesn't say anything, I see her snooping
> in my refrigerator in a condescending way. She can't believe that we
> spend extra money on butter when we could buy margarine. She has a
> thing about chicken. I've heard this line a hundred times: 'I used to
> make a chicken last for three meals. We'd have it roasted the first night,
> then we'd have sandwiches the next day, and then I'd make a delicious
> soup out of the carcass. All you do is spend twice as much money buy-
> ing frozen chicken and pizza.'"

Faking it undermines the relationship. With the best of inten-tions—in fact, after hearing "rules" like the ones above—many moth-ers begin to fake it in order to help the relationship along. In subtle and not-so-subtle ways they agree with their daughters, do what their daughters ask, hold back their own feelings, needs and beliefs. They try to please their daughter. In the role of friends your rights are equal, and it is not a favor to either of you to pretend that you like Japanese food just because your daughter does. Faking it creates mixed messages and confusion and a tendency to always second-guess each other. Tell the truth, again! It works better to be straight.

> 🙊 "I wanted so much to have a good relationship to my daughter
> that I became as accommodating as I could, as appreciative and
> complimentary of her as I could, as like her as I could be. I was a
> chameleon. I was sure this was the only way to bridge the gap that had
> been created in high school. When I realized that I was beginning to
> resent her, I knew it wasn't going to work. I've been expressing some of
> my ideas lately and it's been working better."

Changing some long-standing behavior patterns does not mean
that you give up loving your daughter. It means that you see her as a
person capable of handling her own life and that you respect her
right to live her life the way she chooses. It also means that you do
not have to pretend to be able to take care of everything anymore. It
means that if you are afraid of thunder, you can say so without wondering how it will affect your little one. It means that you let your
daughter know that you love her because she is who she is, not
because she is your baby. Playing by some new rules will allow you
both to be fuller people. Both of you will find that you have rights
and they can be respected, you have needs and they can be honored,
you have preferences and they can be negotiated, adult to adult.

Guidelines for an Ex-Child

Stepping out of the role of daughter into the role of independent
woman and ex-child involves gaining control of your own story and
also giving up some of the perks of having mother there to do for you
and give you the things that you want. While it is clearly difficult to
give up the role of mother, it is equally difficult to give up the role of
daughter. At least it is difficult to give up the goodies in that role.
Many adult women try, unconsciously, to have their cake and eat it
too, to be an adult and still have mother as the safety net, to do what

they want and still have mother help foot the bills. Truly being an adult will require letting go of the "little" and taking on the big.

Take her off the pedestal. If advice is offered, before you react in old ways (probably as if mother were telling you how badly you are doing) ask yourself, *How would I respond if my best friend said this to me?* Think about the value of what has been said by mother. Might some of what she says be true? Don't automatically imagine that she is treating you like her little girl because she doesn't trust you or sees you as less than a grown woman. And let her know where and how you are open to hearing about her perspective on things. You might even try asking for her advice on occasion, knowing that it may or may not fit for you.

> "I have run as far as I could away from my mother's 'interference.' In fact, I am beginning to see that some of the choices that I made were made just to get away from her opinions. But the other day, in desperation with my own daughter, I called Mother and asked her how she had handled temper tantrums. I really appreciated what she said. More than anything, she made me feel that I was doing okay in a tough situation. It has changed my attitude about her."

Don't interpret! You are as likely to read old feelings and ideas into your mother's actions as she is to treat you in old ways. Don't interpret her actions, words, requests without checking out what they mean. "Why did you do that?" "What do you mean?" "What's going on when you say that?" These and other questions designed to gain clarity will let you know what your mother's side of something is. When you know that, you can react appropriately. Trust her intentions and look for the positive in what she is doing rather than the negative. This will go a long way toward creating an adult-to-adult experience.

⮚ "Every time my mother asks me about the kids, I have assumed that she expects me to be failing, to tell her of some tragedy or problem that I can't handle. One time I yelled at her about it. She was shocked and I was forced to look at my own stuff. I expected me to fail. She was just being casual and concerned. If she hadn't asked about the kids, I would have been equally upset."

Don't carry expectations. If you've decided to be an adult, then you can't still be a child. You have to give up the perks of being your mother's little girl. She won't bail you out, fill in for you, fix things in the way she did when you were a child. Don't expect your mother to be your baby-sitter, housekeeper and financier. Ask for her time, money and effort only with the same courtesy and lack of demand that you would ask a friend. Don't expect her to approve of all the things you do with your life. Be willing to have her disagree. She needs to be her own person and you need to let her be. Respecting her is as important as being respected by her.

⮚ "I live my life very effectively, as do my four sisters, but this issue of going home to Mom makes us all act like kids. We all expect Mom to pay for our trip and then we feel slighted if any one of us stays longer. We have this credit-card routine. Mom lets us go shopping with her credit card. And we play these games about who gets the most, who was most responsible with Mom's credit card (read: who was less greedy). It's ridiculous. We're all over thirty-eight years old. Mom doesn't push this on us. We do it. We want to be little for all the goodies—but big as well. I'm going to my parents' home this week and I went shopping before the trip. I bought myself new clothes so I wouldn't feel tempted into the credit-card trip. I think this will really help."

Create boundaries. Daughters often invite their mother's interference by not letting it be known who they are and what they want. Creating boundaries isn't about becoming armored, it's about defining yourself. Mother knows you best as a growing girl. The twenty, thirty, or forty years of her knowing you has been mostly as a child. Cleaning your room for you as a girl was probably an appropriate action. Cleaning your house may or may not be. How will she know, if you don't tell her? Knowing yourself, and being willing to own that to your mother, will help her know how to be with you respectfully.

> Gloria came from a conservative family. Her mother's values were quite different from hers, especially around issues of being "feminine." She often bought Gloria dresses and offered to take her to the beauty parlor when they visited. It took Gloria a long time to make clear to her mother who she was and how she was different from what her mother wanted her to be. For a while, Gloria would just brush off her mother's advances and secretly resent her. When she finally told her mother that she liked her hair straight, that she preferred pants to dresses, that she'd rather eat at a casual than a fancy restaurant, her mother heard her. The level of friction lessened markedly. Mother was able to accept these boundaries when she knew what they were.

Guilt hurts! Daughters can lay guilt trips on mothers as powerfully as mothers can on daughters. All sorts of covert behavior can be used to try to fix old and "little" feelings. Mother is likely to respond, but it will be in an unclear way. She certainly knows that she hasn't done her job perfectly and probably wishes she had. This fact leaves her wide open to trying harder, to feeling bad, to trying to make up for it. It also leaves the relationship wide open to staying "hooked" and hurt. Don't compare what mother does for a sibling with the things she does for you. Don't play "poor me" games with your mother in an effort to get her sympathy or help or anything else. Don't make "loaded" statements, designed to pull mother into your own problems. Talk straight, be honest, let her know your feelings and wants. Be prepared, as well, to have her not be available in all the ways you want.

> The bulk of one mother/daughter relationship that we encountered was composed of the daughter's unconscious need to make mom feel bad. Sally herself felt bad inside. She felt little and scared. Her initiatives with her mother were often about her pain, her inability to get on with life, her "neediness." Mother was always right there, trying harder and harder. Of course it never worked for either of them. Mom felt guilty and like a failure. Sally felt like a victim who was never quite saved.

"Oh, Mother. . . ." This is not much better a start to a sentence than "Well, in my day. . . ." The daughter's version of "My way is better" comes down to a slightly rebellious and condescending approach to mother and her "old" ways. We may be overt or covert in our put-downs of mother. We may embarrass her by emphasizing our differences especially where she is sensitive—or we may discount her with our "greater" knowledge. When we act out of a feeling of superiority we are covering up our own feelings of insecurity. When we are certain in our knowledge about anything, we are not likely to need to proclaim it loudly or to make anyone else "bad" for their way. If valid differences exist, we do need to state our version, but not with any assumptions or intimations about mother's limitations. Respecting mother will lead to a great deal of growth.

℘ Mary, at some unconscious level, loved to make her mother uncomfortable with her liberal ideas and radically different lifestyle. She was, for instance, a vegetarian, and a good cook as well, but when mother came to visit she managed to make the skimpiest, least appealing vegetarian meals she could think of. She often laughed at her mother's opinions, frequently in front of her friends, and generally felt herself and her "new age" ways to be superior.

The final blow to mother came when Mary invited her to come over for a Sunday afternoon and had her hot tub going with lots of naked friends roaming around. Mother was embarrassed and distressed. She felt put down and disrespected. She put on a good face, but when she got home she broke down and felt a deep hurt. She wrote to her daughter and said she would not visit her anymore. Mary needed to take a good, hard look at her own intentions and her mother's needs before this relationship would be able to grow.

Daughters, as well as mothers, need to change some old behavior patterns. It is quite surprising to note how easy it is for us as young women to act out adolescent behaviors with our mothers long past our adolescent years. We struggled for independence as adolescents and yet we need to struggle, too, to transcend that stage and become full-fledged adults no longer playing tug-of-war with our mothers!

So we are left to consider what advice we need to give ourselves and what advice to take. How will we handle the good times and the bad, the ups and downs, the loves and the hates that we will surely encounter in our whole lives and in our relationship to this very important other? We may console ourselves with the knowledge that the difficulties can lead to greater strength, the pain to greater love, and the obstacles to greater growth. Mothers and daughters attest to this over and over.

WORKBOOK

No relationship is without its share of problems, internal and external. Each set is unique. We are, finally, lucky that there is no Doctor Spock for adults, because we are left with the challenge and the gift of being ourselves in the face of problems. In fact, it is in the face of problems that we may discover much of who we are, and often it is here, in the fire, that we can burn away our limitations and conditions and free ourselves to be the best we are able. As we climb the mountain of our lives, each obstacle will present a challenge. Each will require us to accept something or offer us the opportunity to learn something new. The attitude that we hold as we face life will make a difference in our efforts to grow.

❧ *What is our attitude about problems in the first place?*

❧ *Do we see each obstacle or crisis as a punishment or as an opportunity?*

❧ *Do we consider hardship to be a proof of our unworthiness or a test of our strength?*

❧ *Are the obstacles felt as blows to our precarious balance or as hurdles by which we will strengthen ourselves?*

❧ *Are they random—the luck of the die, the deal of the deck—or are they purposeful, having meaning for us?*

❧ *What is the worldview that we each live by?*

If it rains on the day of our picnic, what *does* this mean to us? More is at stake than a solution to the actual dilemma. We can have the picnic indoors, plan it tomorrow, wear a raincoat, build a dome over the meadow, yell at God, become a weather forecaster or give up. What is finally at stake is the challenge of attitude: finding acceptance, giving meaning to life, and taking life as an opportunity to grow.

ﷺ Difficult as It Is ﷺ

It is important to acknowledge the difficulties and challenges in our lives and in our relationships. This helps us both to see clearly and put a perspective on our "problems." It is as much a problem to deny our difficulties as it is to get lost in them.

As we have worked in the past on unhooking from painful inner dynamics, so too must we come to a relationship with problematic external circumstances. When mothers age, when daughters change, when families intervene, when crises occur, all of these are problems that need to be considered. What, if any, is the circumstance in your relationship at this time that is problematic? Or what can you foresee down the road that will be an issue to deal with? What is the puddle in your path?

When you have come to recognize a circumstance that seems problematic or frightening, limiting or confusing, painful or threatening, write it down in totally objective language.

ﷺ "My mother is eighty-eight and her health is failing. I am the only living relative and I will need to make a choice about her living situation when she can no longer take care of herself."

Note that your statement, like this one, is factual, nonemotional and has no interpretation. Now make the statement from your emotions, from your "little," or scared, confused self. Let all the feelings associated with this event be recognized (no need to use responsible language here).

ﷺ "I can't bear the thought of this. What will I do? I can't have her live with us and I can't afford a decent nursing home. I'm desperate. Anything I do will be a disaster for someone I love."

Finally, make a statement as if this event were a challenge, a chance to grow, and a unique opportunity for you to be creative, adult and successful.

❧ "I have yet to figure out what's next with my mother, but we are beginning to talk about options. I know that it will be difficult to find a perfect solution, but everyone involved will be able to give a little and so create a workable situation. I do have faith that this next challenge can be met in a healthy and loving way!"

What a difference! How do you want to face your particular problem/challenge?

❧ Hate Hurts ❧

We have worked throughout this book on letting go, getting unhooked, being free of conditions that limit us. Here is one more designed specifically for that most painful experience of hate, and perhaps applied as well to other extreme and dangerous feelings. If you feel hate as an emotion, see if you can simplify it, down to its origins. Consider the person whom you hate and ask these questions. Writing down your answers may help.

- When I feel that hatred, what's underneath?
- Am I angry? hurt? sad?
- Do I feel wounded? threatened?
- Do I want retribution for all that has happened?
- Do I long to strike back and am afraid to do so?
- What is it that I hate most about this person?
- Do I feel as if she victimizes me?
- What would need to change so that I would let go of hate?
- If hate disappeared what would replace it?

- Is there longing, neediness, feelings of desire, neglect or envy that are covered with this hate?

Try this brief process on for size; see if it helps you get a clearer picture of what is going on when you feel hate. "I hate her because

_____."

"I want her to _____."

Go through this question over and over, until a clear picture emerges of what you want that you are not or have not been getting. Remember Erma? Her hatred came from wanting to be hugged for many, many years.

- What is it that I want that is hidden under this hate?
- Could I deal more directly with my want?
- Can I own my wanting as my need and not be left hanging, waiting for the other to change?
- Can I find ways, with or without my mother/daughter, to heal the wound caused by this unfulfilled wanting?

Give yourself the gift of letting go of that hate. It keeps you powerless and waiting. Take your own needs and wants seriously and with great love. Meet your needs. Go for your best.

2e The Best Advice **9e**

The best advice you can give yourself is yours. Guidelines given by others cannot truly "fit" you. Only the words, values, beliefs and the uniqueness of your true self will be able to make the right intervention, teach the right lesson, answer the questions rightly. And here is your chance. You may want to glance again at the guidelines we offered for mothers or daughters—or you may not want to.

Based on everything that you know about yourself, your growth and goals, your morality and values, your best, become the advice giver. Remembering that you are a compassionate, wise and gentle teacher, write down the advice that you need to hear about your relationship to your mother/daughter and about yourself.

Suggestions: Write short, pithy statements that are easy to remember and then elaborate, if necessary. Watch for a critical voice. If you feel it, dump it and find a loving place from which to begin again. Be specific. Global advice like "Be good always" won't be very helpful.

May you have the joy of following your own best advice!

CHAPTER TWELVE

Enduring Love

FOR ONE HUMAN BEING TO LOVE ANOTHER:
THAT IS PERHAPS THE MOST DIFFICULT OF ALL OUR
TASKS, THE ULTIMATE, THE LAST TEST AND PROOF
THE WORK FOR WHICH ALL OTHER
WORK IS BUT PREPARATION.

—Rainer Maria Rilke

CHOOSING/CHANGING

To change is to grow. To be all that we are, to be ourself, to give and receive love requires change. It is necessary and inevitable. Nothing can remain the same. Change can be graceful and smooth, like swimming downstream, or it can be painful and rough, fighting the downward current. *Choosing* to change is the author's prerogative, not the victim's response. Paradoxically, this choice to change, to grow and be all of who we can be is predicated on first accepting who we are as we are. Acceptance and change are sisters. When we can look squarely in the mirror and accept who we are—with all the layers, with all the faults and weaknesses, with all the strengths, with all the love—we will be able to truly change. True change comes from that place of acceptance of ourselves, that place of our uniqueness and essential okay-ness, our true self.

As we have grown all our lives from infant to child to adult, so now as adults we will continue to grow. We will mature in inner ways. As we choose to make the most of our growth, we will choose to change. In exploring our mother/daughter relationship we may already have seen the ways that we could change, to heal and support that valued relationship and to heal and support our own growth. If so, we are in a powerful position. We are potentially ready to author the changes that will enhance our lives. If, on the other hand, you are quietly thinking, *I'm going to underline parts of this book and see that Mother (Daughter) reads it, then she'll change,* please know that you will be better served by letting go of that idea. Maybe our mothers or daughters could change and maybe they will change, but it is not our role to see that they do. We must not wait for any other person or circumstance to change in order to make that choice to change for ourselves. "Ifs," "whens," "soons," "laters," "afters" leave us hanging, waiting for an external something to shift, so that we can get on with our lives. We need not ever be at the mercy of people, places and things.

Choosing to change is an exciting and hopeful project. It is rather a mystery how change finally occurs: sometimes in effortless leaps to new levels of experience, sometimes in painfully slow and difficult steps toward these new levels. Change can be internal or external. Circumstances may change or I may change. While we may devote most of our energy to changing circumstances (or people), the change that is most profound is internal. It is the change I make. I may change at many levels. I may change a behavior or a feeling or a belief or an entire way of seeing/being in the world. The vaster the change, the more impact it will have on my whole life. And any change will create more change. Consider the pebble tossed into the still lake. The splash is followed by the ripples that radiate ever outward until the whole lake is changed. When I change, my world will feel that ripple effect as well. Even those with whom I relate will begin to change.

> "For twenty years, our anger kept us distant and cold. When she began to change I can't be certain, but along the way her change began to rub off on me. I could feel her softer edge, the caring in her voice, her willingness to give in. I held to my own old feelings for a long time. I was buried deeply in them. But I, too, began to soften—without even a choice to do so. When I finally felt the stirrings of love again, after so many years, I took charge of my own change as well. Having felt that long-lost love, I would never let it go again."

The process of change, finally, is a natural one, but like the natural growth of the flowers or the acorn that we have spoken of before, that growth can be supported, encouraged, relished, or it can be sabotaged, blocked and resisted. We have told several stories of the change that happens when life demands it: A mother's or daughter's illness or death will force a change in any status quo. The gradual maturing of both mother and daughter will also create change, more or less slowly.

Consciousness and choice, however, are not dependent on the vagaries of life. We can choose to change now and, in so doing, we choose to support, encourage and relish the natural process of life.

As you consider your ability to change, ask yourself the question *Have I ever changed?* and ask, as well, *Have I ever not changed?* We are always changing and, at the same time, we may not change in some very important and major ways. We may not be able to leap into a desired change overnight. But we can take one sure step after another, whether the change we want is in relationship to ourselves or to our mother or daughter, or, more likely, both.

Change comes about in several ways and at several levels, involving thinking, feeling and behaving. Thoughts may change, feelings may change, and actions may change and each of these plays supporting roles to the other. This can work for or against us. We may change an action ("No more criticizing my daughter!") without changing the belief behind it ("She is living her life irresponsibly!"), and this will leave us feeling incongruent. We may change a feeling ("I'm really happy to be with my mother now") and not the action that corresponds ("Why am I still acting grouchy?"), and this will leave us acting in ways that don't resonate. In our choice to change we will need to create change in all arenas.

How common it is to have a thoughtful revelation "Ah, Mother did the best that she could," only to find yourself behaving in the same old and limited way. That new thought will need a corresponding change in feelings and behavior. As your thinking changes, what is the feeling that corresponds? "Mother did the best she could. I feel my love and caring and appreciation for her now." And what actions resonate with this thought and feeling? "Mother did the best she could. I feel my love and caring and appreciation for her now. I will behave toward her from a compassionate and giving place." The strength of this change—in feelings, thought and action—will stand against old feelings, thoughts and behaviors until it is a fully realized change. When we present a united front honoring the pull toward our best, our world will begin to move in alignment with our presentation.

Julie and Dorothy's Story

"In the midst of our alienation toward each other, we both knew something needed to change. The first step for us was a choice: 'This relationship is worth it. Let's go for it.' The second was learning about what was in the way of going for it.

"All the old wounds were obstacles to change: this hurt and that, my littleness, her neediness, our fear, etc. Each had to be considered and dealt with. Most of that we did on our own, each dealing with our own 'stuff.' The third step was allowing ourselves to feel our real feelings about each other, letting down our blocks and defenses and taking in and giving out love—as well as telling the truth about our other feelings. The last step, still in process, is refining how we do that: learning skills . . . opening at new levels . . . not forgetting what we know. The original change we set out to create has happened. We have a good relationship. Now comes the icing on the cake, everything we do to make it better!"

Change can happen without choosing and without conscious effort, yet it will be more effective when choice is added. We are choosers. In every moment, we choose. We can choose to go with the best or the least within us. We can choose to stay with pain or move toward letting go. We can choose to see, believe in and act on the negative, limiting aspects of others, or we can choose to see, believe in and act on the positive, expansive aspects of others.

What is important to me? This choice for change starts with our values, our hopes and desires, our goals. When we articulate and honor our values, then we can choose in relationship to them.

Choosing. This ideally follows from values. We do not choose without a context, a reason why, and when we know our values, our truth, our self, then the choice that follows will be right.

Power. Power can flow from our choice, and must, in order to see it through to realization. The choice we make will need to be affirmed, emphasized and stated with conviction, as a reminder to ourselves of what we do value and what we want to go for.

Often, unfortunately, what we value and want to make true will be blocked by the old within us. Every person is constantly faced with a pull toward maintaining the status quo, no matter how limiting or painful it is. At the same time, we are pulled toward growth and transcendence of the old. How will we make the pull of the new more powerful than the pull of the old? What can we do to maximize the value and potential that awaits us, while minimizing the risks and fear inherent in each new step? This will be an ongoing task. Once we get our foot in the door of change, we may well find that we have learning to do.

The "how to" comes next. It is an oft-repeated mistake to try to figure out the how before we have truly and powerfully chosen. "Where there's a will, there's a way" is good folk wisdom. If I say, "Gee, I value my relationship with my mother, but I don't know how to make it work," I'll be giving in to the old. There's not much power in that—just a wistful statement, which will fade away. If I say, "I do value this relationship. I choose to make it work. I am capable of creating the needed change," then my next step will be "What will I do to make it work?" This consideration of "how to" will be placed in a context of deep commitment, and while we still may not have an easy answer to the "how to," our motivation will help us find the way.

When we begin to realize our power to change, we can see that the possibilities are endless. Learning the "how to's" of any desired change will be a trial-and-error proposition at times, but then so is life. Committing to those changes and to the process that is involved in seeing them through will be an act of will and an act of love. When you commit to the changes that have value to you and follow through on the process involved in making those changes happen, you will be a willer. Your self will be creating that resonance, bringing to fruition the seed that it has planted, conducting for all the world to hear the symphony that is you.

LOVING AND LETTING GO

Finally, there is love. Philosophers, preachers, poets have sung its praises, plumbed its depths, painted its picture. Psychology has tip-toed around its mystery, not knowing what to say or do with this strange commodity. Science can't approach it. But people build their lives around it, rise and fall with it, pray for it, long for it, live for it, die for it, struggle to create and hold it. And, in our changing, we will grow closer to that love.

Mother/daughter love can be love at its highest: pure, selfless, giving and compassionate. Or it can be love at its worst: clinging, greedy, possessive. As we clear away the layers of old baggage, hurts and false fronts that have covered us, we will find our way surely and rewardingly to love at its highest level. Love is not something we build or create; it is something that we are. We do not add it to our resume as another skill; we find it beneath all that has blocked it. When free, our love pours forth as a direct expression of ourself. This is not "mushy" love; often it is not even personal. The love that is our self is altruistic, compassionate and impersonal. Love responds to selves, it does not get caught in personalities. Love is harmless, it has no limiting intent. Love has goodwill, it is not greedy.

"The greatest love is a mother's, then comes a dog's, then comes a sweetheart's," goes an old proverb. What does this strange idea point to? Perhaps we can see in the ideal of mother love the basic, unconditional love and acceptance that is the transformative element of life. When love holds on, needs, demands, exacts payment, requires change and is conditional, then it is a trap. It is everything that we have talked about freeing ourselves from. We are little, hurt, lost, blaming. We have no autonomy, nor are we honoring our own self. And yet so much love is just like this. We don't need to look far into the world of adult relationships to see that this is true. No longer do we love "till death do us part," but until something better comes along.

When a mother and daughter face a reunion, it will be transformative if it is infused with the love that is beyond the hurt. The mother will reach back into herself to the act of giving birth, the act of giving of her body and soul to the life of another human being. The daughter will reach forward into her maturity, her wisdom, into the moment of her mother's death, when she too can be freed of all hooks. In these two moments that bind and hold us—the birth and the death that create this mother/daughter pair—there is the potential for love that is pure.

If we are ready to go for it, then we will turn to that very special other, in life or in death, and we will embrace her self. We can see, as if by magic, through all the layers that cover her and we can know our love for her, unfettered by demands, expectations, needs, fears, hurts. If you take a moment to experience the love that you feel for anyone or anything, you will notice that it fills you up. There is no room for anything else when you allow love. Everything less fades from awareness. Blocks and limitations are washed away. Fear is erased.

Julie's Story

❧ "As I was preparing to leave this country for many months on an exciting adventure, I felt all of my love for my children welling up in me. And yet in moments the love and the fear become entangled. Love turns to fear and guilt and concern so easily and I questioned my choice to leave. After all, first and foremost I was a mother. (Or was I?) What if something went wrong? They needed me. (Or did they?) Stepping on to that airplane was an act of faith and an act of real love. For I knew that I could love them and let them go. This is harder than any task I have faced as a mother or as a person: loving, without holding on."

Our love will never be perfect. We do well to remind ourselves of our humanness. Only saints can love with a purity that is untainted. And yet each of us can and deeply wishes to love more fully, more clearly. And each woman who has picked up this book longs to love her mother or her daughter and herself with more purity and more joy. Love is sitting right around the corner from choice. The two will serve and support each other. My love will help me choose, my choice will help me love. When I choose to:

❧ *remember my love for my mother/daughter, act with compassion and empathy, give my best effort to understanding the other, be cooperative and have goodwill, live by my highest principles,*

❧ *honor love over fear, risk rather than staying safe, face pain and doubt in order to find love, let go rather than holding on, honor my self wherever that may lead . . . then I will be open to love.*

❧ Two hundred people felt the movement of love not so long ago, when a group of women acted out the stages of the mother/daughter relationship. There was the birth, the mother's pain and joy, the daughter's entrance into her mother's waiting arms, the first hello. There was the child, growing and risking, returning to her mother for safety, and mother feeling the poignant loss of her infant. There was the struggle, the push and pull, "I love you, I hate you, I need you, I don't," which represented the daughter's perilous journey toward independence, the mother's need to let go. There were the adults, hand in hand, equal, sharing and caring, coming and going, touching and releasing. And there was the ending: Mother is dying, she is held by her daughter, the scene has repeated/reversed—one is held, the other holding. The mother has let go and, now, so too must the daughter. The final goodbye.

Throughout it all there is love. We have never met a woman who did not long for the reconnection to loving and being loved. We have never met a woman who was unable to move closer to that love, and so to her own wholeness.

To love is to give and to take. It is not a sacrifice. When I allow love to come into me, I will allow it to go forth from me. When I allow it to go forth from me, I will allow it to come into me. This is the gift of the mother/daughter relationship. It is the hope of every woman and it is every woman's right.

Your journey will have already taken you far. You will have felt love and pain. You will have known anger and joy. You will have succeeded and failed. In your autonomy, in the integrity of your true self, you will continue this journey through all the highs and lows that still await you. You need never be without love. It is your birthright. It comes from within and without you. You don't need a mate, a child, or a parent to know that love. You need only yourself and the world—of which you are a part. When you next look out your window, see the love that awaits you. When you next look into your mirror, see the love that you are. When you next look into the eyes of another human being, see the love that invites you. And when you next feel the presence of your mother or daughter, know the love that is there.

Conceived by your loving,
formed from your substance,
I sucked from you life-giving milk.
Rocked in your arms lulled by your singing,
I mirrored your smiles mimicked your phrases.
Sensing your joys and your unspoken angers,
I tested with you what a person could be.
Together we loosened the silver cord.
I gathered confidence, made my own journey.
Chose my own love, had my own daughters.
Watched them grow strong, let them go freely.
My arms push your chair, my eyes read your mail,
Your queries ask for my confirmation.
I drew from you strength for my living.
Can you draw from me courage for dying?

—*Alice Johnston Brown*

THE FINAL WORKBOOK

LOVE DIES ONLY WHEN GROWTH STOPS.

—Pearl S. Buck

We come to the end of this work and the beginning of everything that awaits us. There is no place to end except with love, and no exercise to do that does not point to love. Finally, you must create your own exercises to help you find and live your love.

Will you choose to write a song about your love, as many have done, or a poem? Will you speak your love to the world or will you hold it in inner peace? Will you look through all the darkness and see the light and will you let your own light shine? Let your last exercise be about love and choice. If your love is important, then choose to love. When you choose to love, then give that love power. As you empower your love, find the "how to" that you will need to let it be fully realized in your world.

About the Authors

Julie Firman, M.S., and **Dorothy Firman, Ed.D.**, mother and daughter, have been in relationship for more than fifty years. For the past twenty-five years they have worked with women on the mother/daughter relationship. They offer workshops and keynote speeches on the subject throughout the country. Their book, co-authored with Frances Firman Salorio, Julie's daughter and Dorothy's sister, *Chicken Soup for the Mother and Daughter Soul*, is a bestseller.

Julie, a retired teacher, school principal and psychotherapist, is now actively involved in learning new things, creating art, taking and giving classes in a wide variety of subjects, and generally enjoying her eighties. She is in her sixty-third year of marriage!

Dorothy is a practicing psychotherapist and counselor-trainer, working in the field of psychosynthesis, a spiritual psychology. In addition she is a life coach, speaker and consultant. She has been married to her best friend for more than twenty-five years, has three children and a grandchild. She is a beginning potter, following in her mother's artistic footsteps.

Both women live in Amherst, Massachusetts. For more on Julie and Dorothy's work visit their Web site at *www.motherdaughter relations.com*. For more on psychosynthesis and Dorothy's work, visit *www.synthesiscenter.org*.

Resources

Assagioli, Roberto. *Psychosynthesis: A Collection of Basic Writings.* Amherst, Mass.: Synthesis Center Press, 2000.

Edelman, Hope. *Motherless Daughters: The Legacy of Loss.* New York: Delta, 1995.

Firman, Dorothy, and Julie Firman. *Chicken Soup for the Mother and Daughter Soul.* Deerfield Beach, Fla: HCI, 2003.

Firman, John, and Ann Gila. *Psychosynthesis: A Psychology of the Spirit.* Albany, N.Y.: Suny Press, 2002.

Franklin, Cher M., and Sherry G. Rubin. *Girls Are Stars in Their Own Lives!* Lionville, Pa.: Girls Star, 2002.

Harris, Thomas A. *I'm OK, You're OK: A Practical Guide to Transactional Analysis.* New York: Galahad Press, 1999.

Imber-Black, Evan, and Janine Roberts. *Rituals for Our Times: Celebrating, Healing, and Changing Our Lives and Our Relationships.* New York: HarperPerennial Library, 1993.

Kirshenbaum, Mira. *Parent-Teen Breakthrough: The Relationship Approach.* New York: Plume, 1995.

Lesser, Elizabeth. *The Seeker's Guide: Making Your Life a Spiritual Adventure.* New York: Villard Books, 2000.

Pipher, Mary. *Reviving Ophelia: Saving the Selves of Adolescent Girls.* New York: Ballantine Books, 2002.

Straus, Celia. *The Mother-Daughter Circle.* New York: Ballantine Books, 2003.

Val-Essen, Ilene. *Bring Out the Best in Your Child and Yourself.* Culver City, Calif.: Quality Parenting, 1999.

Courage to Change

By offering practical solutions for the real day-to-day issues that confront you, *The Power of Focus for Women* helps you build the life you deserve.

Code #1142 • Paperback • $12.95

Powerful profiles of prominent women including Oprah Winfrey and Sandra Day O'Connor will show you how to create the life you really want and ought to have.

Code #0545 • Paperback • $12.95

Positive Thinking

Change Almost Anything in 21 Days provides both the inspiration and motivation needed to make important changes—from careers and relationships to parenting and health.

Code #0677• Paperback • $12.95

This beautifully written book will open your eyes to the liberating power of forgiveness and provide you with the ability to find true joy.

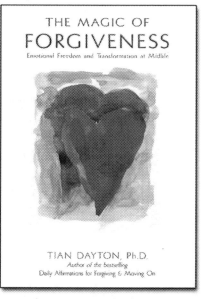

Code #0863 • Paperback • $12.95

Health and Wellness

Healthy Living

Never Be Sick Again

One Disease • Two Causes • Six Pathways

**Health Is a Choice
Learn How to Choose It**

Raymond Francis, M.Sc.
with Kester Cotton

Foreword by
Harvey Diamond
Coauthor of the
#1 *New York Times*
Bestseller *Fit for Life*

Code #9543 • Paperback • $12.95

By exploring provocative case studies and cutting-edge scientific research, you will learn an entirely new way to look at health and disease.

Containing practical advice, easy-to-follow tips, reference sources and Web sites, this is the one book on health every family needs.

"I recommend this book to all people who want to know how to navigate the confusing world of medicine. Whether you intend to use alternative therapies or to integrate them with conventional medicine, the information in Own Your Health will guide you to making the right decisions."
—**Andrew Weil, M.D.**, *author, 8 Weeks to Optimum Health*

OWN YOUR HEALTH

Choosing the Best from
Alternative & Conventional Medicine

EXPERTS TO GUIDE YOU,
RESEARCH TO INFORM YOU,
STORIES TO INSPIRE YOU

ROANNE WEISMAN WITH BRIAN BERMAN, M.D.

Code #0111 • Paperback • $16.95

Available wherever books are sold.
To order direct: Telephone (800) 441-5569 • Online www.hcibooks.com
Prices do not include shipping and handling. Your response code is BKS.